IT Governance

Also by Peter Weill

Leveraging the New Infrastructure
(with Marianne Broadbent)
Harvard Business School Press, 1998

Place to Space
(with Michael Vitale)
Harvard Business School Press, 2000

IT Governance

How Top Performers
Manage IT Decision Rights
for Superior Results

Peter Weill and
Jeanne W. Ross

HARVARD BUSINESS SCHOOL PRESS
BOSTON, MASSACHUSETTS

978-1-59139-253-8 (ISBN 13)

Library of Congress Cataloging-in-Publication Data
Weill, Peter.
    IT governance : how top performers manage IT decision rights for
superior results / Peter Weill and Jeanne W. Ross.
        p. cm.
    Includes bibliographical references and index.
    ISBN 1-59139-253-5
    1. Information technology—Management. I. Ross, Jeanne W.
II. Title.
    HD30.2.W4495 2004
    658.4'038—dc22

                                                            2003025726

Contents

Preface and Acknowledgments   vii

1. IT Governance Simultaneously Empowers and Controls   1

2. Five Key IT Decisions: Making IT a Strategic Asset   25

3. IT Governance Archetypes for Allocating Decision Rights   57

4. Mechanisms for Implementing IT Governance   85

5. What IT Governance Works Best   117

6. Linking Strategy, IT Governance, and Performance   147

7. Government and Not-for-Profit Organizations   185

8. Leadership Principles for IT Governance   215

Appendix A: Research Sites   237
Appendix B: Measuring Governance Performance   239

Notes   241
Index   255
About the Authors   265

Preface and Acknowledgments

IT'S HARD TO PINPOINT when the importance of information technology (IT) governance became clear to us. It wasn't like a bolt of lightning that struck and left us first stunned but then seeing more clearly. Rather, gradually over a period of years, involving hundreds of conversations with managers and multiple research studies, we became convinced that IT governance is the most important factor in generating business value from IT. Our conviction—slow to develop but now heartfelt—is that IT governance can actually deliver on the longtime management paradox of encouraging and leveraging the ingenuity of all the enterprise's people while ensuring compliance with the overall vision and principles.

Although this book is about IT governance, we place IT in an organizational context as one of the six key assets (human, financial, physical, intellectual property, IT, and relationships) that must be governed to create value. Too often books and discussions focus on one piece of the organizational puzzle. Value comes from integrating the enterprise's key assets. That said, to be practical and limit the book to only one volume, we focus on providing concepts, frameworks, and lessons from top-performing enterprises on how to get more value from their IT investments via better IT governance in the firm's strategic context.

Unsuccessful quests for business value from IT often exasperate senior business managers. For five years, the MIT Sloan School of Management Center for Information Systems Research has presented thrice-annual programs for non-IT executives struggling to manage IT better. In this program we address capable business executives who recognize that they cannot hand off responsibility for IT value to their IT units. Typically, they are concerned officers of an enterprise (CEO, CFO, COO, and other senior managers) looking for practical guidelines for what they can do tomorrow to improve their returns from IT investments. The more than one thousand executives who have attended this course often feel frustrated, insecure, bewildered, and even angry about the high cost of IT and its limited measurable benefits. One executive implored: "What can I do? I don't understand IT well enough to manage it. My IT people work hard but there is a disconnect somehow . . . with the real business I manage. They don't feel my pain." This book is designed for these executives and the CIOs and other IT professionals who will work together to generate increasingly strategic benefits from IT.

IT governance is an idea whose time has come. Information and IT are the least understood of the key assets in the enterprise. With the huge growth of IT spending in enterprises and the strong evidence that significant bottom line premiums reward better IT decision making, it is time to make IT governance more professional. There has been little field-based research on IT governance, and few publications help managers understand the issues involved in designing effective governance structures and processes. Our objective in writing this book was to addresses that gap.

Looking ahead, the influence of IT on enterprise performance will continue to grow. Whether an enterprise is focused on efficiency, innovation, growth, customer responsiveness, or business integration, IT has become an essential ingredient for business competitiveness. IT supports standardized process components, shared knowledge, instantaneous communications, and electronic linkages—the foundations for new business strategies. In an environment demanding faster responses and increasing agility, management teams must ensure that IT is an enabler of, not an obstacle to, organizational change.

The Research

The insights here come from a series of research projects exploring IT governance in more than three hundred enterprises in over twenty countries during the period 1999–2003. Most of the research was done at the MIT Sloan School of Management Center for Information Systems Research (CISR). The research consisted of three main studies:

1. A CISR study (2001–2003) led by Peter Weill of how enterprises govern IT, which provided the framework for the book. We studied 256 enterprises spanning the Americas, Europe, and Asia Pacific, and conducted several in-depth case studies. We studied who had input to and who held decision rights for five key IT decisions. We also measured governance and financial performance and the effectiveness of the mechanisms used to implement governance. The study and survey was designed at CISR. Marianne Broadbent and her colleagues at Gartner created an interactive Web site (during 2002) and facilitated distribution of the survey electronically and on paper to CIOs of Gartner EXP member enterprises and other organizations who attend CISR programs. Gartner also contributed to the research by conducting ten case studies on IT governance.

2. Forty case studies developed for a series of CISR research projects (1999–2003) led by Jeanne Ross. The cases explored the relationship between IT architecture and busines strategy and identified governance issues associated with IT and organizational change efforts. Firms in the studies were building IT architectures as part of ERP implementations, e-business initiatives, Y2K remediation, and business transformations. CISR research team members included Peter Weill, Richard Woodham, Natalia Levina, George Westerman, and Nils Fonstad. Michael Vitale, then at the University of Melbourne, also participated in the case research. David Robertson at IMD in Switzerland contributed ten European cases, including ING Direct and Panalpina, which provided the background for some of our vignettes.

3. A number of related projects, including:
   - A CISR study (2001) by Jeanne Ross, Cynthia Beath (University of Texas), and Mani Subramani (University of Minnesota) involving interviews of thirty CIOs to explore IT management practices.

- An exploratory study of IT governance (1998–1999) by Peter Weill and Michael Vitale at the Melbourne Business School.

- An examination of IT governance arrangements and performance of twenty-four *Fortune* 100 firms at MIT CISR (2000) by Peter Weill and Richard Woodham, using data collected as part of "Justifying and Funding IT Infrastructure," the Results Research Project ITI, The Concours Group.

Who Should Read This Book

We wrote this book for all executives who have ever celebrated, worried about, or cursed IT—including CIOs. We discuss the roles of senior business and IT managers in fostering effective and empowering use of IT through IT governance. The language, style, data, examples, and lessons concern business issues that rely on technology. We discuss the strategic governance decisions with enough detail to guide implementation of governance mechanisms—the structures and processes that make governance happen. We encourage senior managers, operational managers, marketing managers, financial managers, and IT managers to read this book and take responsibility for IT governance design and implementation in their enterprises.

People We Would Like to Thank

We gratefully acknowledge the support of CISR's patron and sponsor firms at the time of writing:

Accenture, Aetna Inc., Allstate Insurance Co., Banknorth N.A., Campbell Soup Co., Celanese, DiamondCluster International Inc., Det Norske Veritas , EMC Corp., Freddie Mac, Gartner, The Gillette Co., The Guardian Life Insurance Co. of America, Intel Corp., Hewlett-Packard Company, IBM Corporation, International Finance Corp., Marsh Inc., Merrill Lynch & Co. Inc., MetLife, Mitsubishi Corp., Microsoft Corporation, Mohegan Sun, National Kidney Foundation (Singapore), Nomura Research Institute Ltd., Ortho Biotech Products L.P., Pfizer Inc., PFPC Inc., Raytheon, Qwest Communications, State Street Corporation, and TRW Inc. Executives from these firms not only inform and fund our research, they probe our assumptions, test our ideas, debate our findings, and implement and improve our work.

During research and writing we have had the opportunity to work with many extraordinary managers and academic colleagues who have influenced our thinking and reinforced our passions. First we would like to acknowledge the managers who shared their insights and in many cases provided the examples for the book. These managers included John Fiore and Joe Antonellis at State Street, Steve Sheinheit at MetLife, Doreen Wright at Campbell Soup, Steve Brown at Carlson Companies, Mike Eskew and Ken Lacy at UPS, Martin Vonk at ING Direct, Monika Ribar at Panalpina, Andre Spatz at UNICEF, Ron Carter at Pfizer, Jim McGrane at Mead-Westvaco, Joe Adamski at Barwon Water, Jim Venglarik at JPMorgan Chase, Bill Kirkey at DuPont, Robbie Higgins at Motorola, and Steve Yates at USAA. Frank Erbrick at McKinsey and Charlie Feld at Feld Associates enlightened us about enterprise architecture and its implications for IT governance. Appendix A lists companies that participated in the research. We want to acknowledge all the managers who participated in case study interviews, as well as the 250+ CIOs who took the time to answer our survey questions about IT governance and add their own insights and further questions. We are grateful to all of them for making this book possible.

A number of people provided important feedback on the manuscript and research insights including Ken Cooke and Michael Brook at PriceWaterhouseCoopers, John Sviokla at DiamondCluster International, Inc., and Tony Scott at GM. Thanks also to the many executives who made comments during our presentations or came up afterward to share their insights and criticisms.

We are especially grateful to Marianne Broadbent and her colleagues at Gartner for participating and for contributing case studies, talent, and insights to the project. We also want to acknowledge Shafeen Charania of Microsoft for his thought-provoking discussions and comments on the manuscript and his strong advocacy of applying IT value research to practice.

Susie Lee, Francisco González-Meza Hoffmann, Chris Foglia, and Richard Woodham—all researchers at CISR—did most of the detailed and painstaking quantitative analysis and data management for this book. Individually and together as a team they added precision, professionalism, collegiality, and insight. We thank them.

During the manuscript development, we received tremendous support from our colleagues at CISR and the Sloan School. David Fitzgerald III adroitly managed the production process; he devised the template, policed version control, tracked down references, formatted text, designed graphics, checked for inconsistencies, and kept us on schedule. We appreciate not only his professionalism but also his dedication and good humor. Chris Foglia contributed wide-ranging skills including project management, data analysis, and proofreading. She proved, once again, to be the model center manager. Julie Coiro took on extra duties to keep CISR running smoothly and to keep us all sane. We also appreciate the interest, ideas, and collegiality of our CISR research colleagues Chuck Gibson, Jack Rockart, George Westerman, Sinan Aral, and Nils Fonstad. They have influenced our thinking and made CISR both personally and professionally a great place to work.

CISR is a research center in the Sloan School of Management at MIT. We feel very fortunate to work in such a rich and exciting research environment. We have benefited, in particular, from the strong support, friendship and encouragement of Dean Don Lessard, whose responsibilities include research centers, as well as Area Head Professor Wanda Orlikowski and IT Group Head Professor Tom Malone.

We feel fortunate to have worked with Carol Franco and Kirsten Sandberg at Harvard Business School Press. Kirsten as our editor championed the book and improved our work greatly by challenging both big ideas and specific text and keeping us focused on the main message.

Working together on this book has been a wonderful opportunity for us to combine the insights of many years of IT management and value research. We have collaborated on a number of projects—sometimes while on separate continents—and this work combines both joint and independent research. We have frequently applied different methodologies to similar questions, leading to richer, occasionally contradictory findings and ultimately lively debates. In writing this manuscript we found enormous satisfaction in the process of bringing together our different skills, challenging our assertions, and learning together. For both of us it has been an inspiring and joyful partnership.

Personal Note from Peter

I want to dedicate this book to Margi Olson, my wife and mate, who managed to be supportive, insightful, and delightful despite observing that every organizational issue we discussed in the last year was, in my eyes at least, a governance problem.

I hope the M.B.A. and other master's students in my Sloan School courses recognize their input into this book. I thank them all as they contributed much in the way of learning, clarity, and focus during the countless discussions in and out of class.

I would like to acknowledge John Alford of the Melbourne Business School at the University of Melbourne who educated me about management in the public sector and provided helpful input to chapter 7. I would also like to acknowledge Erik Brynjolfsson at the Sloan School of Management for the many helpful and collegial discussions about IT value. And a warm thank-you to Mike Vitale at the Australian Graduate School of Management. We worked together on IT governance in 1998, trying to understand why IT governance was important and how it could be done well.

To my new godson, James Quinn Diamond: Welcome to the world, and I hope you grow up to be just like your parents; I look forward to participating. Thanks, as always, to my mum who is brave and loving. And thanks to my brother Steve, as well as to Lois, David, and Simon, who together complete my family and are always loving and supportive.

Personal Note from Jeanne

My acknowledgments must start with my parents, who raised independent-thinking girls before it was fashionable to do so. I am enormously grateful for their love and encouragement. I also want to thank Pat, Jo, Barb and Mark, Russ and Diane, and Dave and Jill for being really cool siblings. I treasure our moments together.

Thanks to my friend and neighbor Janet Helgeson for sharing her enthusiasm for life and for keeping the garden green while I was writing, and to Ann Little, Cindy Crimmin, and Peggy Berko for their ongoing friendship despite distance and distractions. I am grateful to Cynthia Beath, Carol Brown, and Mike Vitale for long discussions that have stimulated and sustained my passion for research. I am also grateful to Kate Kaiser for getting me started and keeping me going. And a special thank-you to Jack Rockart for believing in me and teaching me how to do what I do—I couldn't have had a better role model.

I want to thank my children—Adam, Julie, and Steffie—for bringing sheer delight into my life in ways that no professional pursuit can approach. I marvel at what wonderful people you are. Finally, I want to thank my husband and best friend, Dan, who, for twenty-six years, has encouraged me to pursue my goals in spite of the added burden it places on him. He has become an unwitting IT expert through his careful editing and patient listening. I dedicate this book to Dan, whose unwavering love and support are the best explanation for my extraordinarily happy life.

Peter Weill
Jeanne Ross

IT Governance

1

IT Governance Simultaneously Empowers and Controls

DO YOUR information technology (IT) capabilities enhance your competitiveness?[1] Do managers throughout your organization recognize their responsibilities for the effective management and use of IT—or do they assume that the IT department will manage IT? Do your IT investments target enterprisewide strategic priorities—or does your firm squander resources on diverse tactical initiatives? Simply put, are you getting acceptable value from your IT investments?

Firms manage many assets—people, money, plant, and customer relationships—but information and the technologies that collect, store, and disseminate information may be the assets that perplex them the most. Business needs constantly change, while systems, once in place, remain relatively rigid. IT implementations involve both up-front and ongoing investments for outcomes that no one can precisely predict. These uncertainties and complexities lead many managers to abdicate their responsibilities for ensuring that their people use IT effectively.

For many years, some organizations could succeed despite weak IT management practices. But information—and consequently IT— is an increasingly important element of organizational products and services and the foundation of enterprisewide processes. The tight linkage between IT and organizational processes means that the IT unit cannot bear sole—or even primary—responsibility for the effective use of information and information technology. Getting more value from IT is an increasingly important organizational competency. Leaders throughout an enterprise must develop this competency.

Our research shows that top-performing enterprises generate returns on their IT investments up to 40 percent greater than their competitors.[2] These top-performing enterprises proactively seek value from IT in a variety of ways:

- They clarify business strategies and the role of IT in achieving them.

- They measure and manage the amount spent on and the value received from IT.

- They assign accountability for the organizational changes required to benefit from new IT capabilities.

- They learn from each implementation, becoming more adept at sharing and reusing IT assets.

Top-performing enterprises succeed where others fail by implementing effective IT governance to support their strategies. For example, firms with above-average IT governance following a specific strategy (for example, customer intimacy) had more than 20 percent higher profits than firms with poor governance following the same strategy.[3] We define IT governance as *specifying the decision rights and accountability framework to encourage desirable behavior in using IT*. IT governance is not about making specific IT decisions—management does that—but rather determines who systematically makes and contributes to those decisions. IT governance reflects broader corporate governance principles while focusing on the management and use of IT to achieve corporate performance goals. Effective IT governance encourages and leverages the ingenuity of the enterprise's people in IT usage and ensures compliance with the enterprise's overall vision and values. This book is intended to alert both business and IT unit executives to the critical role they play in defining IT governance processes—a role that ultimately determines how much value the enterprise receives from IT.

All enterprises have IT governance. Those with effective governance have *actively* designed a set of IT governance mechanisms (committees, budgeting processes, approvals, and so on) that encourage behavior consistent with the organization's mission, strategy, values, norms, and culture. In these enterprises, IT can factor significantly into competitive strategy. For example, David Spina, CEO of State Street Corporation, a world leader in global investor services, defined the firm's corporate vision in 2001 as "One State Street." This vision shifted the focus of the enterprise from the individual accomplishments of business units such as investment research and management, trading and brokerage services, and fund accounting and custodial services, to the firmwide demands of the customer. Desirable behaviors changed to include optimization of enterprisewide as well as business unit objectives. State Street established and refined a set of governance mechanisms, including enterprisewide IT budgeting and an Office of IT Architecture, to encourage the new behaviors.[4]

In contrast, enterprises that govern IT by default more often find that IT can sabotage business strategy. One financial services firm was pursuing a cost reduction strategy. Rather than create a comprehensive set of mechanisms that would encourage cost saving, this firm relied on a new chargeback system to curtail demand for IT services. When the chargeback system led to bickering among IT and business managers, the CIO assigned relationship managers to restore internal customer satisfaction. They improved satisfaction scores but did not lower IT or business process costs. Without a cohesive IT governance design, enterprises must rely on their CIOs to ameliorate problems through tactical solutions rather than position IT as a strategic asset.

To understand IT value creation, we studied IT governance in over 250 multibusiness unit for-profit and not-for-profit enterprises in twenty-three countries in the Americas, Europe, and Asia Pacific (see appendix A). Our research revealed that top-performing enterprises governed IT differently than did other enterprises. Mindful of competing internal forces, the top performers designed governance structures linked to the performance measure on which they excelled (for example, growth or return on assets), thereby harmonizing business objectives, governance approach, governance mechanisms, and performance goals and metrics. The net effect: Good governance design allows enterprises to deliver superior results on their IT investments. We conclude that *effective IT governance is the single most important predictor of the value an organization generates from IT.*

ME.

What Is Governance?

Before we dive into IT governance, we must look at the broader issue of corporate governance in enterprises. Corporate governance became a dominant business topic in the wake of the spate of corporate scandals of midyear 2002—Enron, Worldcom, and Tyco, to name a few. Interest in corporate governance is not new, but the severity of the financial impacts of these scandals undermined the confidence of both the institutional and the individual investor and heightened concerns about the ability and resolve of private enterprises to protect their stakeholders. The crisis in confidence in the corporate sector contributed to the downward pressure on stock prices worldwide and particularly in the United States. In the first six months of 2002 the S&P 500 fell 16 percent; the technology-heavy NASDAQ fell 36 percent. The U.S. government intervened, and new legislation required CEOs to personally attest to the accuracy of their firms' accounts and report results more quickly.[5] Simultaneously, corporate America increased the level of self-regulation.

SO.

Good corporate governance is important to professional investors. Major institutions rank corporate governance on par with the firm's financial indicators when evaluating investment decisions. A McKinsey study found that professional investors are even prepared to pay large premiums for investments in firms with high governance standards.[6] Premiums ranged from an average of 13 percent in North America and Western Europe to 20 or 25 percent in Asia and Latin America and even higher in Eastern Europe and Africa.[7] On average, when moving from poorest to best on corporate governance, firms could expect an increase of 10 to 12 percent in market value.

ROI
13-25

% 10-12%

A number of bodies have published guidelines for good corporate governance.[8] One we found very useful was the Organization for Economic Cooperation and Development's 1999 publication "OECD Principles for Corporate Governance," which defined corporate governance as providing the structure for determining organizational objectives and monitoring performance to ensure that objectives are attained.[9] The OECD emphasized that "there is no single model of good corporate governance," but it noted that in many countries corporate governance is vested in a supervisory board that is responsible for protecting the rights of shareholders and other stakeholders (employees, customers, creditors, and so on). The board, in turn, works with a senior management team to implement governance principles that ensure the effectiveness of organizational processes.

We propose a framework for linking corporate and IT governance. The top of the framework (figure 1-1) depicts the board's relationships. The senior executive team, as the board's agent, articulates strategies and desirable behaviors to fulfill board mandates.

FIGURE 1-1

Corporate and Key Asset Governance

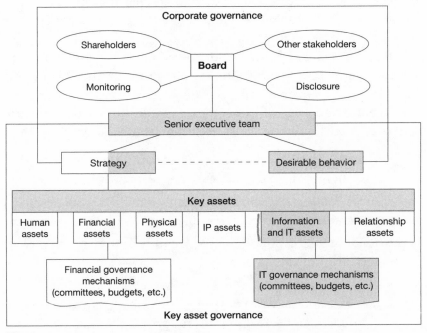

☐ IT governance.

Q₅ We see strategy as a set of choices.[10] Who are the targeted customers? What are the products and service offerings? What is the unique and valuable position targeted by the firm? What core processes embody the firm's unique market position?

Desirable behaviors embody the beliefs and culture of the organization as defined and enacted through not only strategy but also corporate value statements, mission statements, business principles, rituals, and structures.[11] Desirable behaviors are different in every enterprise. Behaviors, not strategies, create value. For example, Johnson & Johnson relied on autonomous business units to create shareholder value for nearly a hundred years. Eventually, however, customers insisted that they wanted to deal with J&J—not a set of individual J&J operating companies. Accordingly, J&J's well-known corporate credo has evolved to specify desirable behaviors such as lowering the cost of its products to customers, creating mechanisms for better understanding the unique needs of individual customers, and transferring employees across J&J companies to enhance individual careers and help them identify with the corporation.[12] Clear desirable behaviors are key to effective governance and are major topics in chapters 3 and 6.

The lower half of figure 1-1 identifies the six key assets through which enterprises accomplish their strategies and generate business value. Senior executive teams create mechanisms to govern the management and use of each of these assets both independently and together. The key elements of each asset include the following:

- *Human assets:* People, skills, career paths, training, reporting, mentoring, competencies, and so on

- *Financial assets:* Cash, investments, liabilities, cash flow, receivables, and so on

- *Physical assets:* Buildings, plant, equipment, maintenance, security, utilization, and so on

- *IP assets:* Intellectual property (IP), including product, services, and process know-how formally patented, copyrighted, or embedded in the enterprises' people and systems

- *Information and IT assets:* Digitized data, information, and knowledge about customers, processes performance, finances, information systems, and so on

- *Relationship assets:* Relationships within the enterprise as well as relationships, brand, and reputation with customers, suppliers, business units, regulators, competitors, channel partners, and so on

Governance of the key assets occurs via a large number of organizational mechanisms (for example, structures,[1] processes,[2] committee,[4] procedures,[5] and audits[3]). Some mechanisms are unique to a particular asset (for example, the IT architecture committee) and others cross and integrate multiple asset types (the capital approval process, for example) ensuring synergies between key assets. Maturity across the governance of the six key assets varies significantly in most enterprises today with financial and physical assets typically the best governed and information assets among the worst.

At the bottom of figure 1-1 are the mechanisms used to govern each of the six key assets. We contend that enterprises with common mechanisms across multiple assets perform better. For example, if the same executive committee governs both financial and IT assets, a firm can achieve better integration and create more value. Some mechanisms will always be unique to each asset—the audit committee for financial assets and the IT architecture committee for IT, for example—but some common mechanisms lead to better coordination of the six assets.

As a sobering exercise, quickly jot down the list of mechanisms used in your enterprise to govern each of the six assets. Could you complete the lists? How many of the mechanisms were common across more than one asset—more than two assets? Coordinating the six key assets of an enterprise is not easy. The average assessment of a group of forty-two CIOs on how well their enterprises integrated IT governance with the governance of the other key assets was less than three on a five-point scale.[13] Creating common governance mechanisms across the assets will not only increase integration but the resulting smaller number of mechanisms will be simpler to communicate and implement. Education of the senior management team about how governance mechanisms combine to work for the enterprise is an essential and ongoing task for effective governance. We contend that many tangible benefits await better IT governance.

What Is IT Governance?

Analogy

In governing IT, we can learn from good financial and corporate governance. For example, the CFO doesn't sign every check or authorize every payment. Instead, he or she sets up financial governance specifying who can make the decisions and how. The CFO then oversees the enterprise's portfolio of investments and manages the required cash flow and risk exposure. The CFO tracks a series of financial metrics to manage the enterprise's financial assets, intervening only if there are problems or unforeseen opportunities. Similar principles apply to who can commit the enterprise to a contract or a partnership. Exactly the same approach should be applied to IT governance.

IT governance: Specifying the decision rights
and accountability framework to encourage
desirable behavior in the use of IT

Disc

clash

This definition of IT governance aims to capture the simplicity of IT governance—decision rights and accountability—and its complexity—desirable behaviors that are different in every enterprise.[14] Governance determines who makes the decisions. Management is the process of making and implementing the decisions. For example, governance determines who holds the decision rights for how much the enterprise invests in IT. Management determines the actual amount of money invested in a given year and the areas in which the money is invested. The senior management team designs IT decision rights and accountabilities to encourage the enterprise's desirable behaviors. If desirable behavior involves independent and entrepreneurial business units, IT investment decisions will be primarily with the business unit heads. In contrast, if desirable behavior involves an enterprisewide view of the customer with a single point of customer contact, a more centralized IT investment governance model works better. More centralized models for HR (and the other key assets) would also assist in achieving a single point of customer contact. Problems occur when there is a mismatch between

Mismatch

−Ex

desirable behavior and governance. In one financial services firm, a key desirable behavior was rapid innovation by business units to meet the enterprisewide objective of an increased percentage of sales from products introduced in the last five years. In contrast to the stated desirable behavior, most of the IT governance mechanisms conspired to discourage innovation. A particular business unit wanted to lead its financial services industry segment with a new IT-enabled service providing alerts to important clients via their handheld devices like pagers and cell phones. To implement this service, the business unit had to pay the entire cost of the wireless infrastructure (the technical foundation for the product) plus the application development cost for the business process that would use the wireless infrastructure for alerts. This up-front payment was required even though other business units and product offerings would probably utilize the same wireless infrastructure. Thus the innovator was asked to bear all the risk and other business units could then utilize the infrastructure if successful. This practice is like asking the first car using the road to pay all the construction costs.

This firm's solution was to introduce a dividend system consistent with the firm's culture. If the enterprise's senior management saw a potential multibusiness unit application for the infrastructure, the CEO would fund some of the cost (typically 20 percent) from corporate funds. Then the innovating business unit would make the remaining infrastructure investment. If other business units later utilized the infrastructure, the innovating business unit received a dividend of one-third its cost from each business unit using the infrastructure. This approach encouraged early adopters and created infrastructure to foster future innovation across the enterprise. The new funding mechanism, implemented via the executive management, capital investment, and IT architecture committees, carefully balanced risk and reward, encouraging rather than discouraging desirable behavior.

R+

This example highlights two complementary sides of governance articulated by the OECD:[15]

- *Behavioral side of corporate governance:* "Corporate governance encompasses the relationships and ensuing patterns of behavior between different agents in a limited liability corporation; the way managers and shareholders but also

employees, creditors, key customers, and communities interact with each other to form the strategy of the company."

- *Normative side of corporate governance:* "Corporate governance also refers to the set of rules that frame these relationships and private behaviors, thus shaping corporate strategy
  formation. These can be the company law, securities regulation, listing requirements. But they may also be private,
  self-regulation."

The behavioral side of IT governance defines the formal and
informal relationships and assigns decision rights to specific individuals or groups of individuals. The normative side defines mechanisms formalizing the relationships and providing rules and operating procedures to ensure that objectives are met. We found that
enterprises often implement a dozen or more mechanisms to make
IT decisions.

Effective IT governance must address three questions:

1. <u>What</u> decisions must be made to ensure effective management and use of IT?
2. <u>Who</u> should make these decisions?
3. <u>How</u> will these decisions be made and monitored?

The goal of this book is to provide frameworks and insights
from top-performing enterprises to help management teams address these questions.

Important IT Governance Concepts

Figure 1-2 provides a grid that addresses the first two IT governance
questions: What decisions must be made and who should make
them? We will refer to this grid as the Governance Arrangements
Matrix. The column heading of the Governance Arrangements Matrix lists five interrelated IT decisions:

- *IT principles*—Clarifying the business role of IT
- *IT architecture*—Defining integration and standardization
  requirements
- *IT infrastructure*—Determining shared and enabling services

- *Business application needs*—Specifying the business need for purchased or internally developed IT applications
- *IT investment and prioritization*—Choosing which initiatives to fund and how much to spend

These five key decisions are all related and require linking for effective governance—typically flowing from left to right on the matrix. For example, IT principles drive the architecture that leads to infrastructure. The infrastructure capability enables applications to be built based on business needs specified often by the business process owners. Finally IT investments (shorthand for IT investment and prioritization process) must be driven by the IT principles, architecture, infrastructure, and application needs. However, each of these decisions has at its core a unique set of issues, which we will describe in chapter 2. One or more people are responsible for making each of these decisions. Typically, many more people provide input to these decisions. IT governance involves defining

FIGURE 1-2

Governance Arrangements Matrix—Which Governance Archetypes Are Used for Different Types of Decisions?

DECISION ARCHE- TYPE	IT Principles	IT Architecture	IT Infrastructure Strategies	Business Application Needs	IT Investment
Business Monarchy					
IT Monarchy					
Feudal					
Federal					
Duopoly					
Anarchy					
Don't Know					

who will be responsible for both input and decision making for each decision.

The row headings in figure 1-2 list a set of archetypes for specifying decision rights. We deliberately chose provocative political archetypes because, although exaggerated, most managers identify with these stereotypes.[16] Each archetype identifies the type of people involved in making an IT decision:

- *Business monarchy*—Top managers
- *IT monarchy*—IT specialists
- *Feudal*—Each business unit making independent decisions
- *Federal*—Combination of the corporate center and the business units with or without IT people involved
- *IT duopoly*—IT group and one other group (for example, top management or business unit leaders)
- *Anarchy*—Isolated individual or small group decision making

Together these archetypes describe all the decision arrangements we found. Most enterprises use a variety of decision archetypes across the five decisions. The question mark in figure 1-2 represents the challenge for every enterprise to determine where it wants to locate both input and decision-making responsibility for each type of governance decision. Throughout this book, we will describe how top-performing companies have allocated their governance responsibilities. In chapter 5 we will report findings from our research on the relationships between various governance arrangements and governance and financial performance.

While the Governance Arrangements Matrix maps out the types of decisions and the archetypes for making the decisions, the third question—how these decisions will be made and monitored—requires design and implementation of governance mechanisms, such as committees, roles, and formal processes. In chapter 4 we look at common mechanisms (business/IT relationship managers, IT councils, service-level agreements, chargeback arrangements, organizational structures, and so on) and discuss their effectiveness.

Given that enterprises are making five types of IT decisions at multiple organizational levels using a variety of mechanisms, it is easy to see how individual actions might work in opposition to each other rather than in harmony. The complexity and difficulty of explaining IT governance is one of the most serious barriers to improvement. We found empirically that the best predictor of IT governance performance is the percentage of managers in leadership positions who can accurately describe IT governance.[17] Contributing to governance woes is the fact the majority of senior executives aren't familiar with their governance. On average, CIOs in our study estimated that only 38 percent of managers in leadership positions in their enterprises could accurately describe their IT governance—so how could they follow it? In above average governance-performing enterprises, 45 percent or more of managers could accurately describe their IT governance. In only a few very top performers were 80 percent of senior executives familiar with their IT governance. What is the percentage in your enterprise? Why?

To help understand, design, communicate, and sustain effective governance, we propose an IT Governance Design Framework in figure 1-3. We present it here in skeletal form so that readers can

FIGURE 1-3

IT Governance Design Framework

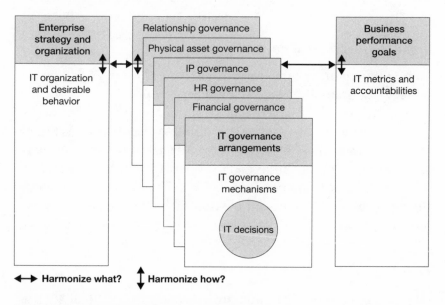

← → Harmonize what?   ↕ Harmonize how?

complete it for any enterprise. The framework maps the harmonization (the horizontal arrows) of enterprise strategy and organization, IT governance arrangements, and business performance goals. The enterprise strategy, governance arrangements, and performance goals are enacted through IT organization and desirable behaviors, governance mechanisms, and metrics, respectively. The framework also illustrates the need to harmonize IT governance with the governance of other key assets. We will return to this framework in chapter 6 to study how enterprises can assign and assess IT governance.

Why Is IT Governance Important?

Effective IT governance requires a significant amount of management time and attention. Is it worth it? Growing enterprise dependence on information and IT suggests that it is. Good IT governance harmonizes decisions about the management and use of IT with desired behaviors and business objectives. Without carefully designed and implemented governance structures, enterprises leave this harmony to chance. There are many reasons why IT decision making should not be left to chance and thus needs good governance. Eight of the reasons follow.

Good IT Governance Pays Off

Among the for-profit firms we studied, the ones pursuing a specific strategy (for example, customer intimacy or operational excellence) with above-average IT governance performance had superior profits as measured by a three-year industry-adjusted return on assets (ROA). The differences varied by strategy of the firm, but the above-average governance-performing firms had ROAs more than 20 percent higher than the firms with poorer governance pursuing the same strategy. Governance was, of course not the only factor, but good governance often comes with effective management practices in all areas.[18]

IT Is Expensive

The average enterprise's IT investment is now greater than 4.2 percent of annual revenues and still rising.[19] This investment results in

IT exceeding 50 percent of the annual total capital investment of many enterprises. As IT has become more important and pervasive, senior management teams are increasingly challenged to manage and control IT to ensure that value is created. To address this issue, many enterprises are creating or refining IT governance structures to better focus IT spending on strategic priorities.

3   IT Is Pervasive

In many enterprises, centrally managed IT is no longer possible or desirable. There was a time when requests for IT spending came only from the IT group. Now IT spending originates all over the enterprise. Some estimates suggest that only 20 percent of IT spending is visible in the IT budget.[20] The rest of the spending occurs in business process budgets, product development budgets, and every other type of budget. In several firms we examined, we even found substantial IT spending hidden in the furniture budgets! Gone too are the days when the IT group was the only place where technically savvy people worked. There isn't a foreign exchange desk manager today who wouldn't get personally involved in making decisions about the technology platform for foreign exchange operations. After all, when 100 percent of your cash flow is on line there is a lot at stake. Personally understanding the technology platform just makes sense. Well-designed IT governance arrangements distribute IT decision making to those responsible for outcomes.

4   New Information Technologies Bombard Enterprises with New Business Opportunities

The rapid introduction of new technologies, including Web-based services, mobile technologies, and enterprise systems, creates strategic threats and opportunities.[21] Witness the rise of mass customization and one-to-one marketing resulting from technologies capable of capturing customer information in a cost-effective and real-time fashion. The fact that information is so readily available, however, means that information assets decay nearly as rapidly as they accumulate. For example, aggregators like Yodalee—which aggregate an individual's financial information from multiple sites—posed a threat to financial services firms such as Citibank

and Vanguard by attempting to intermediate their customer relationships. Financial services firms responded within six months by
absorbing aggregator functionality into their own offerings. Many
firms now hold information about their customers' entire financial
holdings on their sites.

To respond so rapidly to the threat of aggregators, Citibank, Vanguard. and other firms needed a flexible IT infrastructure. Infrastructure must balance the dual needs of cost effectiveness in meeting
current business requirements and the flexibility to support future
business needs. Foresight in establishing the right infrastructure at
the right time enables rapid implementation of new electronically
based business initiatives as well as consolidation and cost reduction
of current business processes. Inability to respond to technology-
induced market changes can threaten a firm's survival, as retailers
such as Barnes & Noble and Toys "R" Us learned in the late 1990s.
Foresight is more likely if an enterprise has formalized governance
processes for harmonizing desirable behaviors and IT principles.

5 IT Governance Is Critical to Organizational Learning About IT Value

As a visiting CEO once remarked to our M.B.A. class, "IT investment is like advertising. I know half of it is well spent. I just don't
know which half."

Enterprises have struggled to understand the value of their IT-
related initiatives because value cannot always be readily demonstrated through a traditional discounted cash flow analysis. Value
results not only from incremental process improvements but also
from the ability to respond to competitive pressures. As the aggregator example demonstrates, it can be difficult to determine in
advance how much a new capability or additional information is
worth. Customers of Citibank and Vanguard value the convenience
of having all their financial information in one place. Would they
be willing to pay separately for this service? Not clear. But aggrega-
tion has become a prerequisite to doing business as a full-service
financial services company. Citibank and Vanguard can more likely
attach a value to the information after it has become available and
they learn more about their customers and how they can ethically
use this information. Effective governance creates mechanisms

through which enterprises can debate potential value and formalize their learning.

Governance also facilitates learning by <u>formalizing exception processes.</u> Enterprises often learn through exceptions—where a different approach from standard practice is used for good reasons. Effective governance makes learning via exceptions explicit and shares any new practices across the enterprise if appropriate. Enterprises in our study reported that 50 percent of new systems involved exceptions to their enterprises' normal policies for architecture or investment. Just over half of the exceptions occurred through the formal exception process, allowing enterprises to learn and update their policies. However, the rest of the exceptions occurred when renegades made decisions independently to meet local needs, effectively preventing systematic enterprise learning. These renegade decisions result from poorly designed, poorly communicated governance arrangements that are not aligned with management incentives.

6 IT Value Depends on More Than Good Technology

In recent years there have been spectacular failures of large IT investments—major enterprise resource planning (ERP) systems initiatives that were never completed, e-business initiatives that were ill-conceived or poorly executed, and data-mining experiments that generated plenty of data but few valuable leads. Some estimates place IT failure rates at over 70 percent of all IT projects.[22] Although some failures result from technical glitches, most represent the inability of organizations to adopt new processes that apply new technologies effectively.

As IT implementations enable increasing standardization and integration of business processes, the roles of technologists and business leaders become increasingly intertwined. IT decision making necessarily becomes joint decision making. When senior managers abdicate to IT executives responsibility for IT success, disaster often ensues.[23] Successful firms not only make better IT decisions, they also have better IT decision-making processes. Specifically, successful firms involve the right people in the process. Having the right people involved in IT decision making yields both more strategic applications and greater buy-in. These more involved people then produce better implementations.

7 *Senior Management Has Limited Bandwidth*

Senior management does not have the bandwidth to consider all the requests for IT investments that occur in a large enterprise let alone to get involved in the many other IT-related decisions. If senior managers attempt to make too many decisions, they become a bottleneck. But decisions throughout the enterprise should be consistent with the direction in which senior management is taking the organization. Carefully designed IT governance provides a clear, transparent IT decision-making process that leads to consistent behavior linked back to the senior management vision while empowering everyone's creativity.

8 *Leading Enterprises Govern IT Differently*

Top-performing firms, in our study, did not follow the most common governance patterns. Instead, leading performers on a particular financial metric had specific governance patterns that encouraged their unique combination of desirable behaviors. For example, firms leading on revenue growth had more decentralized governance arrangements designed to promote customer responsiveness and fast innovation. In contrast, firms leading on profit had much more centralized governance arrangements designed to promote sharing and reuse and asset utilization. Top performing firms balancing multiple performance goals had governance models that blended centralized and decentralized decision making. All top performers' governance had one aspect in common. Their governance made transparent the tensions around IT decisions such as standardization versus innovation. We will explore the governance design implications of these patterns in more detail in chapter 5.

How Effective IT Governance Impacts IT Value: A Case Study of UPS

United Parcel Service (UPS) illustrates how an enterprise can transform IT from a strategic liability to a strategic advantage through effective IT governance.[24] When Oz Nelson became CEO of UPS in 1986, he was concerned about the firm's competitiveness given its existing technology competence. His CIO described the concern as follows: "The strength of Federal Express's tracking system and the things they were doing with technology were eroding what little share of the market UPS had in air services. The UPS board was immensely concerned that Federal Express would not only take the air business away but also start doing daily ground business. The board also saw the profitability of the air business and said, "We just can't continue as we are. We [must] put a lot of money into technology."[25]

Under Nelson's leadership, senior management invested $11 billion over ten years to build a state-of-the-art data center, hire technical experts, create a global network, develop sharable databases, implement enterprisewide applications, and construct a redundant operations environment to protect against disaster. But UPS invested more than money: it invested management time and attention to target spending at key business objectives and to generate benefits from the investments. While creating its new systems environment, UPS designed and implemented IT governance processes that ensured effective IT-related decisions.

UPS's IT governance had its roots in a senior management IT Steering Committee, which established the role of IT at UPS and approved key investment decisions. The IT Steering Committee mandated the firm's highly centralized and standardized IT environment to ensure reliability, cost effectiveness, consistent customer service, and easy access for customers to their package data. These principles have consistently guided other key IT decisions at UPS. For example, UPS's IT Governance Committee (a team of top IT leaders) enforces Steering Committee mandates related to the design, implementation, and management of the IT architecture. The CIO—a member of the IT Steering Committee—heads the Governance Committee. The Governance Committee is responsible for enforcing architectural standards, but members of the committee also work to ensure that UPS's commitment to standards does not unintentionally restrict the firm's flexibility. This flexibility has become increasingly important as the firm has diversified into businesses like supply chain financing and service parts logistics, which have different technology needs from the package delivery business.

But the Governance Committee represents only one step in the debates about technology standards. The top IT architect—who reports to the CIO and is also a member of the Governance Committee—heads a Standards Committee of key technologists who determine when specific standards have become obsolete or cannot meet the requirements of a specific application. This committee handles most of the daily negotiations on standards, but it refers decisions to the Governance Committee when members believe that a standards decision has implications beyond the application in question. Similarly, in cases where the Governance Committee believes that a standards decision will have long-term strategic implications for the firm, the CIO can refer the decision to the IT Steering Committee. The objective is to gain the benefits of standardization without stifling business opportunities.

While IT-only committees shepherd architecture and standards decisions, business leaders take responsibility for identifying IT priorities. UPS's executive team has defined the firm's four cross-functional core processes: customer relationship management, customer information management, package management, and product management. A senior executive heads each core process and has full-time staff responsible for designing subprocesses and identifying IT requirements. Anyone in the firm can submit a project charter to a process team. The project charter spells out the expected costs and benefits of a potential project. The process teams review the charters and refer their highest priority projects to the Steering Committee.

These multiple IT governance mechanisms continuously align IT-related behaviors with corporate strategy at UPS. In the mid-1990s existing governance mechanisms helped key managers recognize the importance of the Internet to UPS's business. Consequently, UPS benefited quickly from its e-business initiatives. The firm continues to aggressively pursue e-business opportunities, cutting operating costs and enhancing customer services. IT governance first helped the firm survive a competitive threat. Now, UPS's governance mechanisms position IT as a strategic weapon.

How IT Governance Simultaneously Empowers and Controls

As the UPS case illustrates, making IT a competitive asset requires senior management leadership. UPS's IT governance structures create strategic control at the top of the firm while empowering decision making at multiple organizational levels. Senior management makes IT governance transparent so that everyone understands and follows the process for proposing, implementing, and using IT. Consequently, UPS can consistently generate desirable behaviors regarding the management and use of IT in the firm, and it shows in the firm's bottom-line performance.

In Figure 1-4, we show UPS's governance arrangements in a simple version of the Governance Arrangements Matrix. UPS has thoughtfully designed IT governance to be transparent to all executives through its four coordinated governance mechanisms: (a) the IT Steering Committee, which vests strategic decisions in four top executives, (b) the IT Governance Committee, which places architecture decisions in the hands of top IT executives, (c) the formal "charter" process, which winnows down the entire enterprise's IT project proposals to those best aligned with strategic objectives, and (d) the referral process for handling exceptions to standards at the appropriate organizational level. Knowing what decisions are made by others and what decisions are under their own responsibility enables managers to make decisions that result in desirable behavior as defined at UPS.

FIGURE 1-4

IT Governance at UPS

		DECISION									
		IT Principles		IT Architecture		IT Infrastructure Strategies		Business Application Needs		IT Investment	
		Input	Decision	Input	Decision	Input	Decision	Input	Decision	Input	Decision
GOVERNANCE ARCHETYPE	Business Monarchy		X								X
	IT Monarchy				X		X				
	Feudal										
	Federal								X	X	
	Duopoly	X		X		X		X			

Governance: Call to Action

Information has always been important in business enterprises, but with recent technological developments, the role and value of information has changed significantly in recent years. Information

- is increasingly easy to collect and digitize
- has increasing importance in products and services
- is very hard to value or price
- has a decreasing half-life
- has increasing risk exposure (e.g., security and privacy)
- is a significant expense in most enterprises

These factors together make information and IT the least understood and most poorly utilized key asset in many enterprises.

This book provides an overview and framework for IT governance, a critical management issue for enterprises concerned with the value they receive from IT. The concept of IT governance has existed for almost as long as computers have been in businesses, but widespread interest and concern is fairly new—resulting from recent business trends such as e-business, globalization, Y2K, business process reengineering, business continuance, and transparency in corporate reporting. In the worst case, probably true in almost all enterprises somewhere, these trends resulted in knee-jerk and unsound IT decision making with no accountability. Little field-based research on IT governance and few publications help managers understand the issues involved in designing effective governance structures and processes.

Recall the study that found enterprises with superior corporate governance to be more highly valued in the market. We found a similar pattern of higher financial performance for enterprises with better IT governance. Thus, we believe a performance premium awaits senior managers who can implement IT governance appropriate to their particular combination of strategy, desirable behavior, and corporate governance. The senior managers that accept that responsibility first will gain the premium—the followers will just play catch-up. This book should help senior managers achieve that premium. We unleashed the "killer app" in the 1990s. Now we must govern the apps that are killing us.

Goals and Overview of the Book

This book proposes an approach to systematically planning IT input and decision rights in key IT decisions. The model relies on two tools: the Governance Arrangements Matrix (figure 1-2) and the Governance Design Framework (figure 1-3). These two tools apply our political governance archetypes (monarchy, feudal, federal, duopoly, and anarchy) for each decision and identify a coherent set of formal governance mechanisms for implementation (for example, committees, approval processes, relationships, and organizational structures). We illustrate the approach with examples from a number of leading enterprises (State Street Corporation, Delta Air Lines, DBS Bank in Singapore, DuPont, UNICEF, and the Metropolitan Police Service–Scotland Yard in the United Kingdom) and explore how their governance patterns evolved to become a strategic tool.

This book is designed for all executives in all types of enterprises struggling to generate additional value from IT. Executive readers will finish the book with specific ideas for management changes that will make a difference in the performance of their enterprise. IT managers will finish the book with a framework, best practices, and clear examples of how to work with their business colleagues to improve their IT governance.

Chapters 2, 3, and 4 review the three questions governance must address: (a) what decisions to make, (b) who should make the decisions, and (c) how to make and monitor the decisions. Chapter 2 explores the five key IT decisions. After delineating the management issues associated with each decision, this chapter raises the question of who should be making each decision in your enterprise. A case on Delta Air Lines demonstrates the interrelationships of the five IT decisions.

Chapter 3 discusses who should make IT decisions. This chapter explores common governance patterns using the Governance Arrangements Matrix. The discussion describes how common IT governance patterns limit the value generated from IT. The chapter reveals how governance differs across the five decision domains. Case studies of DuPont, DBS Bank, and Motorola describe the approaches of three leading firms to aligning governance with business objectives.

Chapter 4 discusses how decisions are made and monitored by focusing on the formal mechanisms enterprises deploy to implement governance. The chapter reviews the benefits and risks of the most popular mechanisms. Examples of governance mechanisms used by Carlson Companies and other leading enterprises describe how well-implemented mechanisms can encourage desirable behavior.

Chapters 5 and 6 discuss the relationship between IT governance and business strategy and how IT governance influences enterprise outcomes. Chapter 5 shows how top-performing enterprises govern differently from the typical enterprise and from each other. We contrast the governance arrangements of exceptional enterprises in the areas of: governance performance, profitability, revenue growth, and enterprisewide asset utilization, using the Governance Arrangements Matrix.

Chapter 6 discusses how enterprises can use the Governance Design Framework to design and assess governance. This chapter identifies the range of strategic objectives enterprises pursue, such as specific value disciplines, and describes how enterprises harmonize individual IT decisions and how governance changes to reflect strategic business changes. The chapter also discusses how governance addresses dueling requirements for business unit autonomy and synergy. The State Street Corporation case study provides an example of how new strategic objectives lead to a new governance approach.

Chapter 7 focuses on the unique environments of not-for-profit and government enterprises. Although research findings reported in this book generally apply to both for-profit and not-for-profit enterprises, the not-for-profit sector has unique objectives that necessarily affect governance. We explore those issues through case studies of the Metropolitan Police Service–Scotland Yard and UNICEF.

Chapter 8 wraps up the key points of the book with a list of symptoms of poor governance that would warrant urgent action. We follow with a list of ten management principles for effective IT governance. We also discuss how incentives and reward systems affect IT governance design and performance.

2

Five Key IT Decisions:
Making IT a Strategic Asset

The significant problems we face cannot be solved
by the same level of thinking that created them.

—*Albert Einstein*

THE DIFFERENCE between management and governance is like
the difference between a soccer team running harder and practicing
longer and the team stepping back to analyze its composition and
game strategy. An analysis may reveal that the team needs to add
coaches or allocate different decision-making responsibilities among
the team leaders. Similarly, extracting greater value from IT is rarely
a matter of just working harder or longer. Achieving more value
may require involving different people in IT decisions, designing
new ways of making IT-related decisions, or developing new techniques for implementing IT decisions. Managers make hundreds of
decisions per week—some after careful analysis and others as part
of the daily frenetic activity. Governance design and analysis requires stepping back from day-to-day decision making, taking Einstein's advice and focusing on identifying the fundamental decisions to be made and who is best positioned to make them.

As noted in chapter 1, effective governance addresses three
questions:

- What decisions must be made?
- Who should make these decisions?
- How will we make and monitor these decisions?

☞ This chapter focuses on the first question: What decisions? After reviewing the five decisions that must be made, we discuss the governance issues that enterprises face—not to describe how to make each decision but to identify the dimensions of these decisions and the key issues to consider when designing IT governance.[1] As you read this chapter, ask yourself, Who is making each of these decisions in my enterprise, and how qualified are they to do so? Also ask, How are we measuring and monitoring decision-making performance and business value?

What Decisions Must Be Made?

Every enterprise must address five interrelated IT decisions: IT principles, IT architecture, IT infrastructure, business application needs, and IT investment and prioritization. Figure 2-1 arranges these decisions to emphasize their critical interconnections. Principles decisions sit atop the framework because decisions on IT principles—by clarifying enterprise objectives for IT—establish the direction for all other decisions. If principles are not clear, it is unlikely that the other decisions will coalesce meaningfully. IT architecture decisions translate IT principles into requirements for integration and standardization and then delineate a technical road map for providing needed capabilities. IT investment and prioritization decisions marshal resources to convert principles into systems.

Decisions on infrastructure and applications can flow "top down" from the principles, the architecture, and the investment criteria. In that case, the infrastructure creates needed IT capabilities, and applications leverage the capabilities. Just as often, business needs and opportunities identify the need for IT applications, which "bubble up" to create new infrastructure requirements. Ultimately, investment decisions select and fund infrastructure and application initiatives, which implement an architecture designed to embody IT principles—and ultimately business principles.

FIGURE 2-1

Key IT Governance Decisions

IT principles decisions		
High-level statements about how IT is used in the business		
IT architecture decisions	**IT infrastructure decisions**	**IT investment and prioritization decisions**
Organizing logic for data, applications, and infrastructure captured in a set of policies, relationships, and technical choices to achieve desired business and technical standardization and integration	Centrally coordinated, shared IT services that provide the foundation for the enterprise's IT capability	Decisions about how much and where to invest in IT, including project approvals and justification techniques
	Business applications needs	
	Specifying the business need for purchased or internally developed IT applications	

© 2003 MIT Sloan School Center for Information Systems Research (CISR). Used with permission.

Decision 1: IT Principles

Enterprises with clarity and focus generally produce better results in any endeavor. Gaining above-industry-average business value from IT is no exception. Study after study demonstrates that enterprises achieving superior business value from IT have a small number of clearly articulated IT principles.[2] IT principles are a related set of high-level statements about how IT is used in the business. Once articulated, IT principles become part of the enterprise's management lexicon and can be discussed, debated, supported, overturned, and evolved. MeadWestvaco, a large manufacturing firm that produces paper, packaging, consumer and office products, and specialty chemicals, provides an example of how a firm derived its IT principles by articulating its expectations for IT to support business strategy.[3]

To compete effectively in its target markets, MeadWestvaco implemented an enterprise resource planning (ERP) system to create efficiencies and a seamless supply chain. Following the ERP implementation, MeadWestvaco management wanted to preserve the efficiencies of the firm's more standardized business processes but at the same time support valuable diversity among business units. Toward these objectives, management listed a number of business principles:

1. Leverage economies of scale
2. Standardize processes and technologies wherever appropriate

SOA 3. Common tools and business diversity (one ERP system)
4. Cost control and operational efficiency
5. Alignment and responsiveness to negotiated business requirements

These business principles led to the following set of IT principles (which MeadWestvaco refers to as its IT governance goals):

1. Benchmarked lowest total cost of ownership
2. Architectural integrity
3. Consistent, flexible infrastructure
4. Rapid deployment of new applications
5. Measured, improving, and communicated value and responsiveness

The hallmark of an effective set of IT principles is a clear trail of evidence from the business to the IT management principles. For MeadWestvaco, architectural integrity (IT principle 2) provides for both standardized processes and technologies (business principle 2) and cost control and operational efficiency (business principle 4); rapid deployment of new applications (IT principle 4) promotes alignment and responsiveness to negotiated business requirements (business principle 5); a consistent, flexible infrastructure (IT principle 3) should enable all five business principles. Combined, MeadWestvaco's business and IT principles provide clear direction for using IT to enable business strategy.

IT principles can also be used as a tool for educating executives about technology strategy and investment decisions. MetLife created a set of seven IT principles to "establish a shared understanding of strategic IT direction and to guide tactical decisions."[4] MetLife's IT principles communicate MetLife's IT values and goals. The principles establish an enterprise position that "can be translated into specific policies, standards and guidelines":

1. Enable the business.
2. Ensure information integrity.
3. Create a common customer view.
4. Promote consistent architecture.
· 5. Utilize industry standards.
6. Reuse before buy; buy before build.
7. Manage IT as an investment. *ROI*

The chief technology officer at MetLife led a team to develop these principles to help the growing number of non-IT managers who needed to make IT-based decisions. The principles reflect the importance of knowledge-sharing across the enterprise, and they have led to increased awareness of how business value is achieved from IT. Each principle is further articulated. For example, for principle 7 about investment, "MetLife will manage IT and associated processes as an investment portfolio, adopting new solutions when cost effective and retiring existing technology that is no longer cost effective or risk acceptable." In the booklet used to articulate these principles and educate managers, each principle is supported by a rationale and a set of implications. For example, the implications for principle 7 include "organizational responsibilities for reviewing, managing, and maintaining the portfolio must be clearly defined" and "a dynamic change management process . . . includes the following stages: emerging, adopted/standard, rejected, exception, retired/sunset, and grandfathered."

IT principles should define desirable behavior for both IT professionals and IT users. For example, at MetLife, systems developers and their business partners learn from principle 6 that MetLife intends to reuse existing IT capabilities rather than buy new system components. Developers understand that proposing to purchase a system with capability similar to an existing system will demand a strong justification. Business users learn to accept that their technology choices are limited.

In addition to IT principles clarifying desirable behaviors, MetLife and MeadWestvaco have specific principles guiding management choices. These principles are specific to individual firm strategies. We suggest that detailed IT principles should clarify at least three expectations for IT in an enterprise:

1. What is the enterprise's desired operating model?
2. How will IT support the desired operating model?
3. How will IT be funded?

The first two questions specify how an enterprise develops and delivers products and services and clarify the parameters for future infrastructure and applications decisions. Answers to these questions evolve to reflect organizational learning and new business strategies. The third question determines the broad criteria for IT investment. Specifically, IT investments can be funded centrally or within business units, or some combination of the two approaches can be applied. The funding model specifies whether enterprise-wide priorities or business unit priorities take precedence in investment decisions.

In our experience, few enterprises provide this kind of clarity through their IT principles. Given that principles provide the direction for all IT decisions, equivocating on principles limits the efficacy of the other four decisions.

Decision 2: IT Architecture

By clarifying how IT supports business principles, IT principles state—implicitly or explicitly—the requirements for process standardization and integration in an enterprise. The IT architecture is *the organizing logic for data, applications, and infrastructure, captured in a set of policies, relationships, and technical choices to achieve desired business and technical standardization and integration.* By providing a road map for infrastructure and applications (and consequently investment decisions), architecture decisions are pivotal to effective IT management and use.

Enterprises need an organizing logic for data, applications, and infrastructure because integration and standardization shape IT capabilities. Process integration allows multiple business units to provide a single face to a customer or to move seamlessly from one function (for example, sales) to another (for example, service). The key to process integration from a technology perspective is data standardization—providing a single definition and a single set of characteristics to be captured with a data element. As standardized data are made available, business owners can effectively integrate their processes. Thus, the architectural requirement is data standardization—no easy task. Data standardization must be planned. This capability never happens by accident.

Process standardization is very different from process integration. The key to process standardization is discipline—adherence to a single, consistent way of doing things. Process standardization provides predictability and efficiency, like the process of cooking hamburgers at McDonald's. For knowledge work, process standardization requires that all individuals performing the process use the same system. Like data standardization, process standardization never happens by accident—it must be planned and explicitly implemented by explaining and demonstrating the value over and over again.

Process and data standardization are the defining characteristics of enterprise architecture. Some enterprises need a great deal of both process and data standardization. More diversified businesses may have much less need for standardization across organizational entities. These more diversified enterprises may nonetheless benefit from technical standardization. Technical standardization facilitates common objectives such as cost-effective processing, negotiated vendor agreements, and enterprisewide security. Choices about technical, data, and process standardization strongly influence IT architecture design.

MetLife's IT principles specify the need for a common customer view—a data standardization requirement. In addition, MetLife wants to ensure information integrity; use industry standards; and reuse before buy, buy before build. These principles determined MetLife's requirements for integration and standardization, forming the basis for MetLife's enterprise architecture. A simplified version of the enterprise architecture is shown in figure 2-2.

Because a common customer view is the key standardization requirement listed in MetLife's IT principles, data is at the center of its enterprise architecture. As an outgrowth of several large mergers,

FIGURE 2-2

MetLife's Enterprise Architecture

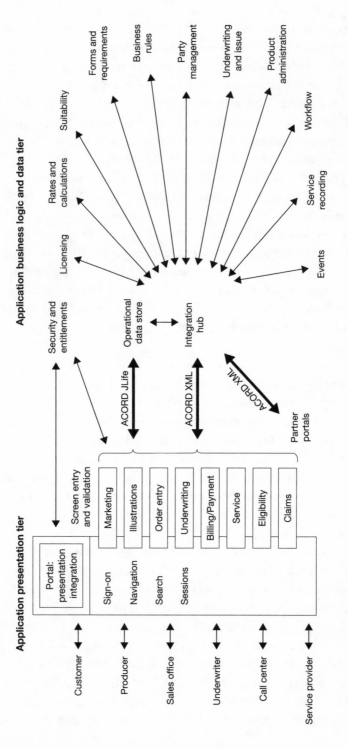

most of MetLife's data is locked into IT applications. The integration hub pictured in the enterprise architecture provides centralized access to data embedded in legacy applications. Together the centralized data and the integration engine provide the common customer view prescribed by the IT principles. Stakeholders will gain access to the data—typically the outputs of applications—using a standardized portal architecture, shown on the left side of the diagram.

MetLife's IT architects use this drawing to communicate with senior managers and business partners the underlying logic for IT development at MetLife. The enterprise architecture guides new application development by explaining how IT will deliver on the firm's IT principles. For example, MetLife's enterprise architecture embodies principles of reuse in its portal architecture—every application will apply the same standards for output to stakeholders. In addition to providing a common customer view, the centralized data stores and integration engine enhance information integrity by reducing redundancy. Thus, the enterprise architecture translates IT principles into a clear vision of how IT will enable business objectives.

Enterprise architectures capture the organizing logic in technical choices and policies. MetLife's enterprise architecture specifies only one high-level technical choice (an industry standard)—ACORD standards for data formats.[5] Most technical choices need not be conveyed to senior managers. They will be elaborated at lower levels of the architecture. MetLife's enterprise architecture elaborates an important policy—sign-on, navigation, and related concerns will be embedded in the portal rather than in applications. This policy has important implications for how new applications will be linked to existing applications.

A critical policy articulated by a high-level architecture is where the shared infrastructure stops and applications begin. The MetLife architecture shows that all applications share the channels, portal, data stores, and integration engine. The presentation and business logic applications are thus distinguished from infrastructure. Communicating where infrastructure stops and applications begin simplifies future infrastructure and applications decisions and promotes shared understanding of IT capabilities in the enterprise.

An enterprise architecture defines data and infrastructure as a stable platform supporting faster-changing applications. Business needs change constantly, so enterprises must build flexibility into their architectures. But applications need a base on which to build. Shared infrastructure and data provide the base. At MetLife the shared customer data and single-portal interface will support future applications without limiting the firm's ability to offer related services or seek new markets. Many manufacturing firms, in contrast, implement ERPs, which establish a set of standardized manufacturing and supply chain processes as the base for future applications. As long as an enterprise does not change its fundamental mission, the infrastructure defined by its enterprise architecture should support its business applications. The distinction between infrastructure and applications thus allows enterprises to leverage economies of scale while retaining flexibility to respond to change.

Currently, most enterprise architectures specify infrastructure, data, and applications. Increasingly, architectures will specify components. Components take an enterprise's applications and infrastructure and turn them into specified, reliable, and modular services. For example, an insurance company might have an underwriting component servicing multiple applications, while a manufacturing firm might develop a pricing service for multiple applications. Component architectures provide another layer of standardization, helping enterprises achieve business objectives for efficiency, economies of scale, and reuse. Early components tend to be enterprisewide infrastructure services, like MetLife's single sign-on. Over time, enterprises will identify the shared, recurring application needs of their processes and create components available to all business units.

The ability to design and build a component-based architecture will grow out of an enterprise's experience with specifying and then implementing technical, data, and process standards. Some enterprises are moving rapidly toward component-based architectures; others have barely begun the journey.

Decision 3: IT Infrastructure

IT infrastructure is the foundation of planned IT capability (both technical and human) available throughout the business as shared and reliable services and used by multiple applications.[6] Foresight in establishing the right infrastructure at the right time enables rapid implementation of future electronically enabled business initiatives as well as consolidation and cost reduction of current business processes. Overinvesting in infrastructure—or worse, implementing the wrong infrastructure—results in wasted resources, delays, and system incompatibilities with business partners. However, underinvesting in infrastructure results in rushed implementations to meet business deadlines, islands of automation meeting local needs without integration across the enterprise, and limited sharing of resources, information, and expertise. Thus, the focus and timing of infrastructure initiatives can have a significant impact on the enterprise's performance.

In the typical enterprise, infrastructure accounts for about 55 percent of the total IT investment. Figure 2-3 shows the various elements of IT infrastructure. At the base of figure 2-3 are the technology components, such as computers, printers, database software packages, operating systems, and scanners. These devices are commodities and readily available in the marketplace. The technology components are converted into useful shared services by a human IT infrastructure composed of knowledge, skills, standards, and experience.

An enterprise's infrastructure services often include telecommunication network services, provision and management of large-scale computing (such as servers or mainframes), management of shared customer databases, research and development expertise aimed at identifying the usefulness of emerging technologies to the business, and an enterprisewide intranet. These services can be provided internally or by outsourcers such as IBM Global Services, Accenture, and Hewlett-Packard. An enterprise's internal infrastructure often links to external industry infrastructures such as bank payments systems and to public infrastructures such as the Internet and telecommunications networks.

The services notion of IT infrastructure is very powerful, as managers can more readily value a service than a technical component such as a server or software package. In addition, the service of providing a fully maintained laptop computer with access to all of the enterprise's systems and the Internet can be specified, measured, and controlled in a service-level agreement. Perhaps most

FIGURE 2-3

IT Infrastructure as a Centrally Coordinated Set of Shared and Reliable Services

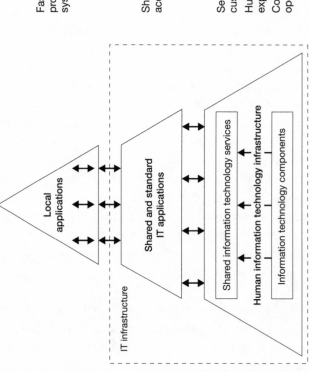

Fast-changing local business applications such as insurance claim processing, Web bank loan applications, customer complaints support system, phone order support systems

Shared and standard applications that change less regularly, such as accounting, budgeting, human resource management

Services that are stable over time, such as management of shared customer databases, PC/LAN access

Human infrastructure of knowledge, skills, policies, standards, and experience binds components

Commodities such as computers, printers, routers, database software, operating systems, credit card swipers

Source: Peter Weill and Marianne Broadbent, *Leveraging the New Infrastructure: How Market Leaders Capitalize on IT* (Boston: Harvard Business School Press, 1998).

importantly, managers can price services in the marketplace for comparison.

An increasing number of enterprises have an additional layer of standard applications used by all business units. We refer to these shared and standard applications as infrastructure applications. They include enterprise systems such as ERPs, customer relationship management systems (CRMs), and supply chain management systems (SCMs) as well as functional systems supporting shared services such as accounting, human resource management, and budgeting. Infrastructure applications are more stable, changing less with evolving business strategies than do the local applications. The local applications, which sit atop the infrastructure, represent the remainder of an enterprise's IT portfolio. These applications change frequently—often every time there is a new product or service feature or when implementing strategic experiments in response to sensing a market opportunity.

An integrated IT infrastructure combines all the enterprise's shared IT capability into a platform for electronically conducted business. An integrated infrastructure has ten capability clusters (figure 2-4) with sets of services in each cluster.[7]

An integrated infrastructure provides capability to the enterprise's local IT applications, depicted by the four short rods near the top of the infrastructure in figure 2-4. The infrastructure connects externally to business partners via agreed-upon standards, as illustrated at the bottom of figure 2-4. Business partners obtain electronic access via *integrated electronic channels.* Usually the channels include all or some of a physical outlet (for example, a store or branch with a point-of-sale device), the Web, e-mail, physical mail (scanned), interactive voice response, wireless devices such as cell phones, kiosks, and a direct point-to-point connection (a private network, for example). In most cases, enterprises try to make their applications "channel independent," meaning that consistent and up-to-date data are available regardless of how a customer makes contact.

All communications pass through a *security and risk* capability, which provides security through technologies (for example, firewalls and encryption) and policies (remote access, use of passwords, and so on), as well as disaster planning and recovery. The

FIGURE 2-4

IT Infrastructure Services in Ten Clusters

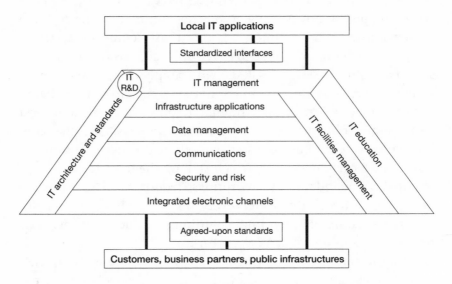

Source: Peter Weill, Mani Subramani, and Marianne Broadbent, "Building IT Infrastructure for Strategic Agility," *MIT Sloan Management Review* 44, no. 1 (Fall 2002): 57–65.

electronic interactions within the enterprise and with customers and partners occur via the set of *communications* services including broadband, intranet, and workstation networks. *Data management* encompasses database management, middleware management, and data exchange translations. Many IT units are isolating in master files enterprisewide data on customers, products, and employees so that critical data elements are accessible to individuals and applications as needed.

Closely aligned with data management are the enterprisewide *infrastructure applications* that capture, update, and access enterprise data. Operations and management of these applications constitutes another set of infrastructure services. *IT facilities management* spans the physical infrastructure layers described so far, providing services such as large-scale processing, server farms, and a common systems development environment.

The six preceding infrastructure capability clusters support the physical elements of infrastructure. The remaining four clusters are the management-oriented infrastructure capabilities. The *IT management* services coordinate the integrated enterprise infrastructure and manage relationships with the business units. Typically the management services include IS planning, project management, service-level agreements, and negotiations with vendors and outsourcers. The *IT architecture and standards* infrastructure services provide the migration plan for the detailed technical standards underlying the enterprise architecture. Architecture services include monitoring the effectiveness of the enterprise's standards and identifying when those standards are outdated or too costly to support. *IT education and training* includes training in the use of the enterprise's specific technologies and systems as well as general management education about how to envision, invest in, and use IT to create business value. *IT research and development* includes the enterprise's efforts in looking for new ways to use IT to create business value and to assess new technologies. R&D sits at the intersection of IT management and IT architecture services because R&D links development of standards to the needs of the business. Infrastructure capability is difficult to create because it is a complex fusion of technology and human assets. These capabilities require long lead times to develop and can therefore be a source of competitive advantage. Enterprises with greater infrastructure capability have faster times to market, higher growth rates, and more sales from new products but lower short-term profitability. In that sense, building a strong infrastructure is like purchasing an option.[8] If leveraged effectively through the implementation of new business applications, infrastructure can generate improved financial performance; otherwise, it will prove an unnecessary cost.

A superior IT infrastructure contains an integrated set of services in each of the ten capability clusters consistent with the enterprise's strategic direction. Enterprises that manage infrastructure as an asset and invest carefully each and every year typically perform better than enterprises that take a "big bang" approach to IT infrastructure. UPS, for example, has an infrastructure renewal strategy to balance infrastructure investment over time:

On the infrastructure I know that we must bite this off and do some each year. You can put things off, but eventually you're going to get caught. So I try to make sure funds are available to refresh continually, which is not a real popular thing.

—*Ken Lacy, CIO, UPS*

Individual IT infrastructure services can be located at an enterprisewide or business unit level. Many enterprises are shifting business unit infrastructure capability to enterprise level to achieve business objectives such as a single point of customer contact or economies of scale. Determining where to locate infrastructure services, how to price services, when to update services, and whether to outsource services are key infrastructure decisions. Getting infrastructure right means providing cost-effective services that position the enterprise for rapid adoption of new business applications.

Decision 4: Business Applications Needs

Although all five IT decisions are concerned with the business value of IT, it is decisions about specific business needs that directly generate value. Even as Schwab, Amazon.com, Cisco, and others demonstrate the potential benefits of strategic IT applications, spectacular failures of large systems implementations at companies like Hershey, Whirlpool, and Allied Waste serve as reminders that defining and delivering value through business applications remains a significant organizational challenge.[9]

Identification of business needs for IT applications often has two conflicting objectives—creativity and discipline. Creativity is about identifying new and more effective ways to deliver customer value using IT. Creativity involves identifying business applications that support strategic business objectives and facilitate business experiments. Discipline is about architectural integrity—ensuring that applications leverage and build out the enterprise architecture rather than undermine architectural principles. Discipline is also about focus—committing the necessary resources to achieve project and business goals. We will discuss the management decisions that lead to creative, disciplined business applications.

Fostering Creative Solutions

Finite resources—including IT skills, management attention, and business unit personnel—demand that new IT applications not only meet a minimum ROI test; they must contribute strategic value to the enterprise. At most enterprises, strategic applications focus on core processes. In large enterprises, core processes often span multiple functions and business units. For example, Partners Healthcare, a Boston-based umbrella organization of major hospitals and local clinics, is developing a Longitudinal Medical Record (LMR) system. Introduced in 1998, the LMR supports Partners' dual missions of medical research and practice. LMR requires physicians to enter electronically, in a standard format, all diagnosis and treatment information so the system can highlight key facts for physicians examining the patient in the future. The device also stores data on treatments and outcomes to facilitate research and inform future practice. The LMR is a strategic system for Partners.

Similarly, manufacturing firms continue to invest in ERPs to enable operating efficiencies and seamless supply chains. Financial services firms are implementing customer relationship management systems to enable a single view of the customer. Retail firms are integrating back-end processes to support their online stores and point-of-sale systems. These systems are all intended to fundamentally improve enterprises' business processes. Value results from their ability to change how the enterprise does business. Decisions about business application needs involve identifying core processes and determining what process and system changes can deliver significant benefits to the enterprise. Successful strategic system implementations demand business leaders with the vision to define and implement the change.

In addition to reinforcing the enterprise's core processes, decisions about business application needs are important for responding to market changes. Enterprises need a constant flow of experiments to seize new market opportunities and avoid obsolescence. Some experiments will develop into strategic systems; others will fold quickly. The flow of experiments generates creative energy and continually alerts managers to changing market conditions so that they can identify the next big thing.

The development of UPS's DIAD, the device that collects electronic signatures, is an example of how experiments can evolve into strategic systems. The initial objective of the DIAD was simply to provide a printed delivery record to replace the driver's handwritten delivery record. Version 1 of the DIAD delivered the intended functionality, but its value was limited because, although it delivered the printed record, it slowed the delivery process. However, the experiment revealed the potential of the DIAD to save drivers time and collect real-time data for other customer services. The DIAD ultimately saved each of more than fifty thousand UPS drivers about a half hour at the end of the day by accumulating information on each driver's deliveries. Subsequent versions of the DIAD tied into the continuously improving UPS tracking systems, eventually making the device a strategic platform for new customer services.

Identifying business experiments that have the potential to become strategically important may be more an art than a science. Enterprises such as Fidelity have created incubators and usability labs to test new technologies and to pilot new concepts. Since some experiments will necessarily fail, enterprises need approaches to identifying, funding, and assessing experiments so that they can sustain a constant flow of creative ideas but back out of unsuccessful projects before they have invested large amounts of money.

Disciplined Execution

Creative solutions can generate interesting technical challenges, particularly when enterprises purchase vendor packages intended to meet their needs. Traditionally, enterprises—and their IT units—were reluctant to establish technical standards that might limit business functionality. Increasingly, however, managers have found that 80 percent solutions can offer significant business value while reducing technical risks and project costs. Successful enterprises consistently demonstrate a willingness to sacrifice functionality to sustain architectural integrity. The CIO at MeadWestvaco described the model: "The role of my chief technology officer is to, in effect, oversee the architecture and to ensure that the architecture over time evolves to achieve our desired results. The default condition is you must choose applications that fit within the context of our architecture. If it's a compelling application, go find one that works with this. We'll have a conversation if you can't find one."

Of course, every enterprise encounters strategic business opportunities that challenge the architecture. Often the challenge helps to establish when an architectural design or technical standard has become outdated. Thus decision makers must recognize when architecture sensibly limits business application choices and when new business opportunities should lead to new architectures or changes in technology standards.

Sustaining architectural integrity, however, is not just a matter of monitoring the adoption of technical standards by individual projects. Large enterprises undertake hundreds of projects simultaneously. An enterprise's project portfolio invariably has multiple projects with similar or overlapping requirements. For example, a number of business units might simultaneously develop applications with requirements for tracking customer interactions, for managing the flow of documents associated with a process, or for computer telephony integration (the ability of a call center representative to view a Web page in use by a customer). The architecture of an enterprise may not address these new capabilities, so a set of applications can result in multiple disparate solutions to the same problem. Most firms have struggled to manage overlapping system requirements, and the net effect has been redundant capabilities, wasted resources, and slow time to market.

Sustaining architectural integrity thus demands coordinating the architectural demands of an enterprise's project portfolio. USAA, a diversified financial services firm, has designed this coordination responsibility into its Enterprise Business Operations unit, which reports to the CEO. This unit works with IT architects to identify common needs across the firm's several hundred business unit and enterprisewide projects. Each IT architect accepts responsibility for defining architecture components that can be shared by multiple projects. The enterprise architecture unit within IT commits to specifying standard products to address new capabilities by a specified date. Projects are then scheduled based on availability of needed infrastructure and business process components.

Specifying the functionality and architectural requirements of an IT project is only the first step in generating value from IT.

Business value results from the organizational changes that IT enables. Thus business application decisions also involve assigning accountability for the organizational change associated with an IT project. At Partners, for example, physicians "owning" responsibility for generating value from the Longitudinal Medical Record invest personal resources to use the system, provide constant feedback on its features, and encourage colleagues to sign on to the project.

The organizational changes associated with many systems are wrenching. They not only require that individuals change their habits, they typically require a new understanding of organizational processes. Changing compensation structures is often a requirement for motivating new behavior, but changing compensation is not enough. Employees implementing change must understand the new processes. They may need both training and structural support. Change management is a difficult challenge in environments where change is constant. New systems and processes may confuse rather than support employees regardless of their commitment to organizational objectives. Key processes in enterprises are often receiving multiple "fixes" at one time. To ensure that an enterprise and its people can absorb ongoing change, many enterprises have organized their projects into a finite set of programs. Typically, programs consist of all projects related to a major process initiative such as customer relations, product development, or financial management. Programs are headed by high-level managers who coordinate the system features, timing, training, and change management requirements of each project. Program managers are accountable for ensuring that new systems have the intended combined effect on the enterprise and that resources are used effectively.

Business application needs decisions require reconciling complex change and opposing organizational forces. Managers responsible for defining requirements must distinguish core process requirements from nonessentials and know when to live within architectural constraints. They must design experiments knowing that actual benefits could be different from anticipated benefits—or if there are no benefits, they must pull the plug. Most importantly, they must know how to design organizational change and then make it happen. Business application needs decisions require creative thinkers and disciplined project managers and are probably the least mature of the five IT decisions.

Decision 5: IT Investment and Prioritization

A leader of a $15 billion retail enterprise told us, "IT investments are like any other investment. You must make a decent return or you go bust. It just happens faster with IT!" The IT investment decision is often the most visible and controversial of the five key IT decisions. Some projects are approved, others are bounced, and the rest enter the organizational equivalent of suspended animation with the dreaded request from the decision makers to "redo the business case" or "provide more information." Enterprises that get superior value from IT focus their investments on their strategic priorities, cognizant of the distinction between "must have" and "nice to have" IT capabilities.

IT investment decisions address three dilemmas: (a) how much to spend, (b) what to spend it on, and (c) how to reconcile the needs of different constituencies. We will discuss each of these dilemmas, noting that IT governance is an invaluable tool for resolving differing views.

How Much to Spend

The IT investment process must determine how much to spend on IT. Given the uncertain returns on IT spending, many executives wonder whether they are spending too much—or perhaps even too little. They often look to industry benchmarks as a way of determining appropriate spending levels. But in the successful companies we have studied, benchmarks are only a starting point. Senior managers focus on the strategic role that IT plays in the organization and establish an enterprisewide funding level that will enable technology to fulfill its objective.

UPS and Federal Express provide a useful example of why benchmarks are only the starting point. Both companies report spending around $1 billion on IT each year, but FedEx, which has annual revenues of around $20 billion, is two thirds the size of UPS. The different spending levels reflect different strategic roles for IT.

The UPS IT strategy, which evolved from industrial engineering roots, focuses on introducing efficiencies into a business that demands consistency and reliability. In contrast, FedEx relies on IT to provide extraordinary responsiveness to unique customer needs. Of course, UPS also uses technology to meet the needs of individual customers, and FedEx uses technology to provide consistent service across customer segments. But the thrust of the two companies' IT and business strategies is different. Both are successful because they have matched their spending levels to their strategies.

How to Allocate IT Dollars: IT Investment Portfolio

As with any investment portfolio, managing the IT portfolio requires providers and consumers to agree on indicators of success. Different strategic contexts lead to enterprises having different levels of IT investment, different IT portfolios, and different indicators of success. We found that enterprises with better returns from IT pay particular attention to these indicators. In these enterprises each year, as part of the investment process, business and IT management agree on the appropriate indicators for the business value of the portfolio.

As a commercial lens on IT investments, many enterprises find it useful to think of an enterprise's IT investments as a portfolio, just as individual investors have portfolios of financial investments.[10] Portfolio management enables decision makers to align their portfolios with enterprise strategy and balance risk and return. Just as personal investment portfolios are reweighted as personal goals change (for example, approaching retirement), IT portfolios are also reweighted as conditions change.

Implementing an IT portfolio management approach requires the dollars for each project or budget line item to be classified into categories reflecting business objectives. Grouping proposed investments by business objective enables management to select projects that shape the portfolio to the enterprise's strategy. Having data on how an enterprise's investments in each category have performed historically helps make more informed future investment decisions—similar to knowing the historical return of bonds versus equities versus property.

One approach to IT portfolio analysis lists four IT asset classes, each supporting a different management objective: strategic (to gain competitive advantage), informational (to provide information), transactional (to process transactions and cut costs), and infrastructure (to provide shared services and integration).[11] Classifying the enterprise's annual investments into these four categories facilitates strategic analysis and raises questions about specific investment decisions. For example, in an economic downturn, do we really want to allocate 40 percent of this year's IT investment to the high-risk, high-return strategic asset class? Instead, should we reweight the portfolio toward the low-risk, solid-return transactional investment asset class? Alternatively, can we afford to have another year of low infrastructure investment?

Growing numbers of enterprises are using IT portfolio approaches as part of their enterprisewide IT investment and prioritization process.[12] These enterprises tailor the definition of the asset classes to fit their specific business and develop metrics to help assess the performance of their IT investments. The IT portfolio concept assists managers in balancing and realigning their investments when the enterprise's strategy or the economic climate changes. Comparisons of portfolios with industry benchmarks facilitate a discussion on how well aligned an IT portfolio is with the strategy and allow managers to make more informed investment decisions relative to the competition. A powerful question to ask is: Can we explain differences between our IT investment portfolio and the industry benchmark by our strategy? If the explanation is credible, the portfolio is a good fit. If the explanation is unconvincing, the IT investment process is failing.

Risks are inherent in any business investment decision, and senior executives are familiar with risk assessment. IT investments can expose firms to four kinds of risk: market, financial, organizational, and technical. Enterprises often have well-developed templates for IT investment proposals that require the articulation of each type of risk. In addition, the portfolio of IT investments carries risk—not unlike the risk of a portfolio of stocks. If well selected, the portfolio of IT investments, like that of individual stocks, can reduce overall risk to the owner.

How to Reconcile Differing Needs—
Aligning IT Investment with Strategic Priorities

Probably the most important attribute of a successful IT investment process is ensuring that the enterprise's IT spending reflects strategic priorities. Investment processes must reconcile the demands of individual business units as well as demands to meet enterprisewide needs. Many enterprises value the independence of their business units and support their efforts to invest in IT according to business unit strategy. Most enterprises also emphasize the importance of enterprisewide efficiencies and even integration. Enterprises that attempt to persuade independent business units to fund shared infrastructure are likely to experience resistance. Instead, business leaders must articulate the enterprisewide objectives of shared infrastructure and provide appropriate incentives for business unit leaders to sacrifice business unit needs in favor of enterprisewide needs.

The IT investment decision-making process can be used to implement strategic change as illustrated at State Street Corporation.[13] Traditionally, IT investments at State Street involved some relatively small funding of central services. Each business then independently assigned additional funding based on business priorities. A disadvantage of this approach is that many similar initiatives could be funded in different businesses. Recognizing this limitation, State Street's senior leadership moved to enterprisewide IT budget management to achieve a better return on IT investment.

In 2001, State Street's Information Technology Executive Committee (ITEC) assumed responsibility for combining IT investment needs of individual businesses into an enterprisewide IT budget. The executives serving on the ITEC included the COO, the Chief Asset Officer (CAO), the CIO, and senior executives responsible for State Street's various business units. In the fall, the leaders of each business and the CIO identified key IT business and infrastructure projects for the coming year and classified them according to their contribution to the corporate growth targets and to the strategy of each business. The result of this analysis created an initial portfolio of all IT projects recommended for the coming year. The ITEC then negotiated to create the optimal enterprisewide IT portfolio that

met the corporate growth targets within the operating budget allocated to IT. A member of the CIO's staff identified several advantages of using the ITEC for budgeting compared with earlier IT investment committees. "The negotiation of an enterprisewide IT
budget encourages value in the use of IT rather than focusing on
the needs of individual businesses. The business executives do not
always appreciate the impact of enterprisewide infrastructure investment. By combining discussion of infrastructure investment
with these business initiatives they understand the value of making
that investment in enterprisewide infrastructure because they're all
going to share in its use."

IT investment and prioritization puts money to work. If senior
management has not clarified or communicated enterprise strategy
or if strategy changes so frequently that it isn't worth investing in
today's strategy, the IT investment process will break down. No
framework or analysis can substitute for clear strategic direction.
When the investment committee understands its business objectives, it can invest IT dollars to generate a significant return.

The five IT decisions we've discussed in this chapter cannot be
isolated from one another. If governance is well designed, the decisions reinforce one another ensuring strategic objectives are successfully addressed. In the next section, we describe an IT-enabled
transformation at Delta Air Lines. This case study provides an example of how one firm designed governance to consider the interactions of all five IT decisions.

Case Study:
Making IT Decisions at Delta Air Lines

When Leo Mullin became CEO of Delta Air Lines in 1997, he took
over the third largest U.S. airline in terms of revenues and passen-
ger miles and the largest U.S. airline in terms of number of departures and passengers enplaned. Delta had 84,000 employees fly-
ing approximately 117 million customers to 45 states within the
United States and 44 cities in 28 countries throughout the world.[14]

Mullin found that Delta's IT capability, which had been outsourced in the early 1990s, was functionally oriented. Each of the
firm's approximately seventeen functional units was developing

and supporting systems in isolation from the rest of the firm. Mullin asked Charlie Feld, former CIO at Frito-Lay and Burlington Northern, to assess the IT capability at Delta. Feld reported that people at Delta could not obtain basic information from their systems. Given the nature of the airline business, the functional orientation of the firm's information systems was limiting the ability of employees to do their jobs. When a flight was delayed or changed for any reason, customer-facing employees could not always determine the whereabouts of planes, passengers, or bags. According to Feld:

> The reason they didn't know where anything was is that the systems infrastructure was so disconnected. There were thirty-five customer databases, dozens of flight databases. If a gate changed, they wouldn't know. The baggage handler would be standing there at the old gate waiting for the plane to show up. The passengers would be standing in the concourse looking at the displays, and they would have the wrong gate. You'd go into the Crown Room and there would be a different gate. And the poor gate agent was standing there and they didn't have any idea, because it was so disconnected from the information in real time. The physical event of a gate change was not reflected in the electronic system in a consistent, timely way.

Faced with imminent Y2K issues, Mullin persuaded Feld to take on the role of CIO at Delta until January 1, 2000. Rather than simply fix the technology to survive Y2K, Mullin and Feld committed to restoring IT as a strategic tool at Delta. They engaged a small team of senior executives—including the chief financial officer, the executive vice president of customer service, and the head of airline operations—to lead an organizational transformation built around the assumption of real-time information.

The executive team, which came to be known as the IT Board, took responsibility for defining the role of IT in the firm. They stated four principles:

- Adopt a process view of the firm.
- Build a corporate infrastructure to support cross-functional processes.

- Build and leverage a standardized environment.
- Focus on the customer.

Consistent with these principles, Feld worked with the Board to create an enterprise architecture (figure 2-5). First, the IT Board specified the firm's core processes: (1) customer experience, (2) airline operations, (3) digital dashboard for revenue management, and (4) wired workforce for administrative functions. Recognizing that they could not develop and implement IT support for all four core processes at one time, the Board chose to fix flight operations and customer experience, the two processes that ran on the firm's outdated airport-based technologies.

Management defined the information requirements for these two core processes in terms of nine databases: location, schedule, flight, maintenance, equipment, employee, aircraft, customer, and ticket. A key component of the architecture was the Delta Nervous System (DNS), a middleware environment that captured and disseminated data to employees and applications. The DNS used a "publish and subscribe" approach—applications subscribe to be notified whenever certain data items change so that employees always have current data, and applications respond to changes as needed. Vicky Escarra, Executive Vice President for Customer Service, explained:

> The whole notion around the Delta Nervous System is if we had a change in our operations control center—let's say a canceled flight—with one or two entries, that information would be pushed into all of the operating and customer groups without an individual or twenty-five individuals having to actually access or send that information. The information would come to the reservations call centers; it would go to the airports, . . . the Crown Room Clubs, . . . [and] customer PDAs, cell phones, beepers, even customers' laptops, giving them the information around the fact that "Flight 222 from Washington to Atlanta has canceled, and we've rebooked you on Flight 223 that leaves two hours from now."

The enterprise architecture in figure 2-5 reflected the core processes, the data driving those core processes, and the channels delivering data to employees, customers, and business partners.

FIGURE 2-5

Delta's Enterprise Architecture

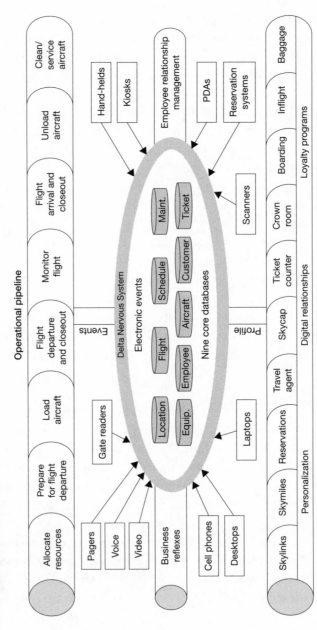

Source: Jeanne W. Ross, "E-Business at Delta Air Lines: Extracting Value from a Multi-Faceted Approach," working paper 317, MIT Sloan School Center for Information Systems Research, Cambridge, MA, August 2001.

From this architecture, IT leaders could develop infrastructure requirements. The key infrastructure requirement was highly centralized, standardized, secure data accessible to a broad set of stakeholders through a wide variety of channels. Delta IT leaders designed channel management, communication, data, and security services to meet these requirements.

Although the enterprise architecture did not detail the applications required to support the core processes, it identified the key activities associated with both the customer experience and flight operations. The IT Board established priorities for application development projects.

The focus on a few projects enabled the enterprise to address Y2K concerns and fulfill their priorities for customer service and reliable operations. Senior Vice President and Chief Development Officer Keith Halbert noted that the IT Board's leadership enabled Delta to avert the Y2K crisis and incrementally address core process improvements: "Through their teaching and through their reinforcement in their staff meetings and through their direction in terms of prioritization, and more importantly, when their teams came through the back door to try to change their priorities, their reinforcement of the plan really made a big difference."

The enterprise architecture was only partly built out by January 1, 2000, but it was sufficient for surviving the Y2K transition. CEO Mullin credited Delta's infrastructure transformation with helping the firm develop strong financials (relative to its competitors). In a few years, Delta moved from last to first on key industry measures such as on-time departures and fewest customer complaints. The IT Board became a permanent fixture, responsible for specifying IT priorities. The Board invested simultaneously in infrastructure and applications. Infrastructure investments supported the cross-functional requirements of the core processes and provided a foundation for future applications. Delta continues to invest in the Delta Nervous System, which has proved a flexible platform for quickly implementing new strategic initiatives such as printing boarding passes at home and proactively rerouting passengers from delayed flights. Delta's success resulted, in part, from a clear strategic vision and from having the right people involved in each of the five key IT decisions.

Linking the Five IT Decisions

The Delta experience underscores the interrelationships of the five key IT decisions. Each of the five decisions requires individual attention, but none of them can be made in isolation. No wonder IT governance is hard! But while all decisions require management attention, a clearly articulated governance approach distributes the decision-making process to persons best positioned to understand the requirements—and their implications. In addition, formalizing input to decisions through governance processes ensures critical communication and feedback on these key IT decisions.

As a chapter summary and primer for governance design, we composed a series of questions representative of each IT decision (figure 2-6). Effectively answering these and similar questions is the job of the people tasked with making the decisions as designated by the governance design. Do you have the right people making these decisions? Are they well equipped to deal with the tradeoff? In the next chapter we discuss the options enterprises have for allocating both decision rights and input responsibilities for each IT decision.

FIGURE 2-6

Questions Key to Each IT Decision

IT principles	What is the enterprise's operating model?
	What is the role of IT in the business?
	What are IT-desirable behaviors?
	How will IT be funded?
IT architecture	What are the core business processes of the enterprise? How are they related?
	What information drives these core processes? How must the data be integrated?
	What technical capabilities should be standardized enterprise-wide to support IT efficiencies and facilitate process standardization and integration?
	What activities must be standardized enterprisewide to support data integration?
	What technology choices will guide the enterprise's approach to IT initiatives?

IT infrastructure	What infrastructure services are most critical to achieving the enterprise's strategic objectives?
	For each capability cluster, what infrastructure services should be implemented enterprisewide and what are the service-level requirements of those services?
	How should infrastructure services be priced?
	What is the plan for keeping underlying technologies up to date?
	What infrastructure services should be outsourced?
Business application needs	What are the market and business process opportunities for new business applications?
	How are experiments designed to assess whether they are successful?
	How can business needs be addressed within architectural standards? When does a business need justify an exception to standard?
	Who will own the outcomes of each project and institute organizational changes to ensure the value?
IT investment and prioritization	What process changes or enhancements are strategically most important to the enterprise?
	What are the distributions in the current and proposed IT portfolios? Are these portfolios consistent with the enterprise's strategic objectives?
	What is the relative importance of enterprisewide versus business unit investments? Do actual investment practices reflect their relative importance?

3

IT Governance
Archetypes for Allocating
Decision Rights

IN A RECENT SESSION of MIT Sloan School of Management's
"IT for the Non-IT Executive" two-day program, one of the authors
asked the attendees what words they would use to describe their
enterprise's IT governance. Following are some of the answers:

What IT governance?

Anarchy!

Depends on the amount of money involved.

Let me ask my CIO.

The business units make all the strategic decisions.

Joint decision making between the business unit heads and
the central IT group.

Senior management lays down the law.

My IT folks manage those things.

Some of the attendees knew how they governed IT. Others did
not. The entire group was searching for a tool they could apply to
design governance for their enterprise and also use to learn from
other enterprises. Representing and analyzing decision rights is
critical to IT governance. The purpose of this chapter is to provide a

set of archetypes and thus choices for IT decision rights. The chapter uses these archetypes to describe how firms make IT decisions and provides three cases of IT governance in growth-seeking firms.

This chapter explores the question: Who should make governance decisions? We focus on "typical" patterns to examine the variety of choices and rationales driving IT governance arrangements. In chapter 4 we will describe the mechanisms enterprises used to implement governance. In chapter 5 we will explore how top-performing firms govern differently.

To understand how enterprises govern, we describe the governance arrangements of the 256 enterprises we surveyed. These enterprises were large, with an average of eight business units.[1] The average enterprise invested 8 percent of its total expenses in IT and employed 850 IT professionals. Ninety percent of the CIOs who completed our survey had enterprisewide responsibility for IT. Nearly half of the enterprises had highly autonomous business units but designed governance arrangements to create or capitalize on synergies across the business units. Most of the rest of the enterprises had less autonomous business units with significant synergy among their business units.

Archetypes

We use political archetypes (monarchy, feudal, federal, duopoly, anarchy) to describe the combinations of people who have either decision rights or input to IT decisions. One of these six archetypes (figure 3-1) could describe how your enterprise makes one or more of the five key IT decisions or provides input to the decision makers.

Business Monarchy

In a business monarchy, senior business executives make IT decisions affecting the entire enterprise. The IT investment process State Street Corporation introduced in 2001, described in the previous chapter, is a business monarchy in action. At State Street the COO, the CAO, the CIO, and the senior executives leading the various business units make up an executive committee. The CIO participates as an equal partner with the other leaders. The senior busi-

FIGURE 3-1

IT Governance Archetypes

STYLE	WHO HAS DECISION OR INPUT RIGHTS?
Business Monarchy	A group of business executives or individual executives (CxOs). Includes committees of senior business executives (may include CIO). Excludes IT executives acting independently.
IT Monarchy	Individuals or groups of IT executives
Feudal	Business unit leaders, key process owners or their delegates
Federal	C-level executives and business groups (e.g., business units or processes); may also include IT executives as additional participants. Equivalent of the central and state governments working together.
IT Duopoly	IT executives and one other group (e.g., CxO or business unit or process leaders)
Anarchy	Each individual user

© 2003 MIT Sloan School Center for Information Systems Research (CISR). Used with permission.

ness executives (the CxOs or C-level executives) decide as a group. Figure 3-2 lists the distinguishing characteristics of the different governance arrangements and how we classified the enterprises.

Typically, business monarchies rely on input for key decisions from many sources. For example, the IT investment decisions at enterprises such as State Street receive input from (a) the CIO's direct reports, (b) the IT leaders from the business units, (c) the enterprisewide IT budget management process, (d) service-level agreements and chargeback, and (e) an activity-tracking system showing all IT resources and how they are deployed.

IT Monarchy

In an IT monarchy, IT professionals make IT decisions. At UPS, for example, the IT Governance Committee, which consists of senior IT managers, makes the strategic decisions that affect IT architecture. Many other enterprises, including State Street, have an Office of IT Architecture that makes architecture decisions. Enterprises implement IT monarchies in many different ways, often involving IT

FIGURE 3-2

Key Players in IT Governance Archetypes

	C-level executives	Corporate IT and/or business unit IT	Business unit leaders or key business process owners
Business monarchy	✓		
IT monarchy		✓	
Feudal			✓
Federal	✓	✓	✓
	✓		✓
IT duopoly	✓	✓	
		✓	✓
Anarchy			

professionals from both corporate teams and business units. DuPont, for example, has an enterprise IT architecture group with representatives from all regions, all strategic business units, and all competency centers. This group proposes architecture "rules" to the senior IT management team, consisting of the corporate CIO and the CIOs of the largest business units. The senior IT management team ensures the clarity of the rules and owns the enforcement of architectural standards.

Feudal

The feudal model is based on the traditions of "merrie olde England" where the princes and princesses or their designated knights make their own decisions, optimizing their local needs. For IT governance the feudal entity is typically the business unit, region, or function.[2] Overall in our study, the feudal model was not very common because most enterprises were looking for synergies across business units. The feudal model does not facilitate enterprisewide decision making.

Federal

The federal decision-making model has a long tradition in government. Federal arrangements attempt to balance the responsibilities and accountability of multiple governing bodies, such as country and states. Charles Handy, among others, has recently identified the federal model's utility in negotiating the interests of both the central organization (typically headquarters) and individual units.[3] We defined the federal model as coordinated decision making involving both the center and the business units. Unit representatives in a federal model could be either or both the unit leaders or business process owners. Business unit and/or corporate IT leaders might also be involved in federal governance as additional participants.

The federal model is undoubtedly the most difficult archetype for decision making because enterprise leaders have different concerns from business unit leaders. Members of a federal organization represent their own unique responsibilities. In addition, incentive systems often focus managers on business unit rather than enterprise results. The impact of shared resources on business unit performance—and specifically the transfer prices charged for the resources—typically raises concerns about fairness. Enterprises in the study often used federal models for input to decisions, perhaps because of fairness and representation issues.

In federal models, the biggest, most powerful business units often get the most attention and have the most influence on decisions. Consequently, smaller business units remain unsatisfied and sometimes secede from the union to meet their own needs. Enterprises enlisting federal governance structures usually rely on management teams and executive committees to resolve inherent conflicts.

IT Duopoly

The IT duopoly is a two-party arrangement where decisions represent a bilateral agreement between IT executives and one other group.[4] The IT executives may be a central IT group or a team of central and business unit IT organizations. The other group may be CxOs, business unit leaders or business process owners, or groups of key system users (see figure 3-2). A duopoly differs from a federal model in that a federal arrangement always has both corporate and local business representation, while a duopoly has one or the other but not both and always includes IT professionals.

IT duopolies often take one of two forms: a "bicycle wheel" or a T-shaped committee structure (figure 3-3). The bicycle wheel describes a duopoly involving the central IT group and the business units. The IT group is at the hub and the business units are around the rim. The spokes are the series of bilateral relationships between the IT group and the various business units. Each business unit gets individual attention along the spokes, but the same hub supports the whole enterprise.

A duopoly involving the central IT group and the senior management team (the CxOs and the heads of the business units) is often implemented by two overlapping committees. The executive committee (the horizontal part of the T) predominantly comprises business managers. The vertical part of the T is an IT committee predominantly comprising technical managers. A small set of peo-

FIGURE 3-3

Bicycle Wheel and T-Shaped IT Duopolies

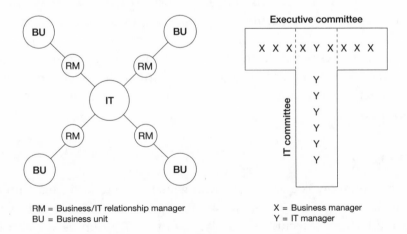

RM = Business/IT relationship manager
BU = Business unit

X = Business manager
Y = IT manager

ple participates on both committees to coordinate and ensure overlap. To improve coordination, the committees may meet on the same day, say, the executive committee in the morning and the IT committee in the afternoon, with some joint meeting time.

Over a third of the 256 enterprises used duopolies to make decisions in the three less-technical IT decision domains: IT principles, business application needs, and IT investment. Duopolies also were frequently used to provide input into architecture and infrastructure decisions. The duopoly archetype is popular partly because it involves only two decision-making parties—it can achieve many of the objectives of a federal model using a simpler management structure. Similarly, duopolies have an advantage over feudal models in that the central IT group is often one of the few groups that sees the enterprise as a whole and can look for opportunities for sharing and reuse. The IT professionals can also manage adherence, either overtly or covertly, to the enterprise's IT architecture. Duopolies often rely on relationship managers or business unit CIOs to represent business unit needs. The IT group can have a series of duopolies with different business units enabling more tailored decisions in less time. These duopolies have the advantage of focusing directly on the needs of the business units, resulting in higher business unit satisfaction. But duopolies with business units can be expensive and ineffective when organizationwide issues are being decided.

Anarchy

Describing the anarchy model always brings back memories of one author's undergraduate days when Artie the anarchist was a prominent campus character. Artie railed against a number of the university's core principles—class attendance, grades, deadlines—but he reserved his most vehement criticism for standards of any kind. All enterprises have their Arties, and our own has more than its fair share! Within an anarchy, individuals or small groups make their own decisions based only on their local needs. Anarchies are the bane of the existence of many IT groups and are expensive to support and secure. Formally sanctioned anarchies were rare but existed in our study and were supported where very rapid responsiveness to local or individual customer needs was required.

How the Typical Enterprise Governs IT

We studied both who made each of the five decisions and who provided input to those decisions. We then categorized the enterprise's approach by archetype (see figure 3-2). Figure 3-4 lists the percentages of enterprises that used each governance archetype for each decision. The percentages in each column add to 100 percent. The darker shaded cells in figure 3-4 indicate the most common or typical governance patterns, with the shaded, bordered cells highlighting the most common decision-making patterns.

The most common governance pattern allowed for broad-based inputs with decision rights allocated to different groups depending on the decision. For the three more business-oriented IT decisions (principles, business application needs, and investment), more than

FIGURE 3-4

How Enterprises Govern

DECISION ARCHETYPE	IT Principles		IT Architecture		IT Infrastructure Strategies		Business Application Needs		IT Investment	
	Input	Decision	Input	Decision	Input	Decision	Input	Decision	Input	Decision
Business Monarchy	0	27	0	6	0	7	1	12	1	30
IT Monarchy	1	18	20	73	10	59	0	8	0	9
Feudal	0	3	0	0	1	2	1	18	0	3
Federal	83	14	46	4	59	6	81	30	93	27
Duopoly	15	36	34	15	30	23	17	27	6	30
Anarchy	0	0	0	1	0	1	0	3	0	1
No Data or Don't Know	1	2	0	1	0	2	0	2	0	0

☐ Most common input pattern for all enterprises. ■ Most common decision patterns for all enterprises.

The numbers in each cell are percentages of the 256 enterprises studied in twenty-three countries. The columns add to 100 percent.

80 percent of enterprises provided inputs through a federal governance model. Committees, budgets, and cross-functional process teams presented opportunities for input and feedback on these IT decisions. Federal structures also supported input to the more technical IT decisions, but enterprise approaches to input on these technical issues were more varied. Duopolies were also a popular approach to input for technical decisions. The duopoly approach to input for technical decisions sought similar objectives as the federal approach, but the federal approach involved all business units together and the duopoly used a set of bilateral business unit IT relationships.

In addition to collecting internal input for decisions, many firms also looked externally. Vendors, business partners, consultants, industry associations, universities, and other groups provided input. We do not generally recommend that external bodies (with the exception of for not-for-profit enterprises, discussed in chapter 7) be given decision rights for key IT decisions, as occurs in some outsourcing arrangements. But external sources often provide invaluable input.

Compared to input processes, decision rights were much less uniformly managed across different enterprises. We describe these variations for each decision domain.

Typical Governance Arrangements for IT Principles

IT principles, which set the strategic role for IT across the enterprise, were decided in a variety of ways. Thirty-six percent of enterprises used a duopoly approach (usually IT professionals and the CxOs in a T-shaped duopoly), but business and IT monarchies and federal approaches were also regularly used. We suspect that duopolies in general and senior management IT duopolies in particular have gained favor in IT principles decisions because senior managers sense that they must take the lead to ensure that IT aligns with business strategies. Working in partnership with IT leaders in the decision process establishes realistic expectations for IT and forces clarification of business strategy. An IT duopoly also secures the IT unit's commitment to business principles. Just as important, senior executives allow IT to shape business principles by reflecting

IT capabilities already in place or under development. Thus, duopolies are structured to leverage IT competencies in future-oriented principles and strategies.

Like duopolies, business monarchies also enhance the likelihood that IT principles will be aligned with business strategy. The leadership of the CxOs greatly enhances the likelihood that principles will be observed. But business monarchies are not without risks. Senior managers can establish principles without providing the governance processes, funding levels, and organizational structures to achieve them. The involvement of IT-savvy senior managers or the presence of a strong CIO on the executive team lessens these risks.

Federal models for IT principles ensure business units a strong voice in defining the role of IT. This voice is particularly valuable where business objectives highlight the importance of business unit autonomy. To balance the different interests of the central core and the business units, some enterprises start with defining the role of IT. Clear principles stating how IT will support both the center and the business units (perhaps via a combination of shared services and local IT units) can ease the difficulty of applying the federal model to other decisions (for example, business application needs).

The 18 percent of enterprises vesting responsibility for IT principles in IT monarchies were assuming significant risk. If business objectives are clearly stated, IT professionals might easily translate strategic objectives into appropriate IT principles. We have seen very effective business/IT relationships that permitted senior management to hand off IT principles to IT leaders. However, an IT monarchy taking responsibility for IT principles is best positioned to develop technically sound but strategically unimportant principles. These principles will lead to an efficient but not a business-enabling architecture. In addition, IT monarchies making decisions on IT principles are positioned to take the blame if systems do not generate anticipated benefits. Worse, because business managers have abdicated responsibility for defining targets, IT may well encounter difficulties in getting business managers to accept responsibility for generating the benefits—which usually means there will be few benefits. Regardless of the capabilities IT delivers, if business leaders do not assume responsibility for converting them into value, the risk of failure is high. With high risk comes the likelihood of frustrated business leaders who often respond by replacing the IT leadership or abdicating further by outsourcing the whole "IT problem."

Typical Governance Arrangements for IT Architecture

Over 70 percent of enterprises rely on IT monarchies to choose IT architecture, suggesting that senior managers view architecture more as a technical than a strategic issue. Most enterprises attempt to incorporate business strategy considerations into architecture decisions via inputs from federal and duopoly arrangements. However, the dominant decision-making role of IT in architecture decisions suggests that business managers feel unqualified, uninterested, or unneeded—they are confident that IT professionals can translate IT principles into an architecture. IT professionals are typically quite comfortable taking responsibility for architecture decisions. At many of the enterprises we have studied, an IT-only team—often with IT representatives from individual business units—is responsible for designing and managing the architecture, which it then communicates to the entire enterprise.

Another 15 percent of enterprises make architecture decisions using duopolies. These duopolies are typically a partnership between the CxOs, who provide the strategic horizon, and IT professionals, who provide the technical and often organizational input—a T-shaped duopoly. The duopoly approach is an overt recognition of the dual business and technical nature of architecture decisions.

Typical Governance Arrangements for IT Infrastructure Strategies

Like architecture, infrastructure strategy decisions are often made within the IT unit. Almost 60 percent of enterprises used IT monarchies to make infrastructure decisions. This arrangement gives IT independence in designing and pricing service offerings. Johnson & Johnson's Networking and Computing Services (NCS) unit provides centralized infrastructure services for many of J&J's operating units. However, because NCS must effectively sell its services to the operating companies, its customers' demands strongly influence it.

At J&J, these demands are most often articulated by the IT people at the operating companies. At many enterprises, however, significant input comes from federal and duopoly arrangements. Effective IT monarchies design infrastructures to address and support the application requirements of business units.

Almost a quarter of the enterprises used a duopoly to make infrastructure strategy decisions. Duopolies are well suited to relatively quick negotiation of the business, technology, and political issues associated with shared infrastructure services. For example, Schneider National, a large U.S. trucking firm, uses regular meetings of senior managers and key IT leaders to define infrastructure requirements. These meetings allow senior managers to share evolving strategies with IT executives, who can identify deficiencies in existing capabilities and propose how the firm might leverage the technology it has in place. The process makes IT people more business savvy and business people more IT savvy.

Typical Governance Arrangements for IT Business Application Needs

People who make business application needs decisions specify the business needs for systems to be acquired or built in the next year or so. Enterprises in our study displayed a wide variety of approaches to these decisions. Federal approaches were slightly more popular than duopolies, and there were also substantial numbers of enterprises using feudal and business monarchies.

Federal models consider enterprise objectives in the process of deploying local business applications. In a federal model, implementations of local business applications may replicate or customize software adopted enterprisewide. For example, one pharmaceutical firm purchased an ERP for the entire enterprise, but except for a small set of firmwide data definitions (for example, financial data), it did not standardize the application across its regional business units. The central team developed a model and then helped local teams configure it according to their unique needs. This arrangement allowed for shared expertise across the firm but opted for the benefits of local customization over global standardization.

IT duopolies, typically bicycle wheels, were used by 27 percent of the enterprises. These duopolies give a stronger voice to IT in business application decisions, which may reflect the greater role of architecture standards in limiting the number of choices considered for purchased applications. For example, at Commonwealth Bank of Australia, Australia's largest bank, with several major business units, the central IT architecture team reviews all business application proposals. During one review, the team observed that multiple business units were proposing similar functionality across multiple front-end customer service platforms. The architecture team extricated the common requirements and proposed a common approach that eliminated U.S. $20 million from the business units' combined application proposal budget requirements. IT involvement in business application decisions increases the likelihood that both technical standards and existing IT infrastructure capabilities influence the choice of applications.[5]

Business application needs is the only decision where a significant number of enterprises (18 percent) use a feudal model—independent business units decide for themselves. Feudal models allow for high business unit autonomy and permit business units to move faster when they find packages or define requirements to meet a unique business need. In some enterprises the feudal model for business application needs was balanced with more centralized governance for IT principles and IT investment (for example, business monarchy).

At 12 percent of the enterprises, business monarchies make application needs decisions. Dow Corning took this approach to the implementation of its enterprise resource planning system. Committed to a global supply chain, management developed a single instance of the software, which was installed at all 109 sites.

Typical Governance Arrangements for IT Investment and Prioritization

Three approaches dominate IT investment and prioritization decision making—business monarchies, federal, and duopolies. The three approaches are almost equally popular, but they offer different views of how enterprises ensure maximum value from IT investments. That only 9 percent of enterprises place IT investment decisions in the hands of IT professionals reflects the growing awareness that IT investment decisions involve business tradeoffs—

decision makers determine which business processes will and will not receive IT support.

Business monarchies are well positioned to define and fund business priorities. Business monarchies are typically also responsible for overall capital budgeting decisions. Thus, vesting responsibility for IT investment and prioritization in a business monarchy allows IT projects to compete for funds with other organizational needs. The competition for funding facilitates an integrated view of the enterprise's key assets (physical, human, relationship) and is aided by an enterprise investment committee that looks at all major investments.

Federal approaches to IT investment balance enterprisewide priorities with business unit priorities. At one enterprise, over 80 percent of IT investment funds were allocated by the senior management team, but the functional units each had an "allowance" for business unit priorities. In contrast, firms with highly autonomous business units fund most IT from their regional offices, using occasional central funding to address strategic global needs.

Duopoly approaches (often T-shaped committees) to IT investment recognize that the IT unit is uniquely positioned to identify the risks posed by the existing IT infrastructure and the opportunities for sharing and reuse across business units. Thus, the involvement of IT in investment decisions provides a longer-term view of the implications of currently funded projects. Senior executives can simultaneously ensure that priority projects are "staged" according to the need for and availability of needed infrastructure. Enterprises with strong duopolies can group projects requiring new infrastructure capabilities. This process allows faster payback on infrastructure because major infrastructure investments are delayed (as are the applications requiring them) until a critical mass justifies the investment.

Analyzing Different Governance Patterns Across Enterprises

This first look at the data from our study reveals some broad patterns. For example, few enterprises govern with anarchy or feudal approaches. Many enterprises allocate responsibility for architecture and infrastructure decisions to IT specialists. Overall, however, we found significant variation in governance patterns. Variations result from a number of factors:

1. *Strategic and performance goals:* Effective governance attempts to reinforce desirable behaviors to achieve the enterprise's strategic and performance goals. Because each enterprise's goals are different, a wide variety of governance approaches are used.

2. *Organizational structure:* Traditionally, enterprises have relied on organizational structure to align decision making with enterprise goals and strategies. However, as enterprises attempt to address competing goals, expanding geographies, rapid change, and intense competition, organizational structures have provided inadequate support for strategy. Enterprises design governance to compensate for the limitations of structure. Given that organizations cannot rely on an organization chart to deliver strategy, they must identify processes and governance that transcend the organization chart.

3. *Governance experience:* Many enterprises are relatively early in the learning curve of IT governance effectiveness. Less-mature enterprises change governance more often and struggle with coordinating all their mechanisms. Individuals within enterprises also contribute different levels of expertise. IT executives learn about business strategy (and often force clarity) and business executives learn about IT capabilities through ongoing involvement in IT decisions.

4. *Size and diversity:* As enterprises grow and diversify—both geographically and organizationally—they introduce competing and even conflicting objectives. Desirable behaviors become less clear and more contingent on circumstances as an enterprise introduces competing objectives. Governance must address the tradeoffs presented by competing objectives. Thus, the governance approach is likely to change as the enterprise becomes more complex.

5. *Industry and regional differences:* Industry and regional differences create unique pressures on enterprises that are reflected in their IT governance. Decision-making cultures

vary considerably across different regions of the world, often complicating governance in global enterprises. The last section of this chapter explores these differences and provides the typical IT governance patterns by industry and region. To aid in comparison, a series of tables summarizing the different approaches to governance by region and industry are available.[6]

Finally, the variation in the governance arrangements reflects varying levels of governance effectiveness. Top-performing firms govern differently. We will explain the differences in chapter 5. Now we will review the governance arrangements of DuPont, DBS Bank, and Motorola—three excellent firms, all pursuing growth, each applying governance arrangements specific to their needs.

Case Study: DuPont

DuPont is a $25 billion manufacturer of science-based solutions in industries spanning food and nutrition, health care, home and construction, apparel, electronics, and transportation.[7] The company, which celebrated its two hundredth anniversary in 2002, has over 79,000 employees in seventy countries. DuPont is organized around six market-growth platforms, which are further divided into strategic business units. Despite difficult economic conditions, DuPont started its third century as one of twenty companies identified by *BusinessWeek* with the financial strength and flexibility to take advantage of the acquisition opportunities available during the bear market.

Financial strength is important to DuPont to fund the firm's oft-stated strategic intent of sustainable growth. DuPont divests product lines that are not positioned to grow, even when performance has been strong. To fuel growth, DuPont purchases smaller companies with unique technology and market know-how.

IT at DuPont is charged with enabling a vision for "One DuPont." This vision brings together the enterprise's diverse expertise to deliver innovative solutions to specific customer problems. "One DuPont" will also provide a single face to global customers who do business with multiple DuPont business units and product lines.

To address the information needs of its diverse business units, DuPont has a global architecture defining points of intersection among the businesses. A small set of "Big Rules" establishes the critical elements of the architecture.[8] For example, one Big Rule specifies: "When creating enterprise communications and data sharing, use chemical industry standards for sharing that data back and forth."[9]

To support the business vision and implement Big Rules, DuPont created enterprisewide infrastructure services such as channel management, telecommunications, security, desktop, and global applications services. Although corporate declared some application standards, such as Lotus Notes for collaboration and SAP for financials, organizational units define most of their application needs. Application needs may be defined at the regional, business unit, or product line level.

Most global infrastructure development at DuPont has been funded centrally, but business units eventually pay for all such services through chargeback processes. Business units make their own investment decisions to fund the significant variations in processes such as R&D, manufacturing, and distribution, and supply chain management.

DuPont's enterprisewide IT governance (mapped onto the Governance Assessment Matrix in figure 3-5 and listing the critical IT mechanisms) reflects global market demands, the diversity of its businesses, and its emphasis on growth. A Governance Arrangements Matrix could also be drawn for each of DuPont's six growth platforms.

IT principles are focused on delivering the "One DuPont" vision. The principles evolved from discussions between the senior executive team and IT leaders. One regional CIO described his role in defining strategy and principles as follows: "Many times I was educating on the potential of IT to play a different strategic role. And many times I was trying to take a piece of strategy and figure out how can we actually develop that and put it on the ground in a business process."[10]

Architecture decisions result largely from the efforts of a global architecture team of forty IT professionals from all regions, business units, and IT competency centers. This team designs the rules and

FIGURE 3-5

How DuPont Governs IT

GOVERNANCE ARCHETYPE \ DECISION	IT Principles		IT Architecture		IT Infrastructure Strategies		Business Application Needs		IT Investment	
	Input	Decision	Input	Decision	Input	Decision	Input	Decision	Input	Decision
Business Monarchy										
IT Monarchy			Arch. team	IT leaders	Comp. center	IT leaders				
Feudal	Business unit							Business leaders		
Federal									Senior execs. Business leaders	Corp. IT Business leaders
Duopoly		Senior execs. Corp. IT					Senior execs. Corp. IT			

▢ Most common pattern for all firms.

Governance mechanisms:
Arch. team—Forty IT experts from across company
Business leaders—Business unit leaders
Business unit—Business and IT leaders in business units
Comp. center—Global IT competency center representatives
Corp. IT—CIO and four direct reports
IT leaders—Corporate IT and fifteen business CIOs
Senior execs.—Senior Executive Team, including CIO

policies embodied in the architecture and makes recommendations to DuPont's IT Global Leadership Team (IGLT), consisting of approximately fifteen of the top IT leaders across the businesses and regions. DuPont IT managers note that every IT leader must work closely with business leaders and must represent the business units as well as the enterprise in architecture decisions. This capability for IT to represent the business stems from the operational and reporting roles of business unit IT leaders.

DuPont's IT leaders make infrastructure decisions offering shared services to business units and forcing any business units that prefer not to leverage the shared services to present an argument justifying their uniqueness. Business units must pay for these services, so they want to negotiate their needs with the central infrastructure team. As with architecture, most of these negotiations occur between local and corporate IT staff, who must represent business needs. Thus, like architecture, DuPont governs infrastructure through IT monarchies for both decisions and input. Infrastructure within DuPont exists at several levels. In addition to the enterprisewide infrastructure considered here, the strategic business units develop their own infrastructure with their own governance arrangements. The firmwide architecture governance ensures compatibility among the multiple levels.

Because business application needs vary significantly across business units, most of the decisions on business applications—as well as the responsibility for implementation—lie within business units. DuPont corporate mandates some vendor packages, but business units have discretion in the implementation. Thus, the feudal approach best describes business application decision making at DuPont. The enterprisewide applications defined by corporate business and IT management influence these decisions, however, making the input process primarily a duopoly.

Finally, IT investment decisions result from negotiations between corporate and business unit executives. These negotiations involve IT executives as well as business executives, but the involvement of both corporate and business unit leaders makes investment decision making a federal process. Business units and corporate also provide input to the investment process, making the input, like the decision, federal.

In summary, DuPont's global scale, growth targets, complex structure, and "One DuPont" strategy have led to feudal decisions on application needs balanced by a federal investment approach. Because of its size and global diversity, Dupont relies more than other companies in the study on IT professionals to represent business needs. DuPont still values alignment between IT and business strategy, but it relies more heavily than other enterprises on IT professionals to define solutions for business opportunities.

Case Study: DBS Bank

DBS Bank is Singapore's leading bank, serving over 4 million customers in Singapore, Thailand, Hong Kong, Indonesia, and the Philippines.[11] Like DuPont, DBS's strategy focuses on growth, specifically positioning the bank to become a leading Asian regional franchise.

DBS intends to facilitate growth, in part, by rapidly shifting acquired banks onto the DBS platform. Accordingly, DBS is building an enterprisewide platform with common technology, data definitions, and metrics. While accountability for performance will remain at the local level, senior management mandates synergies across the banks. Management's vision for the future is a "network of relationships" rather than bricks and mortar. The enterprise platform is central to enabling the banks to provide a consistent set of DBS services according to local needs.

IT efforts at DBS are guided by a set of principles encompassing governance, data ownership, and architecture. DBS's new architecture defines fifteen infrastructure services to be provided enterprisewide. An exception process enables development teams to occasionally go outside architecture standards, although the architecture is expected to then incorporate the new requirements. Development teams are centralized and work with architecture "case workers" to ensure an architecturally sound approach to all application development.

IT investment falls into three investment tiers—the same way DBS handles all capital investments. Business unit heads have authority for investments under Singapore $1 million. Regional project councils, comprising key IT and business managers, review projects in the S $1 million to S $5 million range. The corporate office handles all projects over S $5 million, although all IT-related investment decisions are made on the recommendation of the group CIO. Every major initiative is assessed on both financial and nonfinancial objectives. IT governance at DBS Bank is mapped onto the Governance Assessment Matrix in figure 3-6.

Despite sharing a vision of growth, DBS and DuPont take quite different approaches to IT governance. Much of this disparity probably relates to industry differences in how firms grow. DuPont in-

FIGURE 3-6

How DBS Bank Governs IT

GOVERNANCE ARCHETYPE	DECISION									
	IT Principles		IT Architecture		IT Infrastructure Strategies		Business Application Needs		IT Investment	
	Input	Decision	Input	Decision	Input	Decision	Input	Decision	Input	Decision
Business Monarchy		Corp. office CIO						Corp. office CIO		Project council Corp. office
IT Monarchy				Arch. office	CIO IT leaders	CIO IT leaders				
Feudal										
Federal							Business leaders Business process owners			
Duopoly	Business leaders IT leaders		Business leaders IT leaders						Business leaders IT leaders BT managers	

☐ Most common pattern for all firms.

Governance mechanisms:

Arch. office—Office of architecture
Business leaders—Business leaders
Business process owners—Business process owners
BT managers—Business technology relationship managers

CIO—CIO office and staff
Corp. office—Corporate office (CEO, CIO, three business heads)
IT leaders—IT leadership group
Project council—Regional project councils

novates and acquires new businesses along business unit lines. Needing to support the individual growth of its strategic business units leads DuPont to a feudal business application governance model and a duopoly for principles that leverage and guide IT behaviors. DuPont uses a federal model for investment, however, to ensure that both enterprisewide and business unit objectives receive IT support. In contrast, DBS grows by replicating standard business components, so strategic business decisions are centralized in the business monarchy while technical decisions are centralized in IT. As a result, DBS can grow rapidly in the region while also competing as a low-cost provider of services.

Case Study: Motorola

Motorola offers an example of a company pursuing growth while managing the inherent security issues.[12] Motorola is a global leader in providing integrated communications and embedded electronic solutions. Celebrating its seventy-fifth birthday in 2003, Motorola consists of six sectors covering telecommunications equipment, software solutions, and services, as well as semiconductor products and integrated systems. Motorola is rebounding from very difficult market conditions over the last couple of years, following the extraordinary telecom and dot-com boom in the late1990s. With 2002 sales of $27.3 billion, Motorola is attempting to return to what the CEO refers to as steady, rational growth with "real products serving real needs in real marketplaces."[13] Motorola is number one or two in its key markets, and management believes the firm is poised for growth as the global economy recovers. Growth for Motorola will result from leveraging strong customer relationships and from continued innovation in software applications and products.

Because the software and telecommunications industries are particularly vulnerable to security risks, Motorola management believes that information security is critical to its growth objectives. Management defines information security as protecting information and systems from failures of availability, confidentiality, and integrity. Motorola has committed to information security in both its operations and its products. This commitment has made information security a senior management issue and an integral part of IT governance at Motorola.

IT governance at Motorola relies on close IT-business relationships at both the corporate and sector level. The CIO is on the executive team and participates in decisions on principles and investment with the Management Board. The CIO's leadership team consists of the heads of architecture, infrastructure, enterprise applications, and security and the CIOs of the six sectors. The CIO's leadership team is responsible for both architecture and infrastructure decisions. Business application decisions involve negotiations between corporate IT leaders, sector IT leaders, and business unit heads in a duopoly arrangement. Motorola's IT governance arrangements are shown in figure 3-7.

Motorola's Corporate Information Security Officer, who reports to the CIO, joins the CIO at quarterly Management Board meetings. In these meetings, the security officer details Motorola's security risks and alternatives for addressing them. A key element of information security governance is ongoing education. The security officer has worked with senior management on how to think

FIGURE 3-7

How Motorola Governs IT

GOVERNANCE ARCHETYPE	DECISION									
	IT Principles		IT Architecture		IT Infrastructure Strategies		Business Application Needs		IT Investment	
	Input	Decision	Input	Decision	Input	Decision	Input	Decision	Input	Decision
Business Monarchy										
IT Monarchy				IT leaders Security leaders		IT leaders Security leaders				
Feudal										
Federal	Business leaders						Sector IT Business leaders		Sector IT Business leaders	
Duopoly		Mgmt. board IT leaders	CIO staff Sector IT		CIO staff Sector IT			Business leaders Sector IT CIO staff		Mgmt. board IT leaders

☐ Most common pattern for all firms.

Governance mechanisms:

Business leaders—Business unit leaders within sectors
CIO staff—CIO staff
IT leaders—CIO's four direct reports, six sector CIOs

Mgmt. board—Senior executive team, including CIO
Security leaders—IT leadership and security staff
Sector IT—Sector CIO staff

about both the likelihood of various security breaches and the potential impacts of each threat on the business.

As with other areas of IT governance, the Management Board establishes security principles and defines priorities. The Board specifies the security budget separately from the rest of the IT budget. Motorola implements its security plans at both a corporate and a sector level. The security officer's staff designs and builds appropriate technology. Security staff members also work with IT architects at both the corporate and the sector levels to ensure that security measures are seamlessly built into infrastructure and applications.

The security-based governance initiatives at Motorola provide an example of how enterprises govern to address strategic issues. Motorola's security concerns are reflected in its organizational structure and roles, governance arrangements, and specific architecture processes. Many enterprises are concerned with security, but Motorola has made it a strategic priority. Its governance arrangements ensure that security considerations are built into desirable behavior.

The three cases also illustrate how different sets of IT mechanisms can be used to effectively implement governance. The Governance Arrangements Matrix for each firm identifies the mechanisms through which the firm implements its governance arrangements. For example, DuPont uses mechanisms like an architecture team of forty experts and global IT competency centers. DBS's mechanisms include an office of architecture and regional project councils. Motorola uses mechanisms including a management board and security leaders. In the next chapter we examine the mechanisms used to implement IT governance and how they work—both independently and together.

Industry and Regional Differences in IT Governance

As the DuPont, DBS, and Motorola cases demonstrate, "typical" profiles of IT governance do not serve as generic guidelines for governance. Many factors influence governance requirements. Industry and region are two of the factors.

To illustrate some of the industry differences, compare the for-profit with the not-for-profit and government sectors. Measuring performance is challenging and much less clear in the government and not-for-profit sectors. This difference affects the organization's culture and each individual's sense of accountability as everyone works to provide service that is justified on legislative or social merits and affordability rather than impact on future sales or profits. The differences in governance between the for-profit and the government and not-for-profit sectors reflect these differences in culture, measurements, and accountabilities. For example, the not-for-profit and government sectors use significantly more business monarchies for IT principles and IT investment decisions than do for-profit enterprises. The heavier use of business monarchies reflects the more centralized decision-making process in some types of government and not-for-profit enterprises, such as emergency response, taxation, and defense. The multiple and often conflicting objectives of not-for-profits demand strong direction from the center. The decision-making power of the CxOs might also result from different attitudes toward risk management and empowerment. Government and not-for-profit enterprises also rely more heavily on federal models for business application needs decisions. Federal models for business applications allow the central leadership to ensure that the enterprise's objectives are considered, while recognizing that functional units have unique IT requirements for fulfilling their respective objectives. Chapter 7 extends the discussion of how government and not-for-profit enterprises apply governance to meet their strategic objectives.

Other industry differences are also apparent. For example, financial services firms rely more on duopolies and, to a lesser extent, IT monarchies for decisions on IT principles than does the "typical" enterprise. The heavy involvement of IT professionals in principles decisions probably results from the nature of the product. In financial services, information is the product. Thus, IT has historically played a strategic role in financial services enterprises. The financial services industry also distinguishes itself from the "typical" enterprise by its significantly lower reliance on federal governance for IT decisions. The federal model is heavily used for input on IT decisions at financial services firms so that both shared functions and individual business units influence decision making. But federal decision-making approaches are rare, probably because many full-service firms are organized around individual product lines. Financial services firms have a significantly higher use of feudal approaches to business application needs decisions than do "typical" enterprises. The feudal approach may be a historical artifact from the product line focus that, until recently, was common in the financial services industry.

Governance arrangements for the telecommunications and utility industries are similar to the arrangements in government and not-for-profit enterprises. The telecommunications and utility industries use business monarchies more than is "typical" for IT principles and IT investment decisions. Use of federal decision making for business application needs is considerably higher in the telco and utility industries than in any other industry.

Manufacturing firms, in contrast, rely more on duopolies for business application needs, probably because business applications in these industries require an increasingly seamless supply chain. IT involvement in business applications can clarify the capabilities and limitations of the existing infrastructure and build new infrastructure to support new applications. Manufacturing firms rely more than other industries on a federal approach to IT investment decisions. This governance probably reflects the unique needs of different product lines, functional departments, and regional offices, while simultaneously ensuring the robustness of the central supply chain and the ability to address the needs of large, geographically dispersed global customers.

We found that regional differences were not as pronounced as industry differences, probably because many of the firms in the sample were global firms, which diminishes the presence of regional differences. European firms tended to rely more heavily on business monarchies for principles, perhaps reflecting the need to clarify how IT would enable coordination across business units. The twenty-seven Asia-Pacific firms in the study demonstrated a greater propensity to adopt federal governance patterns and lower use of IT monarchies. American firms had a stronger business unit influence, particularly in business application needs.

Making Sense of "Typical" IT Governance Design Profiles

Comparisons are a starting point to IT governance design. To commence the process of assessing governance design, we have found that the most useful approach to using our results is to ask the question: Can you explain the difference between your enterprise's governance and the most common approach? You might also want to compare your governance design to the most common approach in your industry or region. Convincingly describing the difference is an indicator of good harmony between your governance and your strategy. An inability to describe the difference indicates a need to rethink governance design in your enterprise.

4

Mechanisms for
Implementing
IT Governance

ONE OF OUR MENTORS often said that there are two things you really don't want to watch being made—sausages and laws. In both cases, a neatly packaged outcome results from messy processes. Similarly, IT governance can be messy. Governance fosters debate, negotiation, constructive disagreement, mutual education, and often frustration. The process is messy, but good governance arrangements enable individuals representing an enterprise's conflicting goals to reconcile their views to the enterprise's benefit.

Enterprises implement their governance arrangements through a set of governance mechanisms—structures, processes, and communications. Well-designed, well-understood, and transparent mechanisms promote desirable IT behaviors. Conversely, if mechanisms are poorly implemented, then governance arrangements will fail to yield the desired results. Chapter 3 showed how DuPont, DBS, and Motorola implemented their archetypes for each decision (see figures 3-5, 3-6, and 3-7). This chapter covers common governance mechanisms and how they implement the different archetypes. We provide detailed examples of these mechanisms and finish with a case study of Carlson Companies as an example of how enterprises assemble a coherent set of mechanisms. We close the chapter with a short list of principles for designing governance mechanisms.

Figure 4-1 lists fifteen of the most common IT governance mechanisms. Effective governance deploys three different types of mechanisms:

- *Decision-making structures:* Organizational units and roles responsible for making IT decisions, such as committees, executive teams, and business/IT relationship managers

- *Alignment processes:* Formal processes for ensuring that daily behaviors are consistent with IT policies and provide input back to decisions. These include IT investment proposal and evaluation processes, architecture exception processes, service-level agreements, chargeback, and metrics.

- *Communication approaches:* Announcements, advocates, channels, and education efforts that disseminate IT governance principles and policies and outcomes of IT decision-making processes.

We will discuss each type of mechanism in this chapter and explain the expected capabilities and limitations of each.

Decision-Making Structures

The most visible IT governance mechanisms are the organizational structures that locate decision-making responsibilities according to intended archetypes. Ideally, every enterprise engages both IT and business leaders in the governance process. Decision-making structures are the natural approach to generating commitment—albeit some executives have been known to wiggle out of their IT governance responsibilities. To review design alternatives, we identify the decision-making mechanisms most commonly deployed in business monarchy, federal, IT monarchy, and duopoly archetypes. Enterprises with effective governance mix and match decision-making structures to implement predetermined archetypes and ultimately achieve organizational goals.

Business Monarchy Decision-Making Structures

IT can enable enterprise strategy only if senior management establishes strategic direction and elaborates an operating model.[1] Enter-

FIGURE 4-1

Common Governance Mechanisms

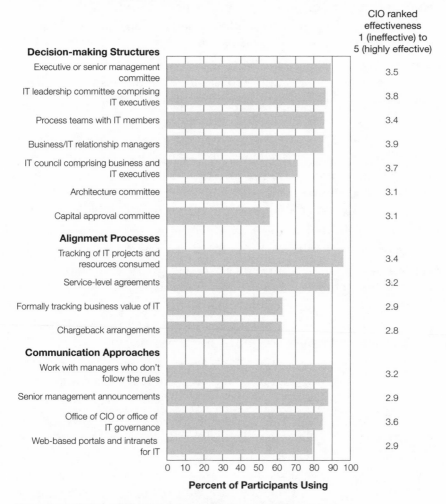

Decision-making Structures	CIO ranked effectiveness 1 (ineffective) to 5 (highly effective)
Executive or senior management committee	3.5
IT leadership committee comprising IT executives	3.8
Process teams with IT members	3.4
Business/IT relationship managers	3.9
IT council comprising business and IT executives	3.7
Architecture committee	3.1
Capital approval committee	3.1
Alignment Processes	
Tracking of IT projects and resources consumed	3.4
Service-level agreements	3.2
Formally tracking business value of IT	2.9
Chargeback arrangements	2.8
Communication Approaches	
Work with managers who don't follow the rules	3.2
Senior management announcements	2.9
Office of CIO or office of IT governance	3.6
Web-based portals and intranets for IT	2.9

Percent of Participants Using

Research conducted at 256 enterprises in twenty-three countries.

© 2003 MIT Sloan School Center for Information Systems Research (CISR). Used with permission.

prises adopt a number of approaches to eliciting this direction. Business monarchies—usually in the form of executive committees—often play a role. Enterprises vary considerably in the design of their executive committees.

In some enterprises the CEO works with a small team of top executives to ensure that IT aligns with corporate objectives. At

DBS Bank, for example, the Corporate Office, which consists of the chairman and CEO, the vice chairman, and the chairman of DBS Hong Kong, ratifies principles and handles IT-related investment decisions greater than S $5 million.[2] (See the DBS case in Chapter 3.) The CEO's visibility in IT decisions at DBS matters because the firm takes a "directed" approach to IT management. DBS does not rely on consensus. The CEO expects the CIO to make and deliver key decisions on corporate objectives. The CEO's direct involvement in setting direction thus strengthens the position of the CIO.

Other enterprises focus the attention of a subset of the senior management team on IT issues. For example, at ING, the Dutch financial conglomerate, three members of the Executive Board sit on the IT Policy Board (ITPB). The ITPB develops strategy, approves technical standards, and sets priorities for group projects. The ITPB also has a role in ensuring systems security, appointing senior IT management, and approving policies in areas such as enterprise applications, infrastructure, and architecture. By having three Executive Board members play such an active role in IT governance and management, ING ensures both that IT fulfills corporate objectives and that Executive Board actions are informed by IT capabilities.

The level of senior executive involvement in IT governance evolves as enterprises become more savvy in using IT strategically. At Dow Corning, a silicon manufacturer, the senior executive team determined the need to transform IT from back-office function to strategic enabler in the mid-1990s.[3] For several years, the executive committee met regularly to redefine the role of IT, articulate the role of the CIO, establish architectural principles, outline key projects— particularly the implementation of an enterprise system—and closely manage IT investment priorities. The full executive committee entrenched IT as a key function with a capable leader and developed both confidence in the CIO and competence in articulating how IT should enable business. Ongoing IT governance responsibilities were then vested in a subset of executive committee members.

Similarly, UPS relied on a seven-member senior management team to direct funding and to shape the role of IT in the late 1980s. Once UPS had built up its IT capability in the mid-1990s, the senior management team was reduced to four members. By reducing the number of senior managers on the steering committee, UPS released some management resources and attention for other strategic needs. Reducing the size of the steering committee was recognition that UPS had created sustainable senior management awareness of the importance of IT. Senior management had incorporated IT issues into a more holistic view of strategy at UPS. The smaller steering committee could represent the senior management team and share learning about IT with other senior managers.

For enterprises like Dow Corning and UPS, including the CIO as a member of the executive team enhanced the ability of a business monarchy to understand the role of IT in business strategy and to map the IT governance role of the executive team. Making the CIO a member of both the business monarchy and the IT monarchy provides a natural linkage between business and IT strategy. For large, complex enterprises, however, embellishing the CIO's role does not address the difficult issues associated with balancing the different needs of diverse business units. Large enterprises often implement federal arrangements.

Federal Decision-Making Structures

Almost 90 percent of enterprises in our study indicated that a senior executive committee played a role in IT governance. Where these senior executive teams drew members from all business units, they implemented a federal rather than business monarchy archetype. Because federal structures overtly work to balance enterprise and business unit priorities, they can provide valuable input to IT governance decisions.

The desire for shared data and IT infrastructures is at the heart of most federal IT organization designs. Mechanisms implementing federal IT governance protect business unit autonomy while developing the standards needed for integrated business capabilities. Management at Brady Corporation, a $500 million manufacturer of identification products, decided in the mid-1990s that success meant that business units would cease competing with one another and start cooperating.[4] Management believed that IT would be instrumental in enabling the change. So Brady created an IT Steering Team consisting of the heads of its three business groups, key business unit leaders, the CFO, and the CIO. This team takes responsibility for principles and investment decisions. Engaging business unit leaders in these discussions has facilitated development of—and commitment to—shared infrastructure and common data definitions.

Similarly, Old Mutual South Africa, a financial services firm with insurance, asset management, and banking operations, aims to operate as one system but with business unit accountability. OMSA's Strategic Investment Committee (SICOM) is chaired by the CEO and includes the CFO, CIO, and three business heads. SICOM makes IT investment decisions and tracks their results—just as it does all other investments at OMSA. The advantage of making IT investment decisions at this level is that the decision makers' combined expertise provides a holistic view of the enterprise. The committee is very aware of the tradeoffs among their investment choices. Thus, they are more likely to target investments strategically than to fritter away investment dollars on "nice-to-have" rather than "must have" business solutions.

While the importance of the involvement of business executives in IT governance is well established, many senior executives acknowledge that they didn't get involvement right the first time they tried. The wrong people were on the committee or committee members didn't always attend meetings, or members didn't understand their responsibilities. More than a few executives consider IT decisions of any kind to be tiresome. But persistence pays. Determined executives eventually learn how to create new business value and own IT through their work on executive committees. And once they understand the value these committees can drive, the work becomes downright compelling.

IT Monarchy Decision-Making Structures

Complementing business monarchies, IT monarchies make most of the world's IT architecture and infrastructure decisions. We will describe the two most common implementations of IT monarchies: IT leadership teams and IT architecture committees.

IT Leadership Teams

In most cases, the IT monarchy is represented, at least in part, by IT leadership teams. Leadership teams may comprise IT functional heads (operations, architecture, applications, and so on), they may be CIOs of business units, or they may be a combination of the two. In many financial services firms, IT leadership teams comprise the IT vice presidents from all the business units and functions (often numbering forty or more). These teams often make infrastructure and architectural decisions.

In many enterprises, business unit CIOs make up a decision-making body. At Old Mutual South Africa, business unit CIOs, who report to the CIO, are decision makers in all key IT decisions except investment decisions. The business unit CIOs approve the recommendations of specialized IT committees on architecture and infrastructure and establish firmwide IT policies. The business unit CIOs identify and address thorny business unit-enterprise tradeoffs.

One of the most difficult challenges facing leadership teams is resolving the different needs of business units that vary markedly in size and thus power. IT leadership teams in firms with business units of vastly different sizes do not give equal weight to the votes of their members. As one CIO noted, "This is not a democracy." Typically, the enterprise would benefit by focusing more resources on and shaping policies around the needs of dominant business units; but such enterprisewide decisions may disenfranchise small business units.

More than 85 percent of enterprises have formal IT leadership teams. In our study, enterprises with an IT leadership team had more effective governance performance than enterprises without such a mechanism. As long as these teams comprise competent, high-level individuals motivated to meet business needs, they can make invaluable contributions to enterprise success.

Architecture Committees

A second type of IT decision-making structure is the architecture committee. Usually made up of technical experts, IT architecture committees are responsible for defining standards and, in some cases, granting exceptions. In most cases, the role of the architecture committee is to advise the IT leadership team on architectural issues, but occasionally the architecture committee is a key governance decision-making body.

At Campbell Soup, the IT leadership team establishes mandates for Campbell's Architecture Review Board, which has representatives from the business units and the corporate architecture team.[5]

The Architecture Review Board prepares a three-year architectural blueprint for the company and monitors technology standards, classifying the status of relevant technologies as research, invest, maintain, or sunset. The Architecture Review Board works with the firm's project management, program review, and compliance teams to ensure that projects conform to architectural standards and meet business objectives. A key concern of the Architecture Review Board is ensuring that Campbell's IT environment evolves consistently with business goals. IT architectures are not static. Aging standards are retired slowly. New standards arrive with new or upgraded applications. The Architecture Review Board sets a technology direction for the firm and monitors implementations to keep the firm on course.

Approximately 85 percent of CIOs in our study reported having an architecture committee. At many enterprises, architecture committees get off to a rocky start, usually because the committees are formed to "impose" technology standards on the enterprise. Because standards limit autonomy, developers and their business partners tend to resist. As long as senior management espouses the standardization for business reasons, however, standards gradually gain acceptance. Application development and business unit managers come to appreciate the simplification and reliability of the standardized technology environment. The growing acceptance allows architecture committees to more effectively define an enterprise architecture and facilitate its implementation.

When architecture committees work closely with business unit managers, they are not only effective in introducing technology standards; they anticipate requirements for new technologies with valuable capabilities. To have impact, architecture committees must work intensely with both business unit leaders and application developers, educating them on the benefits of architecture and becoming increasingly familiar with their needs. Like IT leadership teams, IT architecture committees can make a significant contribution to enterprise objectives. Badly designed and implemented, however, they create obstacles to enterprise success.

Coordinating Business and IT Monarchies

IT monarchies are a natural and valuable approach to applying the enterprise's IT expertise. But the risk of IT monarchies is that, in coordinating IT efforts, they can become isolated from organizational reality. Enterprises waste considerable resources making technical improvements that no one converts into business value. Overlapping membership in IT leadership teams and senior executive teams, often in the person of the CIO, can align the activities of IT and business monarchies. Business unit CIOs are a second popular link for maintaining connections between IT monarchies and business leaders. In many cases, business unit CIOs sit on both the IT leadership team and the management team of their business units. The effect of these IT monarchies is then similar to a federal arrangement, though it is simpler to implement.

Duopoly Decision-Making Structures

The typical role of business leaders in IT governance is to clarify business objectives and incorporate IT capabilities into strategy formulation. The typical role of IT leaders is to help envision IT-enabled strategies, clarify architectural standards, and design shared infrastructures. The responsibilities of these two groups are obviously intertwined. Formal governance linkages often result in better performance, as we will see in the next chapter.

Linkages are sometimes accomplished through overlapping memberships on IT and business monarchy mechanisms, as described in the previous section. Alternatively, some enterprises establish duopoly governance arrangements that comprise joint IT and business members. Over 70 percent of the enterprises in our study had IT councils with joint business/IT membership. Around 85 percent of enterprises had process teams with IT members, and a similar percentage had business/IT relationship managers. These three mechanisms support duopoly archetypes.

IT Councils with Joint Business/IT Membership

One approach to ensuring business/IT interactions is through a joint decision council. For example, at Abbey National, the United Kingdom's sixth largest banking group, the IM leadership group includes representatives from both IT and business. In addition, many of the group's members have both IT and business responsibilities. The firm's IT director, for example, also has responsibility for business functions such as debt management and procurement.

The mix of business unit and IT skills represented in both individual skill sets and the membership of the committee enables the team to align business strategy and IT in making architecture, infrastructure, and business application decisions. The team's composition also helps identify and resolve the very different IT requirements for businesses ranging from the firm's large U.K. personal financial services business to its smaller wholesale banking arm.

Process Organizations

Increasing emphasis on cross-functional business process has led many enterprises to focus on process governance mechanisms. The marriage of process and IT is a natural in most enterprises because cross-functional business processes depend on information flows that cross organizational boundaries and are supported by the IT infrastructure. We found process councils—made up of process owners—working with IT executives to make business application decisions at organizations like DBS and ING. Process councils also have input into other IT decisions because they drive infrastructure needs at the enterprise level.

Much of the emphasis on business process is reflected in organizational units structured around projects. Project-oriented organizational designs facilitate management of cross-functional, multi-business unit processes and redirect management focus from business unit to enterprise objectives. These designs also position an enterprise for the organizational change requirements of IT projects.

As an example, MeadWestvaco has as many as 275 projects running simultaneously, and most have an IT component.[6] MeadWestvaco designed its IT Stewardship Model to organize IT governance around projects (figure 4-2). Following up on its enterprise resource planning (ERP) implementation, the firm is creating performance teams for each of its core processes. Process owners head up the performance teams. The process owners assign project teams drawn from multiple functional areas to staff process improvement initiatives. Project team members retain their functional responsibilities in MeadWestvaco, but they are accountable (responsible to each other) for the success of their project. Project teams closely monitor their projects, coding them red, yellow, or green to indicate their status. Projects are red when something goes wrong so

FIGURE 4-2

IT Stewardship Model and Roles at MeadWestvaco

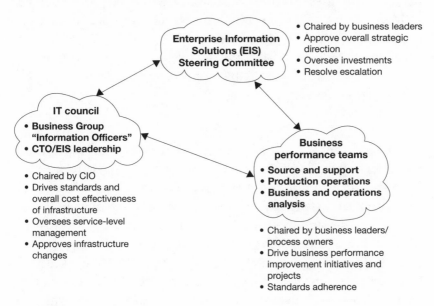

Enterprise Information
Solutions (EIS)
Steering Committee

- Chaired by business leaders
- Approve overall strategic direction
- Oversee investments
- Resolve escalation

IT council
- Business Group "Information Officers"
- CTO/EIS leadership

- Chaired by CIO
- Drives standards and overall cost effectiveness of infrastructure
- Oversees service-level management
- Approves infrastructure changes

Business performance teams
- Source and support
- Production operations
- Business and operations analysis

- Chaired by business leaders/ process owners
- Drive business performance improvement initiatives and projects
- Standards adherence

Source: MeadWestvaco corporate records. Used with permission.

that team members address the problem and senior management can investigate. When a project turns yellow, it gets attention so that it doesn't turn red. Everybody on the team is responsible for noting when something goes wrong and then changing the project code from green to yellow.

This closely monitored project arrangement operates in parallel with MeadWestvaco's IT Council. The IT Council is chaired by the corporate CIO, and its members have high-level IT responsibility within business units (such as business unit CIO or CFO). The Council makes standards decisions and approves infrastructure changes to address the needs of the business performance teams. The Council also works with the Enterprise Information Solutions (EIS) Steering Committee, which sets overall strategic direction. Comprising executive vice presidents, the senior vice president of research and technology, the CFO, the CIO, and one division president, the EIS

Steering Committee approves major IT investments. By designing governance to engage both business and IT leaders in its decision-making structures, MeadWestvaco has transcended formal organizational boundaries in pursuing process improvement and leveraging its ERP. Decision-making structures teaming up IT and business decision makers for process governance, particularly around projects, offer a particularly tangible opportunity to focus IT and business executives on strategic objectives.

Business/IT Relationship Managers

Local business units and functions can find centrally coordinated mandates onerous or confusing. Business/IT relationship managers play an important role in communicating mandates and their implications and supporting the needs of business unit managers while helping them see benefits rather than inconveniences. Effective relationship managers must be true hybrids—equally comfortable discussing business issues, such as effective market segmentation, and technical issues, such as the best design of a distributed database to collect customer segment information. When they succeed, relationship managers make any governance archetype more effective.

Commonwealth Bank of Australia (CBA) retained internal relationship managers when it outsourced its IT services. These managers facilitate the relationship between the business and the contractors to help the business units articulate business needs, maximize value, and minimize the cost of IT to their units. CBA has found that the key to successful relationship management is to have high-level IT managers who can gain the respect of senior business unit managers.

The Tennessee Valley Authority's IT unit assigns account managers to support business units, acting as their advocate in discussions with corporate IT. The account managers facilitate IT governance processes by ensuring that IT standards and the related buy list are understood and followed. Simultaneously, account managers communicate business issues to their IT coworkers. Account managers facilitate the exception process and assist in advancing business cases through the approval process. As a result, the effectiveness of the account managers depends a great deal on their ability to make the infrastructure responsive to business unit needs.[7]

In firms like DuPont, Campbell Soup, and Marriott, business unit CIOs play the role of relationship manager. They meet with corporate IT and with business unit heads to negotiate IT principles, architecture, and investment decisions. The organizational status of business unit CIOs empowers them to make decisions binding both business units and the enterprise.

Duopolies are particularly effective for enterprises experiencing problems aligning business and IT. In duopolies, business and IT interests are connected via joint decision making but still focused on meeting the single business unit's needs. This connection and focus increase the likelihood that IT will be strategically aligned and business executives will understand their role in generating value from IT. Duopoly decision-making mechanisms, however, often require large memberships with unique capabilities. Duopolies also typically rely on the central IT group to implement firmwide initiatives such as shared services or common platforms for business processes. The key to effective duopolies is to find a mix of senior leaders representing both business and IT with the status to enlist the entire enterprise in IT-enabled initiatives while recognizing the needs of each business unit.

Alignment Processes

Decision-making structures are the first step in designing IT governance. But effective governance is as much actions as decisions. Alignment processes are IT management techniques for securing widespread involvement in the effective management and use of IT. Alignment processes should bring everybody on board both by providing input into governance decisions and by disseminating the outputs of IT decisions. Key alignment processes include the IT investment approval process, the architecture exception process, service-level agreements, chargeback, project tracking, and formal tracking of business value from IT.

IT Investment Approval Process

The objective of the IT investment approval process is to ensure that IT investments generate significant returns to the enterprise relative to alternative investment opportunities. Most enterprises formalize their IT investment proposal process to ensure that creative ideas and strategic priorities are considered by investment decision makers. Many enterprises use standardized IT investment approval application templates to estimate metrics such as ROI, NPV, and risk for each project. Without investment templates, decision makers struggle to compare projects and can miss opportunities for value from investments with less certain benefits.

While standardized project proposals expose the relative benefits and risks of individual projects, they are less effective in establishing how a proposed project contributes to an enterprise's strategic objectives. Most enterprises rely on business units and functions to establish their priorities based on business unit and function objectives. Investment committees typically determine the set of projects that together provide the greatest strategic benefits to the enterprise.

UPS focuses on strategic priorities by organizing the investment process around its core processes. IT investment proposals emanate from the firm's four cross-functional process teams. The process teams submit formal project charters to the IT Steering Committee. Because the processes are cross functional, the charters transcend organizational boundaries. The processes embody the firm's strategic priorities, making it easier for the IT steering committee to assess the strategic impact of IT investment opportunities.

USAA relies on its Integration Steering Committee to assess strategic priorities of all IT and non-IT projects.[8] This nine-member committee has senior-level representatives from major business units and functions including IT. Headed by an executive officer of Enterprise Business Operations, who is a direct report to the CEO, the committee considers factors such as shared requirements across proposals, potential value to the firm, the availability of needed infrastructure, and the readiness of the organization to effectively implement the project. The charter of the Integration Steering Committee is to implement the firm's operating model—a model based on a single view of the customer. Because the operating model demands integration across business units, a growing percentage of USAA's investment dollars are funding enterprise projects such as customer relationship management, e-commerce applications, workflow management, and employee intranet. But at USAA, even business unit–specific projects must pass the test of strategic importance to the enterprise.

Without an effective IT investment approval process, IT investments invariably build toward localized rather than enterprise
goals. In doing so, project proposals often overestimate benefits because they fail to consider the combined impact of the full set of an
enterprise's projects. One investment committee reviewed a set of IT
project proposals that, according to their estimated benefits, could
have combined to reduce the firm's headcount by over 100 percent!
The IT investment approval process is a critical determinant as to
whether IT is a strategic enabler or simply a huge expense.

Architectural Exception Process

Few enterprises can afford to support every technical platform
that the business might find useful. Technology standards are critical to IT—and business—efficiency. But occasional exceptions are
not only appropriate; they are necessary. The question is how you
can identify the occasional exception. The answer is the architectural exception process.

Exceptions are how enterprises learn. Enterprises use the exception process to meet unique business needs and to gauge when
existing standards are becoming obsolete. Exceptions act as a release valve for reducing organizational pressures. We are often im-
pressed by the passion with which managers advocate their exception positions. Without a viable exception process, business units
ignore the enterprisewide standards and implement exceptions
with no approval. This approach raises organizational tensions that
build over time as more unauthorized exceptions occur. Other business unit managers who follow the rules get frustrated. We have
heard stories of heated debates and the occasional table thumping.
The result is typically more vigilant IT architecture enforcement
that we have heard described as "here come the IT police again."
Worse still, the unauthorized exceptions rob the enterprise of the
opportunity to learn.

Architecture committees usually have responsibility for establishing standards. In many cases the architecture committee also
takes responsibility for granting exceptions to standards. These
committees, however, can easily become mired in insignificant bat-
tles, which create a bottleneck in IT implementations. To avoid this
dilemma, most architecture exception requests should be resolved
before they reach the architecture committee.

The most successful exception processes resolve most issues at the project team level, while quickly escalating any potentially strategic exception requests. One approach is to put an IT architect on every project team. The architects clarify standards and eliminate minor debates. They can also help a project team make the case for valuable exceptions.

In firms where standardization is a fairly comfortable fit—for example, an enterprise emphasizing low-cost operations—exception requests are necessarily rare. Project architects understand the expectation that systems implementations must conform to standards. CIOs at Air Products and MeadWestvaco note that, because exceptions are rare, they can personally handle the occasional request for an exception. Architecture committees need not become involved.

In financial services, logistics, and other enterprises for which IT is part of the product, exception requests are more frequent. If the project architect senses the need for an exception, the case is often referred to an architecture committee. Effective architecture committees have a high threshold for the quality of the business case that must accompany an exception request. This threshold helps reduce the number of exceptions to only those of particularly great importance to project teams—and the enterprise.

At State Street Corporation, the local IT manager or the project manager working on the initiative has responsibility to justify an exception to the standard and then bring it to the owner of the standard and the enterprise Office of Architecture. The project manager and the owner of the standard discuss the advantages and disadvantages of going "off standard." If the project manager and the standard owner cannot agree on the exception, it is immediately referred for arbitration to the CIO, COO, and business unit leader. This appears to be a steep escalation process, but as the former CIO explains, there are some inherent advantages to this approach. "It definitely sounds severe to immediately escalate to this level but it's the easiest way of dealing with the responsiveness issue, because if you do not respond quickly the business will be concerned about the potential delay and may circumvent the process altogether."[9]

The effectiveness of the architecture exception process depends on the ability of the IT unit to research and define standards and on the enterprise's commitment to technology standards. Where technology standardization is effectively implemented, a rapid exception escalation process reinforces the enterprise architecture and helps the enterprise build an enabling IT capability.

Service-Level Agreements

Service-level agreements (SLAs), used by 90 percent of the enterprises in our study, list available services, alternative quality levels, and related costs. Through negotiations between the IT services unit and business units, an SLA leads to articulation of the services IT offers and the costs of the services. These negotiations clarify the requirements of the business units, thereby informing governance decisions on infrastructure, architecture, and business application needs.

SLAs often encourage comparisons with external providers. The comparisons should result in either cost-effective internal service provisioning or a decision to outsource some infrastructure services—in either case a desirable outcome. Commonwealth Bank of Australia, for example, estimates annual IT cost savings of about 20 percent as a result of repackaging and eventually outsourcing infrastructure services. SLAs also encourage business units to be conscientious in their IT requests. Guaranteed split-second response times on Web transactions typically cost more than three-second response times. Similarly, a thirty-minute guaranteed response time to a workstation going down is costlier than a four-hour guaranteed response time. A customer service representative in a call center can justify the extra cost of a guaranteed thirty-minute response time because of the potential for lost revenue. An administrative assistant in the accounting office probably could not.

SLAs force IT units to think like external providers. They "sell" their services and thus must constantly look for ways to save money. The challenge of the SLA process is in translating business service-level requirements into IT services. IT costs result from labor and from processing time, storage capacity, and the like. Business units require services such as processing of invoices, Web access, and rapid response to online queries. Increasingly, IT units are translating their costs into charges business managers can understand. An SLA listing IT costs in IT terms will not help business units make choices on IT service levels or use the services wisely.

Nor will it help IT service committees design shared services. The SLA has value when communications about business needs and IT services facilitate decisions that lead to lower costs and better utilization of IT resources.

SLAs should help IT and business managers make better choices—choices about how to buy, sell, and price. Well-designed SLAs encourage professionalism on both sides of the supply-demand chain. The result is better IT services and better understanding by both business and IT of the business value generated.

Chargeback

Chargeback is an accounting mechanism for allocating central IT costs to business units. At first glance, it does not seem related to IT governance decisions. However, we found that some enterprises use chargeback successfully for aligning decisions on infrastructure, business application needs, and IT investment with business objectives.

The purpose of chargeback is to allocate costs so that business unit IT costs reflect use of shared services while the shared services unit matches its costs with the businesses it supports. Chargeback may work with SLAs as the charging mechanism for services delivered or it can be an alternative to SLA for IT services for which there are no alternative service levels. Like SLAs, management usually anticipates that chargeback will lead to effective use of IT. Most managers reflect market-based behaviors in response to IT chargeback, adjusting their demands according to the value they receive and pushing back on IT unit charges when they seem out of line.

The fixed nature of many IT costs—and the variable needs of IT's internal clients—complicate IT cost computations and obscure some cost savings. As a result, IT charges often lead to internal, typically nonvalue-added debates. Instead of promoting informative discussions about IT and business value or leading to more responsible buyer and consumer behaviors, chargeback often leads to undesirable outcomes—endless complaints, lack of trust, averting formal approval processes, or not using shared services.

When IT understands its costs and charges out accordingly, chargeback processes demonstrate the cost savings resulting from shared services. Enterprises with effective costing mechanisms find that chargeback can foster useful discussions between IT and business units about IT charges.[10] These discussions lead to better-informed IT governance decisions.

Project Tracking

A critical step in implementing IT governance is to develop the discipline to track the progress of individual IT projects. Over 90 percent of enterprises in our study indicated that they are tracking project resources consumed. Enterprises use a variety of tools to support project tracking. Dashboards—some like the red-yellow-green system at MeadWestvaco, others more quantitative—highlight when projects are off target. Dashboards alert management to potential problems early and enable actions to forestall delays or cost overruns.

At top-performing enterprises, tracking is just one element of a standard project management methodology. Some enterprises rely on the Capability Maturity Model, a highly standardized process for certifying organizational project management.[11] Other enterprises apply an internally developed project management methodology. There is little evidence that one type of metric or project management methodology is more successful than another, but any attempt to measure implementation milestones and to quickly identify and address problems greatly enhances the likelihood of implementation success.

Formal Tracking of Business Value

Much of the challenge of effective IT governance results from the difficulty of assessing the value of IT. IT decision makers make more effective decisions as they better understand the value the enterprise receives from IT. Formally tracking the business value of IT enhances organizational learning about the value of IT-enabled initiatives.

Approximately 60 percent of respondents in our study indicated that their enterprises formally tracked business value. Tracking includes determining whether expectations for a project's cost reductions or revenue increases actually materialized. One CTO noted that the first time her firm conducted post-implementation reviews they found that 0 percent of the firm's projects the prior year had met objectives. In one year, the percentage of projects meeting business objectives increased to 40 percent—mostly the result of focusing the attention of managers on expectations. The value-tracking process helps both business and IT executives to understand the sources of and obstacles to generating value from IT investments. With practice, it also leads to more realistic estimates of the proposed benefits of a system.

Because project outcomes are difficult to isolate—particularly when projects are part of larger program goals—increasing numbers of enterprises are formalizing intermediate objectives. For example, JPMorgan Chase tracks the number of projects introducing non-standard technologies as an indicator of the viability of its standard-setting process. Many IT units track the cost of infrastructure services with a goal of constantly decreasing unit costs. These intermediate objectives often apply six sigma or related quality management techniques. The additional metrics growing out of intermediate objectives clarify management accountabilities and provide another basis for assessing IT outcomes.

IT governance is about empowering all an enterprise's employees. The decision-making mechanisms focus on hammering out business strategy and the implications for IT. Alignment processes allow strategic decisions to guide daily actions. In addition, alignment processes allow daily experiences with IT to feed back into the strategy process. A third type of governance mechanism—communication approaches—is essential to make governance arrangements known.

Communications Approaches

Communication mechanisms are intended to "spread the word" about IT governance decisions and processes and related desirable behaviors throughout the enterprise. Firms communicate their governance mechanisms in a variety of ways. We found that the more management communicated formally about the existence of IT governance mechanisms, how they worked, and what outcomes were expected, the more effective was their governance.

Senior Management Announcements

Senior management announcements clarifying priorities and demonstrating commitment usually get a great deal of attention throughout an enterprise. Eighty-seven percent of responding enterprises indicated that they communicate governance through senior management announcements. Many firms tested governance communications in the late 1990s as they put in enterprise-wide systems or major new infrastructure platforms. For example, Dow Corning announced that during its two-year ERP implementation process, no other IT implementations would be considered. Similarly, management at Delta Air Lines committed to rebuilding infrastructure for airline operations and customer experience and explicitly refused to consider other functions or processes. Commitment to this kind of clarity about what will and will not be done helps everyone in an enterprise focus their attention on strategic objectives.[12]

As IT becomes more strategic in enterprises, IT governance grows more important. Developing a communication strategy to announce and explain new IT governance processes contributes to achieving the objectives of the governance design. A number of firms use rallying themes to keep everyone focused on their governance objectives. Management at DBS has spread the gospel about Asia21, a program to create the infrastructure for the next generation of DBS services and products. Anchored by a technology foundation, Asia21 incorporates new approaches to process innovation, risk management, performance measures, people and organizational structures, and data management.

Many current IT initiatives intend to create more integrated enterprises. Integrating formerly autonomous functions or business units involves changes in not only IT but also business processes and organizational culture. Well-circulated, persistent themes like "One State Street" prepare organizational members for the change. Communicating governance processes facilitates the change and provides a road map for what could otherwise be perceived as an idle threat or promise.

Formal Committees

Despite concerns about committee meetings demanding too much time, much IT governance is committee work. Ideally, IT governance requires few new committees; especially at the executive level, governance decisions can be folded into ongoing responsibilities. Ad hoc committees, however, are often important mechanisms. The decision-making bodies described earlier in this chapter are often committees. Committees also make lower-level governance decisions and carry out high-level decisions. For example, project work often relies on committees of stakeholders to define requirements, monitor progress, and identify potential issues. As Chase Manhattan Bank (now JPMorgan Chase) implemented e-business initiatives, the head of e-business met with stakeholders of all initiatives for forty-five minutes each week.[13] The participants in the meetings discussed progress on the project and related efforts, including infrastructure development and architectural issues. These large gatherings led to greater understanding of the governance decisions around enterprise architecture and shared infrastructure, and their implications for individual business application projects.

Committee meetings are important too because informal mechanisms such as water cooler discussions have proved to be sadly ineffective. In our study, extensive use of informal communications was the only communication approach not associated with high governance effectiveness. Careful committee assignments are required to involve executives in decisions important to them. Electronic tools can overcome geographical barriers, making it possible to staff committees that can make decisions, accept accountability, and monitor implementation. Communications within and across committees align the efforts of the committees with other governance initiatives.

Office of CIO or IT Governance

IT governance needs a recognized advocate, owner, and organizational home. Eighty-six percent of participants in our study used an office of IT governance or the office of the CIO to communicate governance arrangements. IT governance needs an owner to ensure that individual mechanisms reinforce rather than contradict one another and to communicate governance processes and purposes. Just as important, the person, team, or committee responsible for IT governance needs to ensure alignment between IT governance and the governance of the enterprise's other key assets (financial, human, physical, IP, and relationship). The office of the CIO or the office of IT governance are effective mechanisms for advocating and educating about IT governance. Who should own and thus be held accountable for IT governance is an important decision we return to in chapter 8.

Working with Nonconformists

Rarely do all affected managers enthusiastically embrace IT governance decisions. When managers engage in behaviors that undermine enterprise architecture, disregard IT investment guidelines, duplicate shared infrastructure, or ignore project-tracking standards, they may be demonstrating lack of awareness of governance decisions or an unwillingness to adopt mandated practices. Working with managers who stray from desirable behaviors is a necessary part of generating the potential value of governance processes.

Eighty-four percent of the respondents in our study respond to nonconforming behavior by visiting with offending managers to explain the rationale for IT governance. The visits usually establish whether managers are ignoring governance arrangements because they do not know them or because they do not agree with them. Then a dialogue can commence to educate, address concerns, make exceptions, or even change ineffective governance or managers. Most IT units find the visits a particularly important mechanism for communicating architecture and its implications. At DBS, IT architects have accepted responsibility for guiding managers toward architecture acceptance. One architect noted: "We are seeing ourselves more as architecture social workers rather than the architecture police."[14]

Web-Based Portals

Much communication around IT governance is to educate organizational members on IT governance processes, including specific procedures for mechanisms such as investment proposals, architectural exceptions, and service-level agreements. Web-based portals provide a central communications channel for many enterprises. IT governance owners use the portals to make announcements and updates. Some portals have examples of IT investment cases with templates. Other portals have lists of approved IT software and hardware with instructions on ordering hardware and software. Portals can also support IT governance by posting metrics from project-tracking systems. Ninety percent of the enterprises in our study used portals to communicate IT governance. Portals also increase governance transparency by making available enterprise policies, standards, performance, and sometimes debate.

Seven of the mechanisms we discussed earlier were high impact but challenging to implement (figure 4-3). When implemented well, they led to better IT governance performance, which we found is related to financial performance. Figure 4-3 describes these mechanisms both when they work well and when they go wrong. Our advice is either to focus on implementing these mechanisms effectively so that they will pay off or to drop them completely. Anything in between creates frustration, noise, and waste.

Ultimately, the effect of any given governance mechanism depends on how well it is implemented and how it fits with other mechanisms. Large enterprises find governance wanting unless they attend to all three types of mechanisms: decision-making structures to clarify who is responsible and accountable for decisions, alignment processes to ensure effective input to decision makers and implementation of their decisions, and communication tools to disseminate governance processes and individual responsibilities to everyone who needs to know. Carlson Companies provides a good example of how firms integrate the three types of mechanisms to effect good governance.

Coordinating Multiple Mechanisms: The Case of Carlson Companies

Carlson Companies (Carlson) is a $19.8 billion privately owned conglomerate in the marketing, hospitality, and travel business. Carlson has grown through acquisition and has operating groups in relationship marketing services, loyalty programs, hotels, restaurants, cruises, and travel services. Among the names in Carlson's portfolio are Regent International Hotels, Radisson Hotels & Resorts, T.G.I. Friday's restaurants, Carlson Marketing Group (specializing in relationship marketing), Carlson Wagonlit Travel (a business travel management company), Radisson Seven Seas Cruises, and Gold Points Reward Network (a consumer loyalty program). Headquartered in Minneapolis, Minnesota, Carlson Companies and

FIGURE 4-3

High-Impact but Challenging Mechanisms

Mechanisms	Objectives	Desirable Behavior	Undesirable Behavior Observed
Executive and senior management committee	Holistic view of business, including IT	Seamless management incorporating IT	IT ignored
Architecture committee	Identify strategic technologies and standards—enforcement?	Business-driven IT decision making	IT police and delays
Process teams with IT membership	Take process view using IT (and other assets) effectively	End-to-end process management	Stagnation of functional skills and fragmented IT infrastructure
Capital investment approval and budgets	Consider IT as another business investment	Prudent IT investing—different approaches for different investment types	Paralysis by analysis Small projects to avoid formal approval
Service-level agreements	Specify and measure IT service	Professional supply and demand	Manage to SLA, not business need
Chargeback	Recoup IT costs from business	Responsible use of IT	Arguments about charges and warped demand
Formal tracking of business value of IT	Measure IT investments and contribution to business value often using balanced scorecard	Makes transparent: goals, benefits, and costs	Separates IT from other assets Focus on money, not value

© 2003 MIT Sloan School Center for Information Systems Research (CISR). Used with permission.

its franchises employ more than 180,000 people in more than 140 countries.

In 2000, Chairman and CEO Marilyn Carlson Nelson articulated a vision of presenting Carlson customers with an integrated view of Carlson's businesses.[15] Traditionally, each operating group functioned independently and was even encouraged to compete with other operating groups. Nelson intended to change the relationship between operating groups from competition to collaboration. She enlisted CIO Steve Brown to map out the technological underpinnings for this change. Brown, who reports directly to the CEO, was given responsibility for defining the role of IT for the integrated enterprise.

Brown defined two IT principles:

1. Application development can continue to take place within operating groups, but applications should be presented to users through a shared portal, and, where necessary, data will be shared across business units.

2. Carlson will have a shared IT infrastructure.

To translate these principles into IT architecture and infrastructure, business applications, and IT investment decisions, Carlson assigned IT governance responsibilities to five decision-making structures: the Carlson Technology Architecture Committees (CTAC) residing in the operating groups, the Enterprise Architecture Organization (EAO), the IT Council, the Carlson Shared Services Board, and the Investment Committee. Our description of Carlson's Governance Arrangements Matrix is shown in figure 4-4.

Decision-Making Structures

Each Carlson operating group has a Carlson Technology Architecture Committee (CTAC) made up of technologists who take an operating group perspective. The CTACs are primarily responsible for meeting the needs of their operating groups within enterprise standards. CTACs also provide input into enterprisewide architecture decisions.

CIO Brown set up the Enterprise Architecture Organization (EAO) to facilitate enterprisewide standardization efforts under Mark

FIGURE 4-4

IT Governance at Carlson Companies

	DECISION									
	IT Principles		IT Architecture		IT Infrastructure Strategies		Business Application Needs		IT Investment	
GOVERNANCE ARCHETYPE	Input	Decision	Input	Decision	Input	Decision	Input	Decision	Input	Decision
Business Monarchy	Chairman and CEO									Invest. comm.
IT Monarchy		CIO		CIO EAO						
Feudal							All business leaders	Business CIOs Some business leaders CTAC		
Federal			CTAC							
Duopoly					EAO CEOs of business units	IT council CSS board			IT council CSS board CIO	

☐ Most common pattern for all firms.

Governance mechanisms:
CSS board—Carlson Shared Services: CFO and CTO of each operating group
CIO—CIO staff
CTAC—Carlson Technology Architecture Group (one in each operating group)
EAO—Enterprise Architecture Organization
Invest. comm.—Investment committee; subset of executive committee
IT council—CIOs and CTO of operating groups

Price, Director of Information Technology. Price works with a team of two architects from each operating group to establish and monitor new technology standards. The Enterprise Architecture Organization sets corporatewide standards guiding the development efforts of all the operating units.

The Executive Committee, including Brown, established Carlson Shared Services (CSS) to build the infrastructure capability designed by the EAO. CSS provides both IT infrastructure and financial services within the enterprise. The CSS Board, which comprises the CTOs and CFOs of the operating groups, examines any new technologies from a financial point of view.

The IT Council is made up of the CTOs and CIOs of all the operating groups. The Council meets monthly to talk about new technologies and ways technology can be leveraged across Carlson. Finally, an Investment Committee, made up of members of the senior executive committee, gives final judgment on all large Carlson Companies investment projects.

These decision-making structures have clarified IT governance responsibilities at Carlson Companies and are consistent with the CEO's vision for how the firm should operate. By soliciting input from additional sources, these decision-making structures align IT decisions with organizational goals. Carlson further benefits from alignment processes and communication tools to implement effective governance throughout the enterprise.

Alignment Processes

The alignment challenge at Carlson involves balancing integration across operating groups with preserving sufficient autonomy to allow each operating group to succeed in its market environment. Key alignment processes at Carlson are its service catalog (comparable to service-level agreements), its IT investment and funding approach, and its architecture exception process.

Service Catalog

To define and manage the portfolio of shared services offered by CSS, Brown solicited input from the CEOs of the operating groups to ascertain their common business needs for infrastructure services. Operating groups had the option to buy services externally, resulting in a mix of internally and externally provided services. After "unbundling" every service used at Carlson, Brown and the IT group collected eighty-nine services into a "service catalog." Each service definition was in industry standard terms and clearly understood by the operating groups. Once the services were defined, the IT group benchmarked them against thirty-six vendors for cost and service-level availability. The firm updates these benchmarks annually, and the service catalog regularly facilitates conversations between the IT group and business unit managers. For example, if a business wants a given network service with 99.99 percent reliability, then the catalog shows how much it will cost in-house or from an outside vendor.

Investment and Funding Approach

Given the feudal approach to business applications, operating groups fund their individual applications. The office of the CIO and the operating groups share funding for enterprise architecture projects proportionally split by expected benefits from the initiative. Every request goes through an Authorization-for-Funding Process. The process requires details about what will be delivered and when, and where the financial or business benefits will occur. Whoever proposes a project is held accountable for promised results. To support development of the enterprise architecture, Carlson's Capital Budgeting Committee allocates some funding for architecture initiatives to the CIO. This discretionary fund allows the CIO to seed projects until operating groups can see benefits from them.

Architecture Exception Process

To encourage collaboration between his office and the operating groups and to best reflect the needs of all the operating groups in architecture decisions, Mark Price seeks input from a variety of individuals in the operating groups. He views his role as that of a facilitator: "Our approach in the Enterprise Architecture Organization is really a facilitation office. We bring ideas and maybe some technical resources to bear, but the work and the design and the people that are delivering come from the business units. We learn where the business units have needs, and, if we architect to that direction, we end up with a more feasible architecture."

If a proposal from a business unit does not fit current standards, the proposal is evaluated by the Enterprise Architecture Organization (EAO). If the application is limited to one operating group, the technology decision stays within the confines of the respective CTAC. If eventually more than one operating group becomes interested, then the EAO puts together a small working group made up of one architect from each interested operating group. The working group then defines the standard for the enterprise.

These three processes—service catalog, investment and funding, and architecture exception—work with Carlson's decision-making structures to provide input to decision making and to delegate ongoing decisions to appropriate individuals and teams throughout the firm. To help individuals understand how governance works and how they make it work, Carlson has implemented communication tools.

Communication Tools

Two key communication tools at Carlson are senior management announcements and formal committees that disseminate their decisions. CEO Nelson regularly shares her vision for Carlson, including her rallying cry for an "integrated Carlson." The "integrated Carlson" concept provides a constant reminder as to how the firm wants to use IT. Simultaneously, committees with both corporate and operating group members—most notably the Enterprise Architecture Office, the CSS Board, and the IT Council—offer recurring opportunities to communicate with key operating group leaders to clarify IT governance and its implications for the operating groups.

Combined, the governance mechanisms at Carlson have supported Brown's efforts to reduce IT costs while moving the company closer to the CEO's vision of an "integrated Carlson." As at Carlson, we recommend that every enterprise needs at least one high-performing mechanism in each category. Having a smaller number of effective mechanisms is superior to having many mechanisms that may vary considerably in effectiveness and introduce confusion about accountability.

Implementing Governance: Principles for Mechanisms

This chapter has reviewed three types of IT governance mechanisms and identified key mechanisms within each type. Individually, mechanisms should exhibit three characteristics:

1. *Simple:* Mechanisms unambiguously define the responsibility or objective for a specific person or group.

2. *Transparent:* Effective mechanisms rely on formal processes. How the mechanism works is clear to those who are affected by or want to challenge governance decisions.

3. *Suitable:* Mechanisms engage individuals in the best position to make given decisions.

Mechanisms, however, do not act in isolation. The impact of governance mechanisms depends on interactions among the mechanisms. We observed five principles for designing effective sets of mechanisms:

1. *Choose mechanisms from all three types.* Decision-making, alignment, and communication mechanisms have different objectives. All are important to effective governance.

2. *Limit decision-making structures.* Decision making in enterprises is not a "more the merrier" phenomenon. Complex organizations require multiple decision-making structures, but the more decision-making structures, the more opportunities for contradictions and disconnections. Decision-making responsibilities should be disseminated throughout an enterprise using alignment mechanisms, not decision-making structures.

3. *Provide for overlapping membership in decision-making structures.* IT governance requires serious input about both strategic business needs and technology capabilities. To ensure that these critical perspectives influence all IT governance decisions, key decision-making bodies need overlapping memberships or clear mandates. IT governance design should avoid disconnects between IT and business decisions.

4. *Implement mechanisms at multiple levels in the enterprise.* Although diverse enterprises may have limited integration and standardization requirements, a single business unit may want tightly integrated processes. Accordingly, IT governance design at the enterprise level reflects only one layer of governance. Enterprise-level governance influences decisions at the business unit level, but business units often need their own governance arrangements and corresponding mechanisms. Good governance in a multibusiness unit

firm requires connections between the enterprisewide and business unit governance. Mechanisms such as architecture committees and IT budget processes often provide these connections.

5. *Clarify accountability.* Multiple mechanisms can inadvertently create confusion over who is responsible for what or limit the ability of managers to manage outcomes for which they are responsible. The design of IT governance should clarify management objectives and metrics.

In the next chapter we focus on high-performing enterprises. We discuss both the governance archetypes they rely on and the specific mechanisms they implement.

5

What IT Governance Works Best

WHAT GOVERNANCE arrangements work best? Senior managers from a variety of businesses told us the following:

> There is a very highly disciplined project management system, well defined, with totally educated users, everybody knows the vocabulary—all the chief executives of the company know phases of project management. We all talk the same language.
>
> *—CIO, financial services firm*

> The governance procedures we developed brought transparency and accountability into the process.
>
> *—CIO, national police force of a European country*

> Everything that you try to accomplish from an enterprise perspective is all about identifying [what is] not unique to any one line of business. We're able to identify something—an application, or a process, or what have you—that everybody can reuse.
>
> *—SVP for process, financial services firm*

When governance flounders, things break down:

> We were not making best use of our opportunities. . . . The business case for an IT initiative included costs for the project itself,

with some infrastructure thrown in. We used a full chargeback model, so the first project needing a particular piece of infrastructure had to pay the entire cost of creating it.

—*CIO, government agency*

The governance board—composed of the corporate controller, eight domestic CIOs (the most senior and seasoned), and three regional CIOs (Asia, Europe, Latin America)—has been meeting for a year, but anyone who has attended the meetings views it as dysfunctional. No one pays attention or takes it seriously.

—*CIO, global manufacturing firm*

We have to rejustify our refresh strategy every year. What should have been a ten-minute pitch took forty-five minutes. . . . The management committee turned into a team of volunteer architects to redesign cheaper desktops.

—*CIO, telecommunications firm*

Do any of these situations sound familiar? These quotations illustrate the multifaceted nature of IT governance for large enterprises. Getting ten managers into a room to discuss their governance challenges will generate at least ten opinions of what works well. To date, there has been little experience-based research to reveal what governance arrangements work best, and yet understanding what works best in general as well as in meeting particular performance objectives informs governance design. This chapter will provide some evidence and propose guiding principles for IT governance arrangements at large, complex enterprises. The principles come from measuring governance performance and financial performance in a large sample of enterprises and analyzing quantitatively and qualitatively which arrangements work best. The resulting set of best practices provides insights into which of the six governance archetypes (business or IT monarchy, feudal, duopoly, federal, or anarchy) best support each of the five key IT decisions (IT principles, infrastructure, architecture, business application needs, and investment). You can use the resulting general governance principles as input, along with the more enterprise specific strategic, organizational, and cultural issues to design the optimal IT governance for their firm.

Three questions best capture these insights:

- How can we assess governance?
- What governance arrangements work best?
- How do leading enterprises govern?

The answers should provide you with the language and evidence to tackle the governance issues in your enterprise. Since historical performance in a large number of enterprises can indicate only what worked elsewhere, senior management must combine these general findings with the firm's unique goals, strategies, and cultural norms. Chapters 6, 7, and 8 address that challenge.

How to Assess IT Governance

We defined governance as specifying the decision rights and accountability framework to encourage desirable behavior in IT usage. Governance performance must then be how well the governance arrangements encouraged desirable behaviors and ultimately how well the firm achieved its desired performance goals. To provide some structure to this multifaceted issue, we use the framework in figure 5-1.

We identified five important factors when assessing governance—enterprise setting, governance arrangements, governance awareness, governance performance, and financial performance. To assess governance performance, we measured each of these factors. We suggest using the framework to compare your enterprise with those described here. Enterprise setting captures the industry, the size, the number of business units, and the relationship among the business units (the level of synergy desired between business units). Governance arrangements describe which archetypes are used for each IT decision and which mechanisms are used for implementation. Governance awareness establishes how well everyone across the firm understands governance and identifies the communications approaches to engaging management. The percentage of projects with exceptions—both formally approved and renegade—indicates how

FIGURE 5-1

Assessing IT Governance Performance

Setting	Governance arrangements	Governance awareness	Governance performance	Financial performance
Strategy: • Operational excellence • Customer intimacy • Product leadership	**Key IT decisions and archetypes** **Mechanisms:** • Councils • SLAs • IT organization • Chargeback • Architecture Committee	**Percent of managers in leadership positions who can describe governance** **Communication approaches:** • Meetings • Documents • Portal **Exceptions:** Percent of projects	Average of four performance measures weighted by importance Score out of 100 **Effective use of IT for:** • Cost control • Growth • Asset utilization • Business flexibility	**Profit:** • Percent margin • ROE • ROI **Asset utilization:** ROA **Growth:** Percent change in revenue **Data measured using:** Three-year average industry-adjusted percent change
Size: Number of BUs				
Synergy and/or autonomy of BUs				
IT intensity: • Money • People				

uniformly people apply the governance arrangements and what learning results from change.

Governance performance assesses the effectiveness of IT governance in delivering four objectives weighted by their importance to the enterprise:

1. Cost-effective use of IT
2. Effective use of IT for asset utilization
3. Effective use of IT for growth
4. Effective use of IT for business flexibility

When assessing governance performance, senior managers first identify the relative importance of these four factors in their enterprises and then rate enterprise performance on each factor. Using a weighted average formula, they can calculate a score out of 100. Appendix B contains the questions and the formula to calculate governance performance; you can pause now to complete it so that you can benchmark your enterprise against the following results.

Asking senior managers to rate the impact of governance on firm performance offers one perspective on the effectiveness of IT governance. But ultimately, we should see IT governance impact business performance metrics. Although many other factors influence financial performance measures, strong performance provides confidence in the firm's IT governance. Assessing financial performance requires financial metrics covering the major categories. We investigated whether leaders in the following three dimensions of financial performance (adjusted for industry differences) governed differently from other firms:[1]

- *Profit:* Return on equity (ROE), return on investment (ROI), percent profit margin
- *Asset utilization:* Return on assets (ROA)
- *Growth:* Percent change in revenue per annum[2]

We found firms that led their industries in each of these three dimensions of performance governed differently from other firms. We explore these differences later in the chapter.

How Governance Varies Across Enterprises

Governance performance varies significantly across enterprises and is approximately bell shaped (figure 5-2). The average governance performance score was 69 out of 100. The minimum score was 20 and the top third performing firms had scores over 74. Only 17 percent of enterprises scored 80 or above and only 7 percent scored 90 or over. Achieving high governance performance meant that the enterprise's IT governance succeeded in influencing the desired measures of success. How does your enterprise compare?

Firms with above-average IT governance following a specific strategy (for example, customer intimacy) had a 20 percent higher ROA than firms with poorer governance following the same strategy. Governance was, of course, not the only factor, but good IT governance often comes with focus and effective management practices in all areas. The governance performance measure also statistically significantly correlates with several three-year average

FIGURE 5-2

Wide Variance in Governance Performance

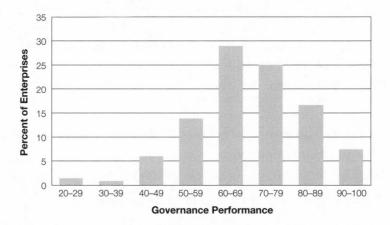

Research conducted at 256 enterprises in twenty-three countries.

industry-adjusted measures of financial performance (for example, ROE and market capitalization growth). We are not saying governance performance caused superior financial performance. However, we can say superior financial performers have high governance performance, and we can study how those enterprises governed.

We suggest that designing IT governance requires working from left to right in figure 5-1 using the IT Governance Design Framework (figure 1-3) and Governance Arrangements Matrix (figure 1-2). To assist managers designing effective governance we now explore what arrangements (a) work best as measured by governance performance and (b) are used by financially top-performing firms. Governance performance is a good broad measure of overall performance, and the lessons from these top governance performers can be applied in any situation. Then we will learn from top performers on a particular financial metric (say, growth) how to target governance to more finely tuned financial goals. If performance balanced across several performance goals is your objective, then focus on the governance performance findings. If you have one clear and enduring financial metric as a target, then carefully consider the findings on financial performance governance arrangements.

Seven Characteristics of Top Governance Performers

We start by teasing out what top governance performers do that is different from the other enterprises. Regardless of their industry, level of IT investment, strategies, or any other factors, the high governance performers differed from other enterprises on seven characteristics. All the relationships with governance performance and financial performance described in the remainder of this chapter are statistically significant and thus unlikely to be due to chance.

The seven characteristics common to top performers are described here in approximate order of impact from highest to lowest. Consequently, we suggest addressing these issues in the order presented when refining or correcting IT governance. Figure 5-3 contains selected benchmarks for best and worst performers.

FIGURE 5-3

Benchmarks for Best and Worst Performers

Governance performance	Bottom 50% of enterprises (score <69)	Top 50% of enterprises (score ≥69)
Percent of managers who can accurately describe governance	29	48
Percent of projects with renegade exceptions on at least one component	23 →	15 ↓
Percent of new systems with agreed-upon exceptions on at least one component	28 ↑	34 →
Average number of changes in governance per year	3 ↑	1 ↓

Arrows represent trends over three years, ↑ increasing, ↓ decreasing, → flat.

© 2003 MIT Sloan School Center for Information Systems Research (CISR). Used with permission.

1. More Managers in Leadership Positions Could Describe IT Governance. The most important predictor of top governance performance was the percentage of managers in leadership positions who could accurately describe their enterprise's IT governance. The higher the percentage of managers who could describe governance, the higher the governance performance. When more managers can accurately describe governance, governance is more likely to become part of the enterprise's management culture—people follow, challenge, and improve it. Without awareness of IT governance, people cannot practice it. Nearly half the managers in the above-average governance performers could describe governance while fewer than 30 percent of managers in poorer performers could do so (see figure 5-3). In only 5 percent of enterprises could 80 percent or more of managers in leadership positions describe their IT governance. How do you compare?

2. Engage, Engage, Engage. Top governance performers achieved a higher percentage of senior management knowledge about governance simply by engaging more often and more effectively. Top performers effectively used the following five communication mechanisms described in chapter 4. Communication approaches are listed in approximate order of impact; however, top performers effectively used all five.

- *Senior management announcements:* Reinforce and alert governance changes
- *Formal committees:* Add weight and cross-functional influence to governance
- *Office of CIO or IT governance:* A recognized advocate, owner, and organizational home
- *Working with managers who don't follow the rules:* Dialog to educate and address concerns
- *Portals or intranets with documented procedures:* A single place for governance information.

Top governance performers typically didn't use informal meetings with colleagues to communicate governance. Somehow the topic of governance doesn't lend itself to informal chats in the corridor, at the water cooler, or in the cafeteria. Informal chats are soon forgotten when participating managers go back to the hurly-burly of e-mail, phone calls, and formal meetings.

3. More Direct Involvement of the Senior Leaders in IT Governance. Top management involvement is such an old chestnut that we often forget its importance. Senior managers in top governance performers were more directly involved in IT governance. The more involvement, the better the governance performance. The managers on the following list appear in the order of the relative effect of their involvement on governance. The numbers in parentheses approximate the leverage of each executive's effective involvement, where the CIO is 1.0 on the index.[3]

- Chief Executive Officer (2.1)
- Chief Operating Officer (1.7)
- Business Unit Leader (1.6)

- Business Unit Chief Information Officer (1.3)
- Chief Financial Officer (1.2)
- Chief Information Officer (1.0)

For effective IT governance the CIO must be intimately involved, and in almost 100 percent of the firms studied the CIO was leading the governance charge. Effective involvement of the CIO in IT governance is a necessary but not sufficient condition for effective governance. The other senior managers provide significant additional leverage when they are effectively involved. For example, we estimate that the CEO provides a leverage of over two times that of the CIO, and the business unit leaders provide a leverage of 60 percent over the CIO alone.

The challenge is to find the right role for each senior manager. For example, involving the CEO a few times a year in high-profile roles such as chairing the investment committee or announcing governance changes is more effective than asking the CEO to attend monthly steering committee meetings. The role of the business unit CIO is also critical to enterprisewide governance. Business unit CIOs often must design business unit IT governance. In addition, for effective enterprisewide governance the business unit CIOs are typically involved in setting high-level architecture. More important, business unit CIOs act as advocates for enterprisewide governance. Business unit CIOs often have dual reporting relationships to the CEO or CFO of their business unit as well as to the corporate CIO. These dual relationships are challenging but valuable for balancing business unit and enterprise priorities. Incentives, transfer pricing, shared infrastructure, and best of all, reduced cost to the business units from economies of scale help make dual relationships work.

4. Clearer Business Objectives for IT Investment. Top governance performers had clearer objectives for IT investment—a few important objectives, not a long, undifferentiated list. The most common objectives were a subset of three or four of the following:

- Reduce costs.
- Improve customer service.

- Provide information to management.
- Enhance customer communication.
- Support new ways of doing business.
- Enable a complete view of the customer.
- Improve product quality.

The more focused the objective, the easier it is to design IT governance. Having a larger number of objectives and thus more desirable behaviors leads to confusing and sometimes conflicting messages and processes. Of all the characteristics of top governance performers, this is perhaps the most difficult to achieve. Complex enterprises have multiple and sometimes competing objectives, and IT governance has to operate in that environment. Nonetheless, top governance performers seem to pick the most important objectives and design governance for them.

5. More Differentiated Business Strategies. Top governance performers had more differentiated business strategies based on value disciplines such as customer intimacy or product innovation.[4] Governance performance was lower in enterprises pursuing operational excellence. Operational excellence is a less differentiated strategy because it focuses on efficiencies, and the vast majority of enterprises are concerned about cost. Our sense is that operational excellence is often the default strategy of enterprises without a clear strategy. Thus, this fifth characteristic is related to the need for strategic focus described earlier. Where operational excellence is the deliberate (not default) enterprise strategy (for example, commodity products and low-cost service providers), managers must drill down to the next level of detail to design appropriate governance. What are the specific desirable behaviors for achieving the enterprise's particular style of operational excellence? How can governance encourage the behaviors? We will explore this question in chapter 6.

6. Fewer Renegade and More Formally Approved Exceptions. The average enterprise in our study reported that the architecture exception process permitted exceptions to agreed-upon IT standards in 30 percent of its new systems. An additional 20 percent of the new systems had unapproved exceptions to agreed-upon IT standards (renegade exceptions). This latter statistic shows the immaturity of the IT architecture processes in most enterprises.

Because of the pace of technology change, exceptions to standards are inevitable. But enterprises manage exceptions differently. Top governance performing enterprises have fewer renegade exceptions and more exceptions that occur through a formal approval process. The arrows in the table in figure 5-3 indicate the trends for exceptions over a three-year period. Top performers had fewer renegade exceptions, and the number was decreasing. They had a fairly constant percentage of new systems with approved exceptions.

7. *Fewer Changes in Governance from Year to Year.* The process of changing governance arrangements, communicating the changes, and institutionalizing the new governance is lengthy. CIOs report that the time to implement a change in IT governance varies from six months to a year. A major change would involve changing who had decision rights for at least one of the key IT decisions. Changes in governance for one decision often have implications for the other four decisions.

Changing governance frequently is confusing to all the managers trying to follow it and often results in managers throwing their hands up in frustration and ignoring governance completely. How often to change governance is therefore a delicate balancing act. Changing governance too often leads to frustration and lower governance performance. But leaving poor governance in place is no better. If an enterprise's existing governance conflicts with how the enterprise wants to make decisions, then senior managers should advocate changing the governance arrangement for a decision or instituting a new committee or process to support a key decision. This kind of major change may also result from a strategic shift or redefinition of desirable behavior. Otherwise, governance design should remain fairly stable to avoid the cost of explaining the change. The enterprise can incorporate new knowledge, new people, smaller changes in strategy, and new organizational requirements by fine-tuning governance design, such as changing key committee members, adding responsibilities to an existing decision-making structure, or revising the parameters of service-level agreements.

What Governance Arrangements Work Best

Beyond the seven characteristics, top governance performers used particular patterns of archetypes in their governance arrangements. Across all the enterprises studied, certain patterns of governance arrangements generally surpassed others. We will first discuss what works best for providing input and then move to what works best for decision making.

Providing Input

In general, enterprises with higher governance performance used federal input models for IT principles and business application needs. In contrast, enterprises with lower governance performance had duopoly input for IT principles and business application needs. For input to the other three decisions, no governance arrangements were generally inferior or superior; the best approach depended on the specific needs of the enterprise.

As a starting point, we recommend federal governance arrangements for input to all five key IT decisions and particularly for IT principles and business application needs. The federal model for input provides a broad-based vehicle for capturing the tradeoffs between the desires of the senior corporate managers and the managers in the business units. The federal model addresses the time-honored tension between what should be shared and what should be locally determined. Sharing can enable economies of scale and standardization as well as delivering on enterprisewide strategies such as presenting a single face to the customer. The governance of Motorola described in figure 3-7 illustrates federal inputs for principles.

Designing a successful federal model for applications is even more difficult than designing one for principles. Business unit heads naturally want their business needs met and are typically less interested in the needs of the center or other business units. The less synergy across business units, the more the business unit heads need independence. Where there are cross–business unit processes (customer relationship management, for example), the pressures for sharing applications increase. Top governance performers heavily used business relationship managers, chargeback, and executive committees to provide input to decisions on principles and business application needs. All three of these mechanisms explicitly balance the needs of the business units and the corporate center.

The duopoly model for input to IT principles and business application needs is typically too restrictive. Limiting the input to IT and one other group often creates a feeling of disenchantment or nontransparency with the process. Worse still, the process can be seen as rigged to benefit the parties consulted for input. The duopoly model proves very effective for decision making but is generally less effective for providing input. Instead, broad-based inputs with mechanisms enabling clear and fair representation work best for providing input.

Making Decisions

Figure 5-4 summarizes the most and least effective governance arrangements for input and decision making to achieve governance performance.[5] Firms with high governance performance typically steered away from federal models for most of their IT decisions and used IT duopolies for the critical decisions of IT principles and investments.

Why Federal Models Struggle

Enterprises using federal decision-making arrangements often scored poorly on governance performance. Many factors explain why federal models are less effective for decision making, including less speed and a tendency to overly compromise and trade away effectiveness. Federal decision-making arrangements often take longer as more people and stages are involved and there is less agreement on the objectives for the decisions. The long cycle times compound the problems faced by enterprises with poor governance because they continue to perform poorly until intervention occurs. Worse still, when compromises are made to "keep everybody happy," neither the business units nor the enterprise achieves what is really needed. Federal models predicted poorer performance in four out of the five key IT decisions.

While federal decision-making arrangements are generally less effective, a few enterprises have overcome their limitations by establishing enterprise success as an important goal for all managers.

FIGURE 5-4

Best and Worst Governance Performers Use Different Arrangements

DECISION / ARCHETYPE	IT Principles		IT Architecture		IT Infrastructure Strategies		Business Application Needs		IT Investment	
	Input	Decision	Input	Decision	Input	Decision	Input	Decision	Input	Decision
Business Monarchy										
IT Monarchy										
Feudal								(−)		
Federal	(+)	(−)		(−)		(−)	(+)			(−)
Duopoly	(−)	(+)					(−)			(+)
Anarchy										

(−) = Poor performers   (+) = Top performers

The chairman and CEO of UPS, reflecting on his thirty years with the company, described the time when he represented a business unit on a federal IT decision-making committee.

> Our culture, traditions, legacy, and length of service gives us a lot of confidence that we can rely on each other . . . you can do things in the best interest of the total. I think about when we built the IT steering committee. . . . I was in air, someone else in engineering, someone else in finance, someone else in HR, someone else in R&D—eight different functions that came together. Each of us would come with orders from our bosses to make sure we got what we needed in our parts of the business . . . somehow along the line we would say, "But the best thing for the company isn't mine; it's the DIAD [handheld computer used by UPS truck drivers] or the delivery record automation." . . . I would go back and my boss would say at the time, "Did you get what we needed?" and I would say, "No, we got something better, something better for the company."[6]

Few enterprises can boast of the longevity of UPS managers on their IT steering committees. Even UPS, whose culture encouraged commitment to enterprise goals, later dropped the federal model in favor of a business monarchy for IT investment. On the other hand, federal models are a viable approach to decisions on business application needs. If business unit representatives are rewarded for achieving both enterprise and business unit objectives, they can work in a federal model to distinguish shared and unique application needs. For business applications needs, enterprises with feudal decision-making arrangements had lower governance performance; even with few synergies among business units, the feudal model underperformed. For business application needs, the appropriate model depends on the enterprise's strategic needs. Highly integrated or synergistic business units thrive under more centralized decision making, such as a business monarchy or federal arrangements. Where fewer synergies exist, IT duopolies work well when the IT group works bilaterally with each business unit to satisfy individual needs.

Why Duopolies Work for Decision Making

Top governance performers often used IT duopolies for both IT principles and investments, the two most strategic of the five key IT decisions, because principles set the role for the enterprise's IT and investments establish commitment and priorities. Some IT and business process standards may be nonnegotiable, but the duopoly approach enables joint decision making between the business leaders and IT professionals, allows for creative business solutions within agreed-upon constraints, but remains focused on the particular business issue at hand. Unlike federal models, wherein managers must balance the interests of the center and all the business units, duopolies maintain strategic focus and typically perform better.

Two popular mechanisms for implementing duopolies are business/IT relationship managers (often the business unit CIOs) and process teams with IT members. Business/IT relationship managers support the bicycle wheel model of the IT duopoly (see figure 3-3). The relationship manager leverages IT for maximum business value and pushes for IT services that address their business unit needs. The process team mechanism implements the T-shaped duopoly.

Process teams work toward an enterprise's desired operating model with IT to enable enterprisewide processes.

Three Successful Patterns of Governance Performance

Among the 256 firms, the governance arrangements varied markedly. For each of the five key IT decisions, management can choose among six governance archetypes, yielding thousands of possible combinations. The ten most popular combinations accounted for 25 percent of the enterprises; the three most successful of these ten arrangements in terms of governance performance appear in figure 5-5. All three of these arrangements balance multiple performance objectives such as cost, growth and flexibility. Arrangement 1 had duopolies (the CxOs and IT, perhaps using T-shaped committees) for principles and investment, IT monarchies for infrastructure and architecture, and a federal structure for business application needs. This arrangement requires IT groups to understand the business needs, and requires business and IT to trust each other. The federal model for application needs can exploit

FIGURE 5-5

Top Three Governance Performers

DECISION ARCHE-TYPE	IT Principles	IT Architecture	IT Infrastructure Strategies	Business Application Needs	IT Investment
Business Monarchy	③	③	③		② ③
IT Monarchy		① ②	① ②		
Feudal					
Federal				① ③	
Duopoly	① ②			②	①
Anarchy					

①, ②, ③ = Top three governance performers (achieving four performance objectives, weighted by importance).

© 2003 MIT Sloan School Center for Information Systems Research (CISR). Used with permission.

potential synergies across business units as would a T-shaped duopoly for investment. Arrangement 2 was similar, with a duopoly for application needs and a business monarchy for investment. Arrangement 2 works well for enterprises with fewer synergies using a bicycle wheel duopoly for application needs.

Arrangement 3 was much more centralized, with business monarchies for all decisions except federal arrangements for business application needs. More centralized approaches are typically used in single business unit firms or where profitability or cost control is more important. Arrangement 3 requires business leaders who care and know about IT issues—often due to the CIO's educating the senior management team. Arrangement 3 is also sensible when major changes are occurring and decision rights must be tightly held (during mergers, major cost cutting, crises, and so on). Figure 5-5 illustrates how the five decision-making approaches fit together into a reinforcing total governance design. For example, an IT monarchy for IT architecture can work well when IT principles set by a business monarchy or a duopoly guide the architecture.

Who Makes Better IT Decisions?

With all the possible combinations, we wanted to understand which managers, on average, make consistently better IT decisions—business or IT professionals. The results from the 256 firms studied indicate that joint decision making is best for many decisions (figure 5-6). The vertical dimension of the table divides the five key IT decisions into the three business-oriented (principles, business applications, and investments) and the two more technical (architecture, infrastructure) decisions. The horizontal dimension of the table divides the archetypes into decisions by business leaders, decisions by technical leaders, and decisions taken jointly.[7] The numbers in the cells add to one hundred and are the percentage of decisions across all the enterprises by each combination. For example, 29 percent of all IT decisions were business-oriented decisions by business people. Twenty-seven percent of all IT decisions were technical in nature and made by IT people. Adding across the rows indicates the percentages of each decision type (business or technical). Adding the columns indicates the percentage by each decision maker (business, technical, or joint). For example, 32 percent of decisions were joint.

FIGURE 5-6

Who Makes Better IT Decisions—Business or IT Managers?

Types of Decisions		DECISION RIGHTS (%)		
		Business	IT	Joint
	Business • IT principles • Business application needs • IT investment	(−) 29	(=) 7	(+) 24
	IT • IT architecture • infrastructure	(−) 5	(=) 27	(=) 8

(+) Top performers*
(=) No difference
(−) Poor performers*

*Statistically significant relationship with governance performance

© 2003 MIT Sloan School Center for Information Systems Research (CISR). Used with permission.

The symbols in each cell represent the relationship between the decision approach and governance performance. The top governance performers were more likely to make business-oriented IT decisions jointly. In the poorer governance performers, business managers were more likely to make business-oriented IT decisions alone. All other combinations of decision and decision maker performed the same.

We derived some general principles from this analysis. Unless there are compelling reasons to do otherwise:

- Business and IT professionals should collaborate on business-oriented IT decisions (investment, principles, and business application needs). Several mechanisms can help to implement this approach: joint committees, process teams with IT membership, budgeting processes with separate business and IT approval stages, and so on.

- Business people should not make business-oriented IT decisions alone. Better decisions require the fusion of business and IT thinking.

- The best arrangement of decision rights for technical decisions depends on other factors such as the synergies
  between business units, the current IT portfolio, strategic
  goals, industry differences, and so on.

How Leading Financial Performers Govern

So far in this chapter we have focused on what governance generally
works best for broad-based multifaceted performance. But beyond
these general principles, governance must be tailored to the enterprise's strategies and performance goals. We now look at governance
design at for-profit firms that lead their peers on particular financial
measures. We considered three different performance goals and associated measures: asset utilization, growth, and profit (figure 5-7).

To determine how leading financial performers govern, we cor-
related governance arrangements with financial performance for
the previous three years relative to competitors.[8] To generate the
governance patterns for top financial performers in Figure 5-7 a
number of assumptions are made (some of which we describe in
the endnotes). As a result, the patterns of top performers should be
viewed as indicative only and not definitive evidence. The next
three sections describe governance at listed for-profit firms who
have higher performance or faster improvements. Not all firms that
led on a particular performance measure governed the same way,
but the patterns were observed and persuasive and supported by
the case studies. For example, firms that led on growth had relatively decentralized IT governance, giving a lot of discretion to the
business units. Firms that led on profit had more centralized governance to facilitate reducing duplication and cost control.

Leaders on Asset Utilization

Firms leading on asset utilization (as measured by ROA) need pro-
active decision makers who look for opportunities to share and
reuse IT across business units, business processes, and regions. For
IT assets, the leading firms typically accomplish this drive for asset
utilization through a pattern of duopoly governance on all five IT
decisions (see figure 5-7). In the duopoly model, the IT group plays

FIGURE 5-7

How Top Financial Performers Govern

		DECISION			
	IT Principles Decision	IT Architecture Decision	IT Infrastructure Strategies Decision	Business Application Needs Decision	IT Investment Decision
GOVERNANCE ARCHETYPE					
Business Monarchy	Profit Growth	Profit	Profit	Growth	Profit Growth
IT Monarchy			Profit		
Feudal					Growth
Federal				Profit	
Duopoly	ROA	ROA	ROA	ROA	ROA

☐ Most common pattern for all firms.

Profit, ROA, Growth = Firms with significantly higher or increasing average three-year industry adjusted profits, ROA, or growth.

© 2003 MIT Sloan School Center for Information Systems Research (CISR). Used with permission.

an important coordinating role as it is one of the few groups that interact with all business units and see firmwide opportunities for sharing and reuse.

Across the five decisions, the two types of duopoly governance described in figure 3-3 are both important for asset utilization. Each type of duopoly brings together business and IT executives; a T-shaped duopoly brings together senior executives to encourage greater synergies across the enterprise, while a bicycle wheel establishes relationships to help business units extract value from enterprise capabilities. Key mechanisms implementing these duopolies include executive committees, process teams, business–IT relationship managers, and IT architecture committees

Citicorp was an early adopter of the T-shaped approach in 1996 and a very successful exploiter of IT. Citicorp's strategic context required that business and IT managers work together in a duopoly to understand their mutual challenges and responsibilities.[9] To create this fusion in the consumer banking area, two overlapping committees that met quarterly provided technology policy and oversight in the bank. The Global Consumer Council, chaired by the senior vice president of marketing, brought together the senior marketing managers and included the senior technology officer, Citicorp's top information technology executive. The Global Consumer Technology Group, chaired by the senior technology officer, brought together the senior technology managers from the consumer banking area and included the senior marketing vice president. The two groups had adjacent meeting times, and some of their meetings were held jointly. Many firms have adapted this model to suit their needs.

Business/IT relationship managers (for example, business unit CIOs) effectively connect the business units to the central IT group, enabling the identification of opportunities for reuse, synergies, and shared services. At the same time, the business/IT relationship managers ensure that the business needs of their business unit are met. Enterprises effectively using business/IT relationship managers mentioned elsewhere in the book include DBS Bank, Abbey National Group, and Scotland Yard.

Process teams with IT members help develop both the process leadership and the IT infrastructure to enable enterprise system implementations and cross-functional business processes. The ERP implementations at MeadWestvaco and Dow Corning highlight the benefits of process teams. Architecture committees are also important for asset utilization. In a duopoly structure, these committees of both IT and business experts encourage reuse to ensure a robust architecture and strict adherence to technical standards. To drive economies, the IT group regularly assesses the set of bilateral relationships for opportunities for synergy and economies of scale. Where can the same system, data, infrastructure, module, capability be shared?

Duopolies are also used for the IT investment decision to ensure that IT spending is balanced between the needs of the business unit strategy and the needs of the enterprise to utilize assets. Leaders on asset utilization often effectively use chargeback. Understanding and exposing costs of IT, particularly infrastructure, supports sharing and reuse. Firms leading on asset utilization don't spend any more or less on IT as a percentage of expenses than other firms. They simply drove for better utilization of their IT assets.

In summary, firms wanting to lead on asset utilization can learn from the top performers that:

- Set IT principles with a strong flavor of asset utilization via duopoly of the CxOs and the IT group. Use duopolies to make investment decisions balances business needs with sharing and reuse.

- Create an IT architecture committee of business and IT people to design an enterprise architecture and manage commitment to shared infrastructure.

- Assign business/IT relationship managers focused on achieving business value from IT for their business units and leveraging enterprisewide infrastructure.

- Establish a technical core of infrastructure and architecture providers who plan and implement the enterprise's technology platform and interact with the business/IT relationship managers.

- Institute a regular review process that brings together business unit and IT leaders to look for synergies, reuse, and trends across operational units.

- Involve IT architects in business unit projects to facilitate education and effective use of shared infrastructure and architecture standards.

- Develop a chargeback system to help business unit leaders see the value of shared services and make effective decisions on IT use.

Leaders on Profit

Enterprises leading on profit (as measured by ROI and ROE) tended to have a more centralized governance approach. Typically these enterprises have business monarchies for IT principles, high-level IT architecture, and IT investment decisions. They use either business or IT monarchies for infrastructure decisions and federal arrangements for business application needs. Leaders on profit using these governance arrangements require IT-savvy business leaders to make decisions—particularly IT architecture decisions. In these firms the business architecture—the linking of key business processes internally and with business partners—drives the high-level IT architecture that is strictly enforced.

Leaders on profit made effective use of executive and senior management committees to achieve cost control and standardization. For architecture, standardization occurs through business decision making with the IT group providing advice, education, and research. Business-driven standardization limits costly exceptions to standards but does not eliminate the importance of an exception process to enable learning. Profit leaders successfully use federal arrangements for business application needs, nicely balancing with business monarchies for IT principles. The federal arrangements ensure a consistency across the operational units with firmwide strategies while recognizing the differences between business units. This type of federal arrangement requires a supportive incentive scheme. IT investments are also centrally controlled via business monarchies that consider IT spending in the context of all spending. There was some evidence that profit leaders on profit actually spent more on IT.

Centralized decision making facilitates standardization and shared services, thereby enhancing profitability via both cost reductions and fast time to market in new regions. For example, Citibank Asia set up a Regional Card Centre (RCC) in Singapore in 1989 as a shared service to support start-up credit card businesses in Southeast Asia.[10] This shared service had a direct impact on the operating performance of each country manager whose credit card data-processing operations were consolidated, so not all existing country managers immediately bought into the concept. Managers who used the shared services demanded exacting performance standards from the center. By 1992, in the midst of heightened cost consciousness, the cost per card was down to 32.5 percent of the 1989 cost. None of the country managers wanted to revert to decentralized credit card operations; who wants cost per card to triple overnight? The cost economies offered by the RCC attracted the countries to use shared services.

The RCC evolved from processing credit cards for ten countries in 1993 to processing credit cards for twenty-six countries in 1999—twelve countries in Asia, seven in Central Europe and the Middle East, and eight in Latin America. Average costs in 1999 were

40 percent less than they were three years earlier. Today many more countries across the world use the shared services. In addition to credit card processing, the RCC provides services including production support, software design for new products, acceptance testing, compliance with the constantly changing rules of Visa, Master-Card, and Diners Club, and dissemination of best practices and corporate quality initiatives. The cost reductions afforded by standardization and centralized processing inherent in shared services are impressive. The existence of "starter kits" also makes adding new countries relatively easy and inexpensive.

In summary, firms wanting to lead on profitability can learn from the top performers that:

- Staff an IT steering committee with capable business executives who take responsibility for enterprisewide IT governance decisions and set IT principles with a strong flavor of cost control.

- Carefully manage the firm's IT and business architecture to drive out business costs. IT monarchies manage and enforce the architecture and work with business monarchies to set architectures.

- Design rigorous architecture exception processes to minimize costly exceptions and enable learning.

- Create a centralized IT organization designed to manage infrastructure, architecture, and shared services.

- Use linked IT investment and business needs processes that both make transparent and balance the needs of the center and the operational units.

- Institute an IT investment process that requires centralized coordination and approval of IT investments.

- Design a simple chargeback and service-level agreement mechanism to clearly allocate IT expenses.

Leaders on Growth

Leaders on revenue growth have governance structures striving to balance the dominant entrepreneurial needs of the operational units with the firmwide business objectives. Business monarchies set IT principles to balance (or at least attempt to balance) operational unit and firmwide goals. These principles typically focus on growth and empower the operational units to be innovative and not too concerned about standardization—that can come later.

IT investments are governed by either feudal or business monarchy arrangements. Feudal governance for investments allows each of the units to independently invest in IT to support their individual strategies. In high-growth firms, the operational units with intimate customer contact typically drive the growth by anticipating and responding to customer needs. The operational units want and need control over their IT investments to enable fast implementations and to experiment with new products and services. Where more firmwide synergies are desired (for example, a single point of customer contact across multiple business units or sharing resources), business monarchies would be used for IT investment. High-growth firms, more than other firms, have effective mechanisms for tracking the business value of IT.

Interestingly, there is no dominant governance approach for IT infrastructure strategies or architecture for high-growth enterprises. Firms use a variety of IT infrastructure governance arrangements to enable fast growth. The key to fast growth is customer responsiveness. Leading firms accomplish this responsiveness with more investment in operational unit infrastructures rather than firmwide infrastructures.[11] Local unit infrastructures are more tailored to the strategic needs of the business units and are usually less integrated in the firmwide systems. The lower integration enables faster time to market for IT-enabled products and services—integration can occur later.

Maintaining IT architectures in high-growth firms is . . . challenging. High-growth firms used no dominant governance arrangement for architecture. Many high-growth firms reported having a number of IT architectures rather than one—perhaps equal to the number of operational units! This proliferation was equally evident whether the growth was achieved organically or via acquisition. The only chance of creating an integrated, rational, scalable IT architecture occurs if the IT group has decision rights. A typical model sends IT proposals from the operational units to IT for architecture screening. To be successful and perceived as helping rather than obstructing the operational units, the architecture process must be very fast and flexible. For example, corporate CIOs in high-growth firms rely heavily on personal relationships involving a one-on-one influence with business leaders and facilitating communities of IT management interest.

In high-growth firms, business monarchies identify strategic business application needs. Typically, demand for IT outstrips available IT resources, so business monarchies identify the key requirements for the processes that will distinguish the enterprise from its competitors. However, high-growth firms often struggle to precisely define business application needs. In their fast-paced environment, the business needs change constantly and often during systems acquisition, construction, or consolidation. To simultaneously define and meet market needs, high-growth firms use prototyping and different types of extreme development. Many high-growth firms report business application needs as the least successfully governed of the five key IT decisions; they are probably creating integration challenges down the road.

Manheim Auctions, the U.S. market leader in business-to-business car auctions, successfully auctions over $50 billion of used cars each year.[12] In recent years, Manheim introduced online auctions and now auctions around 150,000 cars each year on line. In addition, the Manheim Market Report, compiled from the firm's countrywide auctions, provides invaluable information to car dealers and other industry participants and is available on line, on personal data assistants, and on paper.

To launch this fast-growth online business and reinforce its dominant position in the industry, Manheim created an independent business unit, Manheim Online. Hal Logan, the CEO of Manheim Online, worked with the senior management team to define principles and strategic business requirements. Like most high-growth start-ups, the firm did not tightly govern architecture or infrastructure, focusing instead on managing projects for rapid development.

Manheim's development teams were responsible for all aspects of deploying a new Manheim Online service: product management, Web server selection and management, and development and quality assurance of the service. Eventually the teams' focus on speed of system delivery became unsustainable. Manheim Online's Director of Software Development Steve Crawford reflected on this situation: "The ability to always respond quickly eventually became a problem. We became very good at scrambling to meet demands very quickly, but that has a cost and eventually we just said, 'Okay, we're out of magic dust now.' We needed to rethink."[13]

At that point, Manheim Online identified a need for greater attention to architecture and to reusable infrastructure services. Today the online business is carefully integrated into the overall Manheim Auctions business model. In addition, system delivery responsibilities have been redefined. The product management team is responsible for defining the product vision and managing the deployment of the product, thereby sheltering the development group so that they can focus on software development. The quality assurance group is responsible for testing new services. The director of software development described the process of introducing greater discipline into the development environment: "There have been a lot of growing pains along with that change. A lot of people liked the small company kind of atmosphere that we had because they got to wear lots of hats and do lots of things. It was a great place to learn a whole lot because it was very fast-paced and there were very sharp business people here."[14]

The example demonstrates the value of focusing governance on defining strategic business needs and application development processes during periods of high growth. As growth slows and enterprises mature, firms need different skills, cultures, and IT governance.

In summary, firms wanting to lead on growth can learn from the top performers that:

- Empower the business units to drive IT investment—often achieved by setting IT principles with a strong flavor of innovation and market responsiveness.

- Create a more decentralized IT organization with structure and capabilities designed to focus on immediate needs of critical business processes.

- Place IT professionals into operational units focused on meeting their internal and external customers' needs.

- Create substantial operational unit–based IT infrastructure capability tailored to local needs and linked into an often less substantial enterprisewide infrastructure.

- Enable a technical core of infrastructure and architecture providers who plan and implement the enterprise's technology platform, identifying any critical integration requirements. These experts should identify the minimal standards necessary for required levels of security, reliability, and integration because the enterprise will largely sacrifice integration for functionality and speed. The technical core of infrastructure providers also needs to be skilled at creating synergies and integrating after systems are operational.

- Implement a regular review process for formal tracking of the business value of IT.

- Work with the operational units to provide education about how to use IT to enable growth.

Designing Governance: Lessons from Leading Enterprises

In this chapter we looked at what works best for multiple performance goals and for leading on a specific metric. Each enterprise must actively design its IT governance, combining its unique needs with the lessons of what works best for other organizations. Following is a checklist of what works best for consideration when designing governance. In the next chapters, we will look at how enterprises craft governance to suit their strategies.

1. How do you compare to the leading governance performers on the seven characteristics they have in common?

   - Can more than 50 percent of managers in leadership positions accurately describe IT governance?

   - Is IT governance effectively communicated across the enterprise using a variety of approaches?

   - Are senior managers thoughtfully involved in IT governance?

- Are there clear business objectives for IT investment?
- Are differentiated business strategies clearly articulated?
- Are there fewer renegade and more formally approved exceptions?
- Is there only one (or fewer) major change in governance from year to year?

2. The following principles should be considered as the default or starting point for governance arrangements (when all else is equal).

- Use federal arrangements for input into all IT decisions.
- Use duopoly arrangements for IT principles and investments decisions.
- Avoid federal decision making for all decisions if possible. If federal models are used, they require the maturity to balance the needs of the center and the business units and a supportive incentive scheme.
- Use joint decision making involving business and IT decision makers for the business-oriented IT decisions of investment, principles, and business application needs.

3. Moderate these general principles according to the enterprise's dominant performance goals.

- Top performers on asset utilization typically use duopoly arrangements.
- Top performers on profit apply more centralized governance, often using monarchies for decision making.
- Top performers on growth strive to balance the entrepreneurial needs of the operational units with firmwide strategies and principles. IT investments are governed by either feudal or business monarchy arrangements with attempted centralized decision making for business application needs.
- Further customize these principles with the enterprise's unique strategy and desirable behaviors.

6

Linking Strategy,
IT Governance,
and Performance

SENIOR MANAGEMENT TEAMS often question the value they
receive for their IT investments. Most have experienced a number
of IT-related frustrations: huge expenditures for multiple customer
service systems that still cannot consolidate all a customer's interactions; large-scale enterprise system implementations that wreak
more havoc than process improvement; rapidly escalating annual
operating expenses without a corresponding escalation in bottom
line results; virus or worm infections shutting down operations;
and multimillion-dollar investments in initiatives like Y2K remediation, which sustain—but do not improve—performance. Among
the many knee-jerk management team responses to these frustrations, firing the CIO and outsourcing all of IT have emerged as
perennial favorites. The problem with these two solutions is that,
for most enterprises, they do not attack the cause of the problem—
poorly designed IT governance, often with a corresponding lack of
business leadership participation in the key IT decisions

IT governance is a senior management responsibility. If IT is
not generating value, senior management should first examine
its IT governance practices—who makes decisions and how the decision makers are accountable. In this chapter, we look at how
to design governance, elaborating on the IT Governance Design

Framework introduced in chapter 1. We explore alternative governance designs intended to reinforce business strategies built around different value disciplines (operational excellence, product leadership, or customer intimacy).[1] We also address how enterprises design governance to transcend organizational structures and encourage the desired level of synergy (or autonomy) between different business units. We describe how governance evolves as IT becomes more strategic and executives better understand the costs and benefits of IT-enabled business processes. Case studies of two financial services firms—JPMorgan Chase and State Street Corporation—illustrate these concepts.

Six Interlocking Components of Effective Governance Design

Enterprises with effective IT governance clearly articulate and then harmonize six components in the Governance Design Framework introduced in chapter 1 (figure 6-1). *Enterprise strategy and organization* define the desirable behaviors motivating governance. Enterprises design *IT governance arrangements* for each of their six key assets including IT to both enable and influence strategy. Governance arrangements assign decision rights for the key decisions guiding each asset individually and collectively. The effectiveness of an enterprise's strategies and its combined governance arrangements are reflected in its ability to achieve stated *business performance goals*. In this book we focus on the IT asset, but parallel (and interconnected) governance processes for the other five assets are needed.

The bottom half of the Governance Design Framework in figure 6-1 shows that, for the IT asset, enterprises harmonize *IT organization and desirable behaviors* with their enterprise strategy and organization. Enterprises harmonize their IT organizational structures with their *IT governance mechanisms*—their decision-making structures, alignment processes, and communications tools. Harmonization ensures that the mechanisms, IT unit structure, and desirable behaviors result in governance arrangements that deliver on enterprise strategy. Finally, *IT metrics and accountabilities* define how IT will contribute to enterprise performance goals and provide the means for separately assessing IT effectiveness. Let's look at the six components of effective governance design using JPMorgan Chase as an example.[2]

FIGURE 6-1

Governance Design Framework

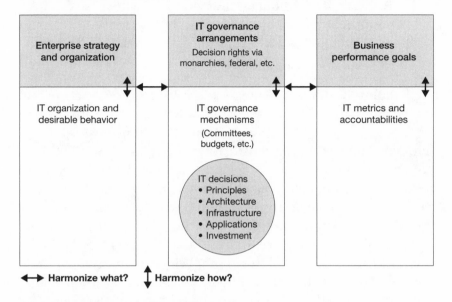

© 2003 MIT Sloan School Center for Information Systems Research (CISR). Used with permission.

JPMorgan Chase, with 2002 assets of $741 billion, competes in five business segments: investment banking, investment management and private banking, treasury and securities services, retail and middle-market financial services, and private equity. J.P. Morgan & Co. and the Chase Manhattan Bank Corporation merged on December 31, 2000, the latest in a long line of mergers and acquisitions of financial giants that included Chemical Bank, Manufacturers Hanover, Texas Commerce Bank, Hambrecht & Quist, and Flemings.

Enterprise Strategy and Organization

Like many diversified financial services firms, JPMorgan Chase had traditionally managed with a high degree of autonomy among its business units. By 2001, however, CEO William Harrison Jr. had shifted the business focus to "one firm—one team." In the firm's

2002 annual report, he summarized JPMorgan Chase's strategy in two principles:

- To be a diversified financial services firm with a leadership position in each of our businesses
- To provide our clients integrated solutions drawing on a wide variety of products and services

Building and maintaining leadership positions in each of JPMorgan Chase's diverse lines of business requires a relatively high level of business unit autonomy. To provide integrated solutions, however, means the firm must garner synergies at two levels: divisions and business units. To reflect the firm's belief that most of the strategy setting and execution for technology should reside in the businesses, management developed an approach deemed the "80/20 rule": 80 percent of the work is done in the businesses and 20 percent is influenced centrally. Thus, 20 percent of IT efforts should secure benefits from scale, simplicity, and integration across the firm. The other 80 percent should continue to focus on adding value to specific efforts of divisions and business units.

Figure 6-2 lists key elements of JPMorgan Chase's enterprise strategy in the top left box. The strategy highlights JPMorgan Chase's need for business unit autonomy with a concurrent effort to cut costs and enable integration through business unit synergies.

For IT governance purposes, enterprise strategy is a set of clear, concise statements clarifying the enterprise's strategic intent. These statements articulate an agreed-upon position that can be readily communicated. The strategy focuses the attention of all employees on simple and achievable messages, whether or not the employees are part of the strategy-making process. Typically, statements of strategy express one or more of the following:

- Competitive thrust of the enterprise
- Relationships among business units (for example, autonomy of business units versus specific types of synergies)
- Intentions for the role and management of information and IT

Parts of an enterprise's strategy are effectively "hard-wired" in the sense that they are built into the organization structure.

FIGURE 6-2

JPMorgan Chase's IT Governance

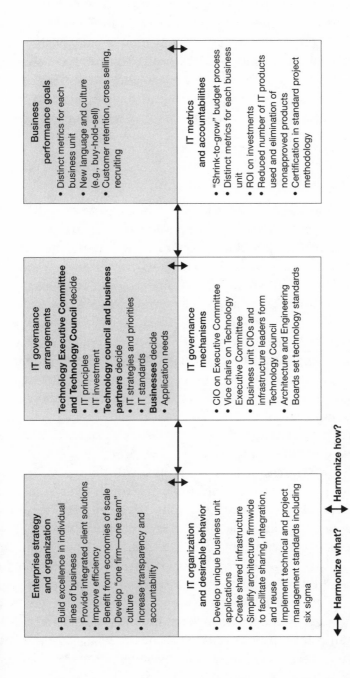

Enterprise strategy and organization
- Build excellence in individual lines of business
- Provide integrated client solutions
- Improve efficiency
- Benefit from economies of scale
- Develop "one firm—one team" culture
- Increase transparency and accountability

IT organization and desirable behavior
- Develop unique business unit applications
- Create shared infrastructure
- Simplify architecture firmwide to facilitate sharing, integration, and reuse
- Implement technical and project management standards including six sigma

IT governance arrangements
Technology Executive Committee and Technology Council decide
- IT principles
- IT investment

Technology council and business partners decide
- IT strategies and priorities
- IT standards

Businesses decide
- Application needs

IT governance mechanisms
- CIO on Executive Committee
- Vice chairs on Technology Executive Committee
- Business unit CIOs and infrastructure leaders form Technology Council
- Architecture and Engineering Boards set technology standards

Business performance goals
- Distinct metrics for each business unit
- New language and culture (e.g., buy-hold-sell)
- Customer retention, cross selling, recruiting

IT metrics and accountabilities
- "Shrink-to-grow" budget process
- Distinct metrics for each business unit
- ROI on investments
- Reduced number of IT products used and elimination of nonapproved products
- Certification in standard project methodology

← Harmonize what?   ↕ Harmonize how?

JPMorgan Chase has a distinctive structure bolstering the enterprise's goal of strong lines of business. The five divisions all consist of semiautonomous business units. The firm also has structures supporting its goals for shared infrastructure and collaboration. For example, division and business unit CIOs have a dual reporting relationship to business management and to the head of technology. The goal of governance design is to both reinforce and transcend organization structure in defining responsibilities for implementing strategies.

IT Governance Arrangements

Governance arrangements identify the archetype used for each of the IT decisions. JPMorgan Chase's governance arrangements (summarized in the top middle box of figure 6-2) reflect the demands of the firm's strategy and organization. IT and business leaders jointly define IT principles and make IT investment decisions. JPMorgan Chase makes infrastructure and architecture decisions with a Technology Council made up of the division CIOs, the technology infrastructure leaders, and the firm's vice chairman for technology. Business application decisions are decentralized to facilitate line-of-business excellence. Within the lines of business, JPMorgan Chase has implemented centers of excellence to facilitate shared projects across business units.

JPMorgan Chase's decentralized structure fosters business unit innovation and responsiveness. The firm's governance arrangements for business applications reinforce its divisional and business unit structures. At the same time, JPMorgan Chase's governance arrangements for principles, architecture, infrastructure, and investment all require collaboration across the business to define how they can foster synergies across the enterprise. These arrangements transcend the formal organizational structure. JPMorgan Chase's combination of (1) relatively autonomous business units and (2) a need for some synergies across business units, managed with (3) decentralized IT applications decisions and (4) joint business and IT leadership for enterprisewide decisions is what we mean by harmonizing enterprise strategy and organization with IT governance arrangements.

Business Performance Goals

The third component in the top half of the Governance Design Framework in figure 6-2 is performance goals. Performance goals establish clear objectives for the governing bodies and a benchmark for assessing the success of governance efforts.

At JPMorgan Chase, each business unit determines business-specific goals for IT-enabled initiatives. The retail and middle-market business, for example, is pursuing an E^2I initiative—efficiency, effectiveness, and innovation—which has led to specific goals of cost reductions and market leadership. Everyone at JPMorgan Chase, however, shares in the goals of the "one firm—one team" philosophy. Related performance goals include eliminating costs through the six sigma organizational quality program, developing a shared language for IT initiatives, and improving results of customer retention and cross selling.

In the for-profit sector, enterprise performance goals such as share price, profitability, and good citizenship are clear. Often, enterprises also specify antecedents of these endpoints to provide more clarity and communication about desirable behaviors and indicators of success. We will look at performance goals in the not-for-profit sector in Chapter 7.

IT Organization and Desirable Behaviors

The three components in the lower half of the Governance Design Framework in figure 6-2 (IT structure and desirable behaviors, IT governance mechanisms, and IT metrics and accountabilities) specify how the top three components will be implemented. Starting on the left, enterprise strategy and organization provides the direction for IT structure and desirable behavior. Our definition of governance—*specifying the decision rights and accountability framework to encourage desirable behavior in the use of IT*—doesn't mention strategy. Instead, we focus on desirable behaviors of the enterprise's people. Behaviors, not strategy, create value. Behaviors are influenced by many factors, such as incentives, culture, internal politics, and organizational history. But desirable behaviors must be in harmony with strategic direction or an enterprise cannot achieve its performance goals.

At JPMorgan Chase each business unit has an IT organization. This structure facilitates the desirable IT behavior of focusing business unit resources on developing and maintaining competitive systems within their markets. But in addition to line-of-business excellence, JPMorgan Chase strategy is concerned with economies of scale, integrated solutions, and a "one firm—one team" culture. Thus, JPMorgan Chase wants to stimulate new behaviors, encouraging collaboration across business units. Accordingly, the firm created Enterprise Technology Services (ETS), a shared services organization for all technology infrastructure. ETS reports to the vice chairman for technology, a member of the enterprisewide Executive Committee. In addition to structural change, JPMorgan Chase has introduced governance mechanisms that clarify new desirable behaviors and establish the means for reinforcing the behaviors. At JPMorgan Chase, these new desirable behaviors include the use of technology standards, centralized purchasing, and a standardized project methodology.

IT Metrics and Accountabilities

IT desirable behaviors are reflected in the IT metrics and accountabilities at the lower right of JPMorgan Chase's Governance Design Framework (figure 6-2). Measurement and accountabilities are critical to any good governance design. Articulating who is responsible for what and how they will be evaluated provides clarity, ownership, and tools to assess governance performance.

In each of its business units JPMorgan Chase has individual IT metrics reflecting the impact of IT capabilities on the business. Firmwide, JPMorgan Chase has IT goals, such as a "shrink-to-grow" budget process that seeks to cut costs through productivity and efficiency improvements in order to free up funds for new investments prioritized by business needs. Reduced operating costs, fewer technology platforms, and certification for its standardized project management approach are among the other goals. Although IT success must ultimately be reflected in business success, these intermediate, function-specific metrics focus JPMorgan Chase's IT efforts and help gauge progress of the IT unit in its ability to contribute to the business.

IT Governance Mechanisms

Well-designed mechanisms convert IT desirable behaviors into the outcomes listed in the Governance Design Framework. Only a few managers see the Governance Design Framework, but most managers interact with one or more of the mechanisms daily. Some mechanisms deal mainly with one decision (for example, the architecture committee makes architecture decisions), while others deal with several or all five decisions (for example, the executive committee makes principles decisions and certain investment decisions). Well-designed mechanisms reinforce and encourage desirable behaviors and lead to outcomes specified in the IT metrics and accountabilities.

At the core of JPMorgan Chase's IT governance is a five-member Technology Executive Committee—a subgroup of the company's Executive Committee. The members of the subgroup are the top line-of-business executives and the head of technology. The decision-making team entrusted with IT principles and investment decisions consists of this committee and JPMorgan Chase's Technology Council.

The Technology Council brings together the division CIOs and infrastructure leaders from Enterprise Technology Services. Defining principles and making investment decisions with the Executive Committee is only one of the Technology Council's charges. Because the Council comprises the firm's technology leaders, it has the expertise and authority to make firmwide architecture and infrastructure decisions. The Council relies on six subcommittees for input into its decisions: Architecture Board, Engineering Board, Financial Performance, People, Strategic Relationships, and Communications. Each subcommittee is headed by a Council member and has representatives from both business unit and corporate IT.

At JPMorgan Chase the Engineering Board has proved to be a key mechanism for implementing the whole-of-enterprise approach to leveraging the firm's scale. The Board's brief is to force greater simplicity in product choices and lay the foundations for greater integration of systems and processes across the enterprise. JPMorgan Chase's history of acquisitions, coupled with its autonomous business unit decision-making model, resulted in nearly two thousand different infrastructure products across the firm. The Engineering Board analyzed each product and put it into one of three categories: buy, hold, or sell. Through these efforts, the Engineering Board reduced the firm's technology product set to 130 component areas with about three hundred product choices. Thus, this governance mechanism has translated desirable behaviors of a simpler architecture and technical standards to a performance outcome—reducing the technical product set. Two other governance mechanisms, the Executive Committee and the Technology Council, are promulgating the buy-hold-sell concept across the firm, fundamentally changing technology procurement.

A new exceptions process complements JPMorgan Chase's new discipline in technology procurement. A business or IT professional seeking an exception must present a strong, quantitatively sound business case for any nonstandard technology. "Everyone knows now that you are dealing with seasoned executives who will ask the hard questions," according to the manager of the Engineering Board.[3] The Board provides a clear, public explanation for every rejected case. This transparency in the decision-making process has reduced the negative impact of the new controls and helped make "buy-hold-sell" part of the business vocabulary for IT.

Another key governance mechanism for achieving JPMorgan Chase's performance goals is the firm's six sigma methodology. Six sigma is central to JPMorgan Chase's firmwide productivity and quality improvement efforts. The director of the six sigma program is a member of the Technology Council. This arrangement firmly establishes the linkage between productivity improvement efforts and the IT investment process. All the firm's divisions and business units have adopted six sigma, enhancing JPMorgan Chase's capability to develop both business unit excellence and firmwide synergies.

The product and price guide and business chargeback are a final mechanism supporting JPMorgan Chase's evolution from a business unit focus to a "one firm—one team" focus. JPMorgan Chase's product and price guide identifies costs for shared IT services. The business chargeback aims to recover ETS costs. ETS intends for the product and price guide to provide the lines of business with a tool for making more informed IT decisions. With the product and price guide, ETS exposes its costs to the business units. So the business units can see savings from consolidating IT operations (such as data centers, networks, common desktops) and from annual productivity gains. Thus, the product and price guide and business charge-back encourage desirable behaviors and lead to the cost reductions targeted in JPMorgan Chase's IT metrics.

Risks of IT Governance Designs

JPMorgan Chase's integrated and disciplined approach to IT governance has started to have a noticeable impact on the firm's new whole-of-enterprise thrust. The head of the Engineering Board notes that the firm has made significant progress in achieving IT metrics: "Purchasing of nonapproved products has now virtually stopped. We are all operating from the same playbook. We are reducing the level of complexity, dealing with vendors differently, and starting to see real teamwork across all our businesses."[4] As expected, these benefits are starting to flow to business results.

Every governance arrangement carries risks. Decisions by IT leaders risk resistance from business managers. Joint business/IT decisions can lead to large and unwieldy decision-making bodies. Decentralized application decisions risk deterioration of firmwide standards and goals. JPMorgan Chase has countered the risks of its governance design in several ways. First, IT decisions are implemented by corporate and business unit IT leaders. The composition of this mechanism ensures that decisions represent business unit needs as well as enterprise needs. But IT decisions are also guided by enterprise objectives, that is, economies of scale and a "one firm—one team" culture. Second, senior managers at the division and line-of-business levels approve their respective IT strategies. These strategies provide input to the principles and investment decisions for the enterprise. Third, performance goals calling for cost savings and business integration motivate adoption of shared infrastructure and architecture standards. Corporate incentive systems motivate divisional and business unit managers to pursue firmwide synergies. Fourth, although business units take individual responsibility for application needs decisions, they must comply with enterprise buy-hold-sell guidelines. And coordination of application development at the division level limits the autonomy of project managers. Without this kind of harmony among the components of the Governance Design Framework, JPMorgan Chase would probably fail in its efforts to implement technology standards and shared services. And without technology standards and shared services, JPMorgan Chase would jeopardize its chances of achieving any kind of synergies across business units.

Designing IT Governance for Different Strategic and Structural Drivers

Although effective IT governance requires harmonization of all six components of the Governance Design Framework, enterprise strategy and organization sets the direction. Thus, we can understand alternative governance designs by focusing on alternative business strategies and organization designs. In this section we review the governance design of firms pursuing different strategies as distinguished by Treacy and Wiersema's concept of value disciplines (see endnote 1). We then review two broad alternative organizational designs: business unit synergy and business unit autonomy. For each alternative, we describe key influences on IT governance design.

IT Governance for Different Strategies: Value Disciplines

Along with many executives, we have found the concept of value disciplines useful in highlighting implications of different strategies for IT governance. Successful organizations, the "market leaders" according to Treacy and Wiersema, usually excel at delivering one type of business value to their chosen customers.

The three value disciplines are:

- *Operational Excellence,* where businesses emphasize efficiency and reliability, lead the industry in price and convenience, minimize overhead costs, streamline the supply chain

- *Customer Intimacy,* focusing on the cultivation of relationships, lifetime value to the company, customer service, and responsiveness and customization based on deep customer knowledge

- *Product (or Service) Leadership,* with continuing product innovation, the embracing of ideas, new solutions to problems, and rapid commercialization

Market leaders excel in at least one value discipline while meeting a minimum threshold of competence in the other two. Each of the three value disciplines has different rules and norms, organization and skills sets, and management systems (figure 6-3).

Operational Excellence

In our study, enterprises focused on operational excellence had larger increases in asset utilization (ROA—see figure 6-3).[5] This relationship reflects harmony between a strategy emphasizing efficiency and reliability and a performance goal emphasizing effective use of assets. Operationally excellent enterprises are process driven, most notably focused on end-to-end supply chain optimization. These enterprises tend to have centralized management structures designing standardized enterprise-wide processes to minimize coordination costs. Standard operating procedures and business processes are finely honed over the years and embedded in the enterprise's information systems. Operationally excellent firms rarely encourage local innovation, relying instead on designing and diffusing innovations from the center outward. Senior managers and corporate staffs make most strategic decisions in operationally excellent enterprises.

Examples of operationally excellent firms include (1) UPS, whose industrial engineering tradition delivers continuous productivity improvements; (2) MeadWestvaco, a manufacturer of commodity paper products, which competes on price, quality, and reliability; (3) BIC Graphic Europe, a small manufacturer of branded promotional products (for example, pens with a company logo) whose success depends on high quality, low price, and a strong distribution network; and (4) ING Direct, a bank that offers lower fees and higher interest rates through standardized, low-cost services. Although all these firms also work to enhance customer service and product and service innovation, they succeed in their markets first and foremost because of their operational excellence.

The IT capabilities of operationally excellent firms reflect their strategic emphasis. IT is highly centralized, designed to enable

FIGURE 6-3

Three Value Disciplines

	Operational excellence	Customer intimacy	Product leadership
Business processes	• End-to-end supply chain optimization • Emphasis on efficiency and reliability	• Customer service, marketplace management • Emphasis on flexibility and responsiveness	• Product development, time to market and market communications • Emphasis on constant innovation
Organization and skills	• Central authority, low level of empowerment • Critical skills at core of organization (e.g., process management)	• Empowerment close to point of customer contact • Critical skills at boundary of organization (e.g., customer service)	• Ad hoc, organic, and cellular • Critical technical skills abound in loose-knit structures
Management systems for coordination (e.g., incentives and IT architectures)	• Command and control, standard operating procedures • Quality management	• Customer equity measures like lifetime value • Satisfaction, share management	• Rewarding individuals' innovative capacity • Risk and exposure management
Information and information systems	• Integrated low-cost transaction systems • The system is the process	• Single view of customer databases • Tools to identify segments and new offerings	• Systems for collaboration • Modeling and simulation tools
Our study	**Larger increases in ROA**	**Lower margins**	**Higher market cap growth and smaller increases in ROI and ROA**

Source: Partially derived from M. Treacy and F. Wiersema, *The Disciplines of Market Leaders* (Reading, MA: Addison-Wesley, 1995).

high-volume, low-cost transaction processing. More important, process design is built into systems. Thus, systems play a key role in ensuring the reliability and predictability of business processes. MeadWestvaco and BIC Graphic Europe establish the process-systems link through purchased ERPs. UPS builds systems in house that converge on a single-package database, protecting the integrity and reliability of both the data and the product delivery process. ING Direct relies on reuse of standard application modules.

The centralized management style and process standardization role of systems gives operationally excellent firms some common IT governance requirements. Typically these firms have highly standardized architectures and a thick layer of shared infrastructure. Operationally excellent enterprises allow few exceptions to standards because exceptions introduce added IT operations costs. They demand broad acceptance of strategies, standards, and metrics to ensure consistent processes. And they tightly align business processes with their standard, enterprisewide applications. Operationally excellent firms need simple low-cost governance arrangements to support their efficient business models. Top performers harmonize the six components of IT governance to facilitate cross-functional, cross-business-unit processes.

Operational Excellence at ING Direct. ING Direct is the international direct banking unit of the Dutch financial services conglomerate ING. Created in 1997, ING Direct offers simple, transparent bank products through multiple channels. By May 2003, ING Direct had assets of 78 billion euros and served over 6 million customers. ING Direct's no/low fees, high returns, and multiple channels appeal to affluent, technology-savvy personal banking customers. Between 2001 and 2003, the firm won numerous marketing and banking innovation awards in Europe, the United States, and Australia.

ING Direct is organized into eight country-based businesses. Each country unit operates autonomously, but the units share a common, "standardized" business model. The bank leverages standardized business solutions as well as standardized technical and infrastructure components in offering a product set featuring savings accounts, term deposits, personal loans/mortgages, retirement savings plans, and a few selected mutual funds.

ING Direct's Information Technology and Operations Council (CIOs and COOs of the country businesses with the head office CIO and COO) makes enterprisewide principles, architecture, infrastructure, and investment decisions (figure 6-4). The Council structure facilitates sharing of best practice and alignment between operations and information technology. The Council holds semiannual meetings in which the CIOs meet on Monday, the COOs meet on Thursday, and the two groups meet jointly on Tuesday and Wednesday. These meetings offer a forum for coordinating the IT Plan with the businesses' Mid Term Plan. The outcome of the meeting serves as input for the ING Direct Council, where the international business strategy is discussed and defined. In doing so, ING Direct allows IT capabilities to influence business strategy just as strategy influences IT.

Unlike many operationally excellent firms, ING Direct looks to its local businesses for innovations. As a country plans to introduce a new product, a product proposal detailing financial and business implications and risks is first discussed by the Product Committee at ING Direct's head office. IT applications are then selected based on a thorough and detailed RFI/RFP process involving all business units. The outcome of this selection process is a global standard rather than an isolated local solution. In addition, the chief architect helps define application specifications so that the new application modules work effectively with existing modules and fit with ING Direct's business, application, and technical architecture.

This arrangement supports ING Direct's desirable behaviors of building modules for reuse, standardizing applications, and achieving a universally compatible architecture. Moreover, it allows for global reusability of expert knowledge through shared and standardized business solutions and architectures. The benefits of module reuse were apparent during the recent launch of ING Direct UK where, besides the head office implementation team, staff from six ING Direct business units contributed.

Customer Intimacy

Customer-intimate firms emphasize flexibility and responsiveness in customer service and marketplace management. Customer intimacy strategies are consistent with performance goals focused

FIGURE 6-4

ING Direct's Governance

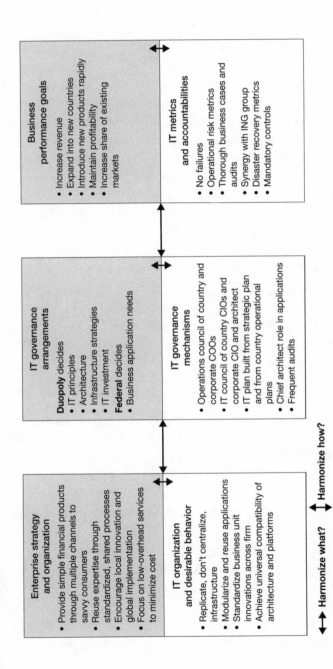

on high profitability (see figure 6-3).[6] Customer-intimate firms require the ability to identify valuable customers and nurture those relationships. Accurately recognizing and developing valuable customer relationships demands a good understanding of both customers and costs. Customer-intimate firms can achieve profitability goals by customizing solutions for individual customers or by identifying discrete customer segments and developing tailored products to serve them. Success in customizing solutions depends on highly capable and empowered employees at the customer interface. Successfully identifying and serving discrete segments depends on powerful data-based systems exposing the segments.

Examples of customer-intimate firms include (1) Federal Express, which takes on the expense of customized services to meet the unique needs of its customers; (2) USAA, a diversified financial services firm focused on serving the financial needs of military personnel and their families; (3) Capital One, a credit card company that segments existing and potential customers into highly specific character sets; and (4) Panalpina, which provides customized freight-forwarding solutions through standardized processes. These firms work hard to cut unnecessary costs while developing innovative products and services. Their competitive edge, however, is in knowing their customers and responding to their customers' specialized needs.

The information and IT requirements of customer-intimate firms center on understanding and serving customers. Customer-intimate firms often strive for a single view of the customer, requiring well-designed and accessible data. Standardized data definitions and naming conventions are critical. USAA, Panalpina, and many other customer-intimate firms are implementing customer relationship management systems to support data standardization and related business processes. Customer intimacy often requires recognizing high-value customers. Analytical tools can expose relationships with the greatest lifetime value and identify life events (for example, sending a child away to college) or support cross selling. Capital One has achieved significant competitive advantage from analytical models that identify demographic segments with unique credit card needs.[7]

IT governance at customer-intimate enterprises requires clarifying desirable behavior regarding responsiveness to customer needs. IT principles should clarify where IT will support individual discretion—and the limits of the discretion—and where IT should support standard processes to provide predictable, cost-effective solutions. To support customer responsiveness, IT governance should clarify responsibility for stewardship of customer data. IT must accept some responsibility for integrating data, but a single view of the customer relies on consistent data definitions and business processes across the enterprise. Just as the CFO owns the financial data in most firms, enterprises need data stewards who own customer data. Customer-intimate enterprises need governance mechanisms that maintain global consistency in the management and use of customer data and interactions. Finally, IT governance mechanisms at customer-intimate firms should clarify responsibility for innovations in customer service and customer segmentation.

Customer Intimacy at Panalpina. Based in Basel, Switzerland, Panalpina focuses on intercontinental air and sea freight services. Panalpina owns no shipping assets but works with transportation companies to meet the end-to-end shipping needs of its global customers. With revenues of approximately U.S. $3.5 billion, Panalpina is one of the world's largest freight forwarders. The company organizes its twelve thousand people into three hundred twenty "houses," each with specific geographical responsibilities. Panalpina's customers can be cost sensitive, but they have varied and often complex shipping requirements. The company's strategy is to provide customized, integrated solutions while minimizing the premium customers must pay for those services. Thus, Panalpina's IT governance focuses on facilitating customization while minimizing nonvalue-added operating costs (figure 6-5).

Panalpina's governance arrangements involve close working relationships between business and IT managers. The Executive Board acts as a global steering committee making principles and investment decisions. The CIO sits on the Executive Board and has responsibility for both IT and process development. The operational head of IT is one of the CIO's direct reports. Her other three direct

FIGURE 6-5

Panalpina's IT Governance

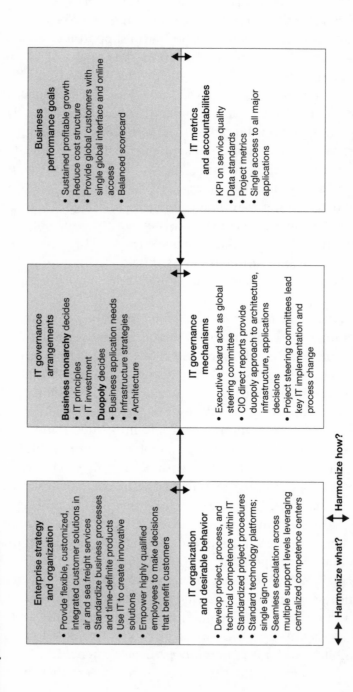

© 2003 MIT Sloan School Center for Information Systems Research (CISR). Used with permission.

reports head information management, business development, and project management. The CIO and her direct reports are responsible for architecture, infrastructure, and applications decisions.

To provide integrated end-to-end customer solutions, Panalpina needs high levels of coordination across its 320 houses. Centralizing both IT and process development under the CIO facilitates this coordination and ensures alignment between IT and business strategy. The CIO organizes around projects, drawing process and IT expertise from her staff while securing business expertise from the field. Major projects have steering committees of IT and business managers. This structure has facilitated implementation of enterprise systems to support standardization of core processes. Panalpina has both technical and process standards. By centralizing process and IT management, Panalpina is able to empower employees to develop customized solutions within the constraints of the standards. Panalpina can therefore deliver customized solutions reliably and cost effectively.

Although Panalpina's centralized IT organization facilitates process and technical standardization, it complicates IT support. Reliable service and support is critical to maintaining constant electronic linkages to customers and business partners. Rather than locate significant IT expertise at each of the 320 houses, Panalpina has distributed some IT professionals in the houses while building substantial support into regional centers. Ensuring adequate support involves designing processes to direct calls from computer users to appropriate technical experts. The CIO has introduced performance metrics to monitor that service.

As a logistics firm, Panalpina's largest capital expenditures are for information technology. The firm's governance arrangements helped the firm realize a small increase in net income in 2002 despite a slow economy. Tight IT/business coordination led to reduced operating costs despite aggressive growth efforts (approximately four hundred additional positions in regions with the greatest growth potential) and a transformation from the firm's traditional local structure to a regional organization structure.

Customer intimacy is a more complex strategy than operational excellence. Checks and balances are needed to ensure that, in addressing complex customer needs, the firm enhances, rather than jeopardizes, profitability. Panalpina's IT governance relies on centralized IT management and business monarchy and duopoly governance arrangements to monitor these dual requirements. Some customer-intimate firms prefer more decentralized organizational structures. To compensate, they typically govern with strong business and IT monarchies to define and enforce shared technology, business processes, and data definitions. The State Street case at the end of the chapter provides an example of this alternative governance design.

Product Leadership

Firms leading on product or service offerings are focused on product development and time to market, emphasizing constant innovation or breakthrough products. Enterprises in our study with strategies focused on product leadership had faster increases in market capitalization (see figure 6-3). Product leadership firms foster innovation by creating productive R&D environments, characterized by knowledge sharing, the freedom to experiment, and organic cells of technical experts. Management practices in product leadership firms focus on encouraging and rewarding innovation while managing the inherent risks of experimentation. Revenue growth from innovation requires success; experimentation inevitably involves some failures. Management focuses on ensuring the right balance of risk taking and control.

Examples of product leadership firms include (1) DuPont, growing through innovation in its global product lines; (2) Pfizer, enabling innovation by separating pharmaceutical R&D into a separate business unit; and (3) Motorola, designing powerful software for telecommunications and other electronic products. These firms cannot ignore requirements for efficiency or customer responsiveness, but their strategies focus first on designing new products and services.

The information needs of product leadership firms revolve around generating and disseminating knowledge about innovations. In core R&D shops, this involves experimentation—increasingly computer simulated—to test compounds and analyze results. Service innovations require customer testing through usability labs or test marketing. For both product and service innovations, IT requirements include collaborative tools for sharing knowledge across (increasingly virtual) teams and modeling tools for actually conducting the experiments. In addition to research support, product leadership firms need technology supporting rapid, cost-effective commercialization of new products. Thus, although the research function of a product leadership enterprise requires an organic environment focused on knowledge sharing, other units in the same firm have needs more similar to operationally excellent or customer-intimate enterprises.

IT governance for product leadership addresses the many faces of a firm encouraging innovation but also attempting to thrive in markets where customers negotiate prices and demand first-rate customer service. Because different functional and organizational units have different needs, governance focuses on clarifying what will be shared across organizational units and how those units will interface. To enable innovation, a product leader's IT governance encourages some autonomy in the applications of innovating units. At DuPont and Pfizer, governance involves feudal arrangements for IT application needs.

Product leaders also require efficiencies in IT operations, so they create shared infrastructures and design enterprise architectures. DuPont and Pfizer rely on IT monarchies to design and implement shared infrastructures. The IT monarchies primarily comprise business unit IT staff and thus achieve the benefits of a federal arrangement. IT staff explore the capabilities of existing technologies as they debate the compromises required of individual business units in adopting shared standards and services. These IT monarchies are empowered by business leaders who are actively involved in principles and investment decisions.

JPMorgan Chase's IT governance design framework in figure 6-2 offers an example of governance design with a product leadership flavor while balancing the need for the other value disciplines. The emphasis on empowering innovators while developing platforms to enable effective delivery of products and services is a constant theme in product leadership firms. Duopolies are useful for ensuring that IT provides the right balance of business unit and enterprisewide support. In chapter 3 we described Motorola's governance design. Despite their very different industries, the similarities in the desirable behaviors of JPMorgan Chase and Motorola lead to similar governance designs.

All firms, regardless of discipline, share the need for IT governance to both reinforce and transcend organizational structure. In the next section we explore how firms coordinate the IT needs of their business units.

Encouraging Business Unit Synergies or Autonomy with IT Governance

A key strategic decision for multibusiness unit enterprises is how to structure business unit relationships. Enterprises in our study had an average of eight independent business units. Over 83 percent of enterprises described significant pressure to capture synergies between their business units. At the same time, over 50 percent of enterprises had significant pressure for autonomy between business units. Forty-seven percent of firms felt significant pressure for both synergies and autonomy. Requirements for synergies across organizational boundaries expose the limitations of organizational structures in facilitating business strategy. A critical role of IT governance is to ensure that organizational boundaries do not constrain strategic objectives.

Despite the desire to develop both autonomy and synergy across business units, we find that more successful enterprises decide which is more important—synergy or autonomy. The answer to this question leads to one of two types of governance objectives: encouraging business unit autonomy with some synergies or encouraging business unit synergies with some autonomy. Figure 6-6 defines these arrangements and lists their management implications, drawing out the differences on four dimensions.[8]

In chapter 2 we noted that enterprise architectures attempt to capture three types of standardization: technology, data, and process. Not coincidentally, these three types of standardization reflect the synergies enterprises seek:

1. Shared technology and infrastructure services to generate economies of scale

2. Shared data, particularly customer, supplier, product, or employee data to facilitate process integration

3. Standardized processes to facilitate process excellence, reusability, and organizational learning

FIGURE 6-6

Business Unit Arrangements

	KEY STRATEGIC DRIVER	
	BU Synergy	BU Autonomy
Business processes	• Some processes standard across several BUs • Some processes integrated across several BUs	• Each BU's processes are distinct and independent • Emphasis on BU decision making
Organization and skills	• Top-down leadership specifying synergies • Remove duplication	• Encourage BU innovative capacity • BU skills focused on local value discipline
Management systems for coordination (e.g., incentives and IT architectures)	• Synergies centrally defined and coordinated • BUs focused on both BU and firmwide strategy	• Few mandated processes • Enterprise financial and risk management
Information and information systems	• Substantial integrated firmwide infrastructure and shared services	• Thin layer of firmwide infrastructure • Each BU infrastructure and systems tailored
Our study	**Higher profit (ROI)**	**Larger increases in market cap and revenue growth**

© 2003 MIT Sloan School Center for Information Systems Research (CISR). Used with permission.

We have found that enterprises that encourage business unit autonomy with some synergies usually focus on shared technology and infrastructure services (number 1 in the list). These synergies offer significant efficiencies without forcing difficult business unit integration, which is often perceived as meddling by business unit leaders. In contrast, enterprises pursuing business unit synergies with some autonomy may gradually work toward developing all three of the synergies.

Encouraging Business Unit Autonomy with Some Synergies

When enterprises want diverse business units to pursue world-class excellence in their specific market or function, they may choose to minimize potential synergies. Their opportunities for synergies are likely to be limited, and the costs and burdens of achieving synergies may be outweighed by the potential for growth from independent business units. Our study provides support for this approach. Firms seeking business unit autonomy had higher growth rates in their industry-adjusted market capitalization and revenues with some weak evidence of lower profits.

To achieve growth, as well as better margins and asset utilization, many firms choose a predominantly autonomous business model but still strive for synergies by removing duplication and achieving economies. For many years Pfizer, now the world's largest and most valuable pharmaceutical company, managed its business units autonomously.[9] The two largest business units, Global Research and Development and Global Pharmaceuticals, have many different but some similar information and application needs. Pfizer has encouraged both to pursue world-class capabilities in their respective functions. These two business units, as well as Pfizer's four smaller business units, have their own IT groups and generally address their own information needs. Because the company has grown rapidly and because the IT groups want to focus their staff on the high-value IT projects, Pfizer has seen value in developing shared services, initially in the area of IT infrastructure, management of enterprisewide data, and enterprisewide applications like human resources and finance. These shared services capitalize on potential synergies, most notably economies of scale and the elimination of duplicate, nondifferentiating services.

To support efforts to capture synergies among business units, Pfizer's management has created IT governance processes. These processes provide a forum for negotiating what can and should be shared, what enterprisewide projects should be undertaken, and how shared resources will be managed. Pfizer created an IT Leadership Team (ITLT) composed of the vice presidents of Information Technology in the six businesses, as well as the vice president of the Corporate Information Technology Group, who chairs the ITLT and has responsibility for building and running the IT infrastructure. The ITLT develops an integrated plan and seeks to share a common set of high-level metrics. The ITLT reports to an Information Technology Planning Group (ITPG) that comprises senior business function heads. This team determines priorities for shared processes, infrastructure, and applications at Pfizer. Each team member assigned a senior staffer to participate in Pfizer's Architecture Council. The Architecture Council designed an enterprise architecture, agreed on technology standards, and developed the enterprise project portfolio for approval by the ITLT. On major projects, an ITLT sponsor then provides high-level guidance to the corporate IT engineering and operations groups, which implement the new services. In addition to these decision mechanisms, Pfizer introduced an architecture exception process, with the Architecture Council making decisions on requested exceptions.

Pfizer has developed an IT prioritization and funding process mechanism to guide the decisions of the IT Leadership Team. We have observed that, like Pfizer, as firms start to seek out synergies, they design IT governance to create those synergies. Pfizer still encourages high levels of business unit autonomy in order to pursue world-class competencies. The firm's IT governance supports its efforts to garner synergies where it makes sense.

Enterprises like Pfizer with predominately autonomous business units but seeking some synergies do need IT governance. But it is governance "light." The light IT governance encourages synergies in enterprise processes, enterprise applications, and technical infrastructure without slowing or retarding business unit innovation. The synergies create efficiencies, thereby enhancing profitability, while business unit autonomy enables growth.

Encouraging Business Unit Synergies with Some Autonomy

While Pfizer continues to encourage business unit autonomy on many IT decisions, other enterprises sacrifice business unit autonomy to gain greater synergies. In our study, enterprises citing high pressure for achieving synergies had higher profits as measured by ROI. But capitalizing on potential synergies is not easy. Organizational boundaries usually cause resistance to any kind of sharing, integrating, or standardizing. Business units argue that "we are different" or "you folks at corporate always slow us down with your bureaucratic procedures." In addition, pursuing synergies introduces coordination costs. Governance is a cost-effective way to manage coordination.

The experiences of MeadWestvaco, Panalpina, Dow Corning, UPS, Delta Air Lines, and other firms suggest that both the number of mechanisms and the number of people involved in IT governance expands as firms pursue technology, data, and process synergies. Without an overwhelming strategic logic, the natural autonomy of business units will prevail. Thus, firms pursuing synergies need senior business executives and business unit heads to make critical decisions, communicate their intentions, and ensure effective implementation.

The mechanisms of IT architecture committees and chargeback were often used effectively by top-performing firms to facilitate synergies. While many firms struggle to deploy these two mechanisms effectively, firms successfully seeking synergies reported that both mechanisms were effective and worked well together. As we saw at Pfizer, IT architecture committees with representatives from the different business units plot a course for IT use by designing and communicating the enterprise architecture. The architecture committee provides the vision for the use of IT and illustrates how business unit synergies will be achieved. A "big picture" architecture illustrating how all the pieces fit together, as in the Delta Nervous System (see figure 2-5), is a very powerful communication tool.

Chargeback adds order to the architecture vision and is used for two purposes. First, chargeback makes clear the cost savings from the shared services model. Transparent chargeback can defuse arguments about transfer pricing by demonstrating the value of shared services. Second, chargeback encourages responsible use of IT consistent with the synergy strategy. Chargeback encourages business unit managers who are accountable for both local and global results to use shared services, such as an enterprisewide customer database. In summary, the architecture committee sets the direction and the chargeback system takes care of the money flow while encouraging responsible IT use.

Summary of the Strategy-Governance Relationship

Business unit arrangements—by reflecting business strategy—have important implications for IT governance. At one end of the spectrum, enterprises consisting of autonomous business units with few requirements for synergies across those business units have little, if any, need for IT governance. Only if business units share some resources—shared infrastructure services, an enterprisewide IT budget, common data—should they govern IT. The demand for synergies aligns somewhat with the value disciplines—product leaders most often demanding only technology synergies, customer-intimate firms often seeking shared data in addition to the economies of scale characteristic of technology synergies, and operationally excellent firms finding value in process standardization, as well as technology and data synergies.

As firms introduce synergies focused on shared and standardized technology, they must govern architecture and infrastructure at the enterprise level. Thus, they start to introduce some governance mechanisms. Firms seeking data and process synergies add more governance mechanisms to ensure the integrity of data and to design and implement global processes. Technology standards require the support of business leaders, but data and process standards force the active leadership of business executives.

These escalating governance requirements suggest that IT governance evolves in enterprises. Throughout this book we have observed that firms such as Panalpina, Pfizer, MeadWestvaco, Campbell Soup, JPMorgan Chase, DuPont, Carlson Companies, and DBS Bank are generally moving from more autonomous to more synergistic organizational designs. As firms evolve toward more synergistic designs, they adopt more complex IT governance. The State Street Corporation case study describes one company's IT governance evolution from minimal governance mechanisms to governing technology synergies and then introducing customer process and data synergies.

Case Study on State Street Corporation: Changing Strategic Objectives

To better understand the complexities of IT governance, we look in detail at IT governance at State Street Corporation, one of America's best-performing financial services firms. To capture the evolution of IT governance, the case study spans more than three years and includes two CIOs.[10] The case demonstrates how IT governance can be used to help implement significant strategic change.

A Top-Performing Financial Services Firm

State Street Corporation is a world leader in financial services, providing investment services, investment management, trading, and research to investment managers, corporations, mutual funds, pension funds, unions, not-for-profit organizations, and individuals. As of March 2003, State Street had $7.9 trillion in assets under custody and $788 billion in assets under management; more than 20,000 employees worked in 22 countries serving clients in over 100 markets. Annual growth rates in both revenues and net income increased on average at more than 15 percent annually from 1996 to 2002. Operating earnings per share experienced over 16 percent compounded growth in the ten years up to and including 2002. In 2002, State Street had total revenues of nearly $4 billion and net income of $719 million. In 2002, annual revenue growth was flat, consistent with the industry downturn, although net income grew 5 percent.

State Street is the world's number one player in each of the following markets: investment servicing, institutional investment management, securities lending, and foreign exchange services. Globally, State Street is one of the leading users and developers of IT, committing on average 20 to 25 percent of operating expenses to technology and technologists. Trademarked information delivery systems, such as State Street's Global Link and In~Sight, and electronic trading platforms, such as FX Connect, Lattice, and Equity Connect, provide clients with critical financial systems. *Computerworld* magazine regularly votes State Street one of the top twenty places to work in IT. Reflecting on the importance of IT, Marshall Carter, former CEO of State Street, often referred to State Street as a technology company with a banking license.[11]

When David Spina became Chairman and CEO of State Street in January 2001, the world's stock markets were in a prolonged slump and a series of structural changes were occurring in State Street's core markets. These changes led State Street to focus on achieving greater returns from all assets and particularly from the IT investments that were crucial to State Street's leadership position.

The structural changes included the impact of the aging population on pension systems. Because people were living longer, policy makers were looking for ways to help individuals build suitable savings to fund their retirements. Governments would need pension fund management services from financial institutions. The aging population, along with increased use of the Internet in the provisioning of financial services, represented a huge opportunity for State Street to expand globally. In contrast, industry-mandated changes—including straight-through processing and going from three days to one day to settle trades—cost millions of dollars that would be difficult to recoup from customers.

One State Street

In response to these and other changes, David Spina articulated his client-focused vision of "One State Street." At internal meetings during 2001, Spina explained: "You've heard me talk about 'One State Street.' That term describes how we must work together to serve our clients. When clients look at State Street, our organizational lines must be completely invisible, and behind this seamless face, we must have industrial-strength lines of communication connecting every part of the company."

Traditionally, State Street operated as a set of separate business units. "One State Street" embodies the strategic imperatives described by Spina at the 2001 annual meeting. "First, we will continue to enrich our relationships with existing clients. We understand that as our clients grow and succeed, we will grow and succeed. So taking care of existing clients is our first priority. Second, we will continue to grow our client base outside the United States. World markets offer almost unlimited opportunity for investment managers and servicers, and our leadership in U.S. markets gives us an advantage over our competitors. We're very excited about the growth we saw last year—particularly in Canada, Luxembourg, the U.K., and Japan."[12]

State Street management believed that shared IT infrastructure was important to enable this single point of contact. Historically, State Street's IT organization had been highly decentralized. A small, central IT organization provided network services, data center operations, and transaction processing for mutual funds, pension funds, and global operations. Each of the four major business units had a self-contained IT operation responsible for operations. Only a small number of infrastructure services, such as the communications network, were provided centrally.

Designing IT Governance

To deliver "One State Street" required a single point of contact and consistent client view of State Street to develop new business and reduce time to market. John Fiore, then CIO of State Street, recognized that the firm needed a new governance structure to facilitate these changes. Because of its traditional business unit autonomy, governance had not been important at State Street. The corporate CIO managed the small set of shared infrastructure services as well as headquarters applications. The new corporate vision introduced a new set of desirable behaviors, including: the development of a consistent view of the customer across State Street; business unit adoption of new technologies; the creation of one IT community across State Street; and the introduction of justification techniques for enterprisewide IT investment, such as pro forma business cases and measurement of IT impact. The new governance design is summarized in figure 6-7.

State Street's new governance arrangement (figure 6-8) focuses on the firm's requirements for customer intimacy and synergy across autonomous business units. A business monarchy makes IT principles and IT investment decisions. IT monarchies assume responsibility for the more technical IT decisions of infrastructure and architecture, receiving broad-based federal input for IT infrastructure. Business application decisions are made with a duopoly involving business unit leaders, IT professionals from the business units (vertical IT groups) and IT shared services (horizontal IT groups). This model provides for both business unit and enterprisewide perspectives in IT governance decisions.

The key mechanism for implementing State Street's business monarchy is the IT Executive Committee (ITEC), composed of the COO, the CAO, the CIO, and senior executives from State Street's various business units. ITEC is responsible for reviewing, analyzing, and synthesizing the IT investment needs of individual business

FIGURE 6-7

State Street Corporation's IT Governance

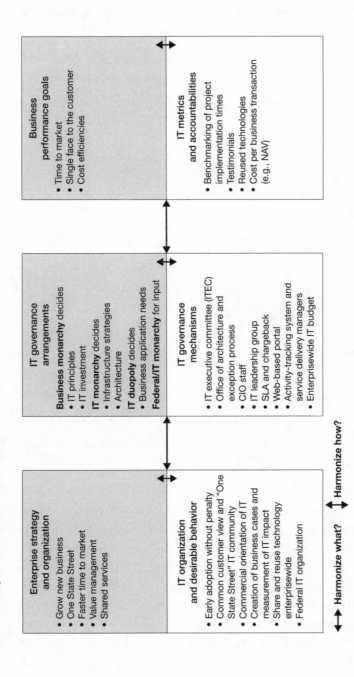

© 2003 MIT Sloan School Center for Information Systems Research (CISR). Used with permission.

FIGURE 6-8

State Street Corporation's IT Governance Arrangements Matrix

		DECISION								
		IT Principles		IT Architecture		IT Infrastructure Strategies		Business Application Needs		IT Investment	
		Input	Decision	Input	Decision	Input	Decision	Input	Decision	Input	Decision
GOVERNANCE ARCHETYPE	Business Monarchy		ITEC								ITEC CIO
	IT Monarchy			Arch. office	CIO IT leaders		CIO IT leaders				
	Feudal										
	Federal	CIO IT leaders IT org. Business leaders				IT org. Arch. office Business leaders				Budgets SLA Activity tracking IT leaders	
	Duopoly								Business leaders IT org. IT leaders		

☐ Most common pattern for all firms.

Governance mechanisms:

Activity tracking—Activity-tracking system
Arch. office—Office of architecture
Budgets—Enterprisewide IT budget management
CIO—CIO staff
ITEC—Information Technology Executive Committee

IT leaders—IT leadership group
IT org.—Federated IT organization (vertical and horizontal IT units)
SLA—Service delivery agreements and chargeback

units in order to create an enterprisewide IT budget. The leaders of each business unit and the CIO identify the key IT business and infrastructure projects for the coming year. These projects are classified according to their contribution to the corporate growth targets and importance to their business unit. The result is a list of all IT initiatives for the coming year. ITEC members negotiate among themselves to create a reduced list of projects and IT infrastructure initiatives designed to meet the corporate growth targets and the agreed-upon percentage of the operating expense budget available for information technology. Once ITEC has decided on the list of projects, the IT organization tracks the allocation and use of the IT budget by project and business unit using an activity tracking system.

ITEC has several advantages over earlier IT business unit-specific investment processes. The negotiation of an enterprisewide IT budget encourages focus on the enterprisewide value of IT rather than on the needs of individual business units. The individual business executives naturally tend to focus on the profitability of their own business. By combining discussion of infrastructure investment with business unit initiatives, the value of making investments in enterprisewide infrastructure for shared use becomes much clearer.

The IT monarchies for infrastructure and architecture rely on two mechanisms: the IT Leadership Group (ITLG) and the Office of Architecture. ITLG, composed of all senior business unit and corporate IT managers, defines IT strategy. This group also establishes linkages with corporate and business unit executives. For example, high-level architectural standards are presented by ITLG to ITEC to get input and buy-in. The Office of Architecture existed prior to the new governance arrangements. Historically, the Office of Architecture had been responsible for reviewing overall architecture frameworks, identifying and recommending technology standards, and conducting research in applied technology. The Office's enhanced responsibilities now include monitoring projects for best use of and compliance with standards. When a standard is not available, the Office of Architecture coordinates with project managers to identify and implement the most appropriate technology to satisfy the business need. The expanded role for the Office of Architecture made it a more effective force both to promote sharing and reuse of technology across the enterprise and to support the deployment of new technology for developing new business. The mission and methodology of the Office of Architecture have been codified in a set of IT Architecture Principles linking technology to the business.

Evolving IT Governance

Early evidence suggested that State Street's IT governance structure encouraged desirable behaviors. Testimonials from project managers indicated that the architectural review process helped deliver solutions more quickly because technology issues surfaced before they critically impacted the projects. The shared infrastructure was evolving to address the joint needs of the businesses. A messaging hub capable of interfacing with a wide variety of platforms began servicing applications for the four different business units. This service was one of several new services reducing IT cost and time to market.

State Street has developed and tracked business metrics influenced by IT. The metric system, using a common baseline of 1997, demonstrates the impact of IT on such key business performance indicators as the number of State Street portfolios, the number of client positions calculated, and the number of daily net asset values (NAVs) calculated for NASDAQ. For State Street, these metrics provide clear measures of the impacts of IT investments on business performance. For example, the number of NAVs calculated has increased nearly threefold between 1997 and 2000. At the same time, the IT cost per NAV has been reduced by 50 percent.

In late 2002, Joe Antonellis, a former line-of-business head, became CIO. He has elected to keep the current IT governance model in place. Joe's focus is on the importance of continuing to align IT strategy with the business strategy, "We are focused more sharply than ever on ensuring that State Street's IT vision and business strategy are aligned with our clients' demands and needs."[13] Monthly Strategy Steering Committee meetings, chaired by David Spina, support the alignment of IT and business. These meetings set the overall business strategies, which then trickle down to provide guidance to ITEC and subsequently IT in terms of priorities.

As part of cost-cutting initiatives in 2002, the IT budget was decreased. At the same time, IT reporting lines changed so that 70 percent of all IT staff reported to the CIO, up from 45 percent in 2001. This change facilitated desirable behavior for "One State Street." The IT organization structure enabled significant consolidation of infrastructure, resulting in significant cost savings and cost avoidance, while still facilitating new offerings to clients such as custom data marts.

This case illustrates good IT governance. Governance evolved as State Street evolved from a set of independent business units to "One State Street" and more recently to a firm operating in a period of a declining stock market. State Street used IT governance explicitly to encourage the desirable behaviors needed to implement its strategies. As State Street strives for additional data and process synergies, it might further adjust its governance mechanisms. Increasing synergies will likely force greater involvement in IT governance on the part of process leaders and business unit heads. In other words, IT governance will evolve as the firm's strategy evolves.

Management Principles for Designing Governance to Address Strategic Objectives

This chapter has discussed how enterprises design their governance. Effective governance design consists of a rational set of arrangements and mechanisms harmonized with strategy, structure, and desired outcomes. Management teams can assess their governance by mapping their governance arrangements and mechanisms onto a Governance Arrangements Matrix and checking whether those arrangements make sense given the enterprise's strategic objectives. Four management principles summarize how IT governance design helps enterprises achieve their strategic objectives:

- *Make tough choices.* IT governance design encourages desirable behaviors, but if management has been reluctant to establish strategic priorities, individuals receive mixed signals about appropriate behavior. IT governance design requires tradeoffs. Thus, management must decide which is more important: autonomy or synergy; operational excellence, customer intimacy, or product leadership? Every enterprise has conflicting goals, but top performers commit to a small set of most critical objectives.

- *Develop metrics to formalize the strategic choices.* IT value can be difficult to measure. By establishing metrics to capture progress toward strategic goals, management can design IT metrics indicating whether IT governance is working.

- *Determine where organizational structure limits desirable behaviors and design governance mechanisms to overcome the limitations.* Even when enterprises succeed in choosing a small set of strategic priorities, tradeoffs remain. IT governance can transcend organizational structures to enable objectives that are inconsistent with the organizational design.

- *Allow governance to evolve as management learns the role of IT and how to accept accountability for maximizing IT value.*

Throughout this chapter we have noted that governance should transcend formal organizational structures and enable strategic objectives. Increasingly, enterprises are seeking the strategic agility to recognize and respond to unpredictable changes in their marketplaces. Agility demands an ability to rethink business strategy based on market changes. But in most enterprises a major shift in strategy would force a change in organization structure because the structure was designed to achieve a particular strategy. By overcoming the limitations of organizational structure, governance can enable greater agility in enterprises. Thus, effective IT governance will become increasingly important as the pace of change accelerates.

7

Government and
Not-for-Profit
Organizations

IN MANY COUNTRIES, more than one third of the economy consists of government organizations, including defense, immigration, utilities, police, education, and health. Add other not-for-profit organizations, such as charities, nongovernmental-organizations (NGOs), and private schools and universities, and the percentage is even larger. For convenience, we will refer to all these organizations including government agencies as not for profits. Not-for-profit organizations are significant users of IT. Similar to for-profit enterprises, IT consumed an average of 8.4 percent of the annual budgets of the seventy-four not-for-profit organizations we studied. However, not-for-profit organizations have poorer governance performance—probably a reflection of broader and more multifaceted strategic objectives. The other chapters in this book are equally relevant to for-profit and not-for-profit managers. However, this chapter deals exclusively with the complex IT governance issues facing senior managers of not-for-profit organizations.

First we will explore some of the complexity faced by not for profits with a case study of the design of IT governance at the United Kingdom's Metropolitan Police Service–Scotland Yard. We introduce a framework that takes account of this complexity and discusses value creation in not-for-profit organizations. With the value framework as a starting point, we have found it easier to design not-for-profit IT governance. Using the data from our study, we will then look at how not-for-profit organizations govern IT compared with for-profit firms. With governance performance as the measure of success, we then look at how top not-for-profit governance performers govern and the mechanisms they use. Finally, we close with a case study of evolving IT governance at UNICEF, using the value framework as a guide.

Metropolitan Police Service–Scotland Yard

The Metropolitan Police Service (MPS)–Scotland Yard provides policing services for London and also has national responsibilities.[1] MPS–Scotland Yard employs over forty thousand people, approximately 25 percent of the total police service for England. Over 1,500 of MPS–Scotland Yard employees are in the Directorate of Information. Ailsa Beaton, Director of Information for MPS–Scotland Yard, also represents the Association of Chief Police Officers (ACPO) on the board of the national Police Information Technology Organization. Policing in England and Wales is funded by both central and local authorities and overseen through a tripartite arrangement between the home office, police authorities, and ACPO.

MPS–Scotland Yard Works with a Strong Committee Structure

MPS–Scotland Yard has six business units and a strong desire for greater synergies across all its operations. The executive body for MPS is the Management Board, which has two top-level committees, one for performance review and one for resource allocation. Under these committees are fourteen strategic committees, one of which is the Information Management Steering Group (IMSG). Depending on the area of operation, the IMSG reports to each of three groups—Management Board, Performance Committee, and Resource Committee.

The underlying value discipline of MPS–Scotland Yard is operational excellence, with a strong focus on streamlining and improving processes. The pressure for synergy is very high, particularly around information for solving crimes. MPS describes its IT principles as follows: Most of the information needed to investigate and solve crimes is in one or more independent systems that are located throughout the MPS. Our challenge is not only to make data input much easier (and not duplicated) but to make it readily available anytime, anyplace, and anywhere.[2]

Ailsa Beaton and her colleagues designed MPS's IT governance arrangements to create value by achieving these and other organization principles, implementing a number of changes in the ways decisions were made. Figures 7-1 and 7-2 are the Governance Design Framework and the Governance Arrangements Matrix for MPS–Scotland Yard.

MPS's business objectives include cost efficiencies, better information access, cultural diversity, and improved operational excellence with streamlined processes. These objectives are reflected in business performance goals and desirable IT behaviors. For example, an important performance goal is to reduce the rate of increase in overall cost base. For IT, the resulting desirable behaviors are reuse of systems and technologies.

IT Investment Process

MPS–Scotland Yard has a structured and transparent process for making IT investment decisions. Decisions are made on the recommendation of the IMSG, which meets every three months and is chaired by the deputy commissioner. IMSG has a budget for IT-related projects and takes a formal IT portfolio approach to IT investment. The IMSG, in its role as an investment committee, decides on funded projects as well as how to start or stop projects and how to fund new work. IMSG also provides input to budgeting. Each proposed project must be linked to a specific strategy, such as e-policing, infrastructure, information management, and call-handling services.

Each proposal has a business sponsor, usually the business process owner. Once a decision is made to fund a project, the accountability for completion and delivering the benefits is placed into the work stream of a senior officer. Each initiative has a program or project board, depending on the scope of the initiative. This board is chaired by the sponsor/senior officer and has a mix of technical and

FIGURE 7-1

Governance Design Framework for MPS–Scotland Yard

Enterprise strategy and organization
- Cost efficiencies as policing in different locales broadly similar
- Cultural shift embracing diversity
- Information to do job wherever you are
- Improved operational excellence
- Greater synergies from BUs
- Streamlined processes

IT organization and desirable behavior
- Joint decision making across businesses
- Disciplined investment
- Business ownership of IT-related programs, projects
- Buy rather than create
- Reuse of systems, technologies
- Tracking of benefits

IT governance arrangements

Federal decides
- IT principles

Business monarchy decides
- IT investment
- business application needs

IT Monarchy decides
- IT architecture
- IT infrastructure strategies

Federal/Duopoly for input

IT governance mechanisms
- Information Management Steering Group (IMSG) reporting to Management Board
- IMSG acts as investment committee, enterprisewide budget for IT-related projects
- Formal IT portfolio approach
- Business owners for programs, projects, program/project board
- Business responsible for benefits realization
- Business/IT relationship managers

Business performance goals
- Reduced rate of increase in cost base
- Increased diversity of workforce
- Extent of integrated decision making across business units

IT metrics and accountabilities
- Known accountabilities for all IT-related investments and benefits
- Greater standardization in processes
- Greater standardization in IT resources
- Lower cost base for current activities
- Increased reuse of systems, technologies, resources

↕ Harmonize what?   ↕ Harmonize how?

© 2003 Gartner, Inc., and MIT Sloan School Center for Information Systems Research (CISR) adapted from Gartner Executive Programs (EXP) Research publication "Effective IT Governance," Marianne Broadbent and Peter Weill, January 2003. Used with permission.

FIGURE 7-2

Governance Arrangements Matrix for MPS–Scotland Yard

GOVERNANCE ARCHETYPE	DECISION									
	IT Principles		IT Architecture		IT Infrastructure Strategies		Business Application Needs		IT Investment	
	Input	Decision	Input	Decision	Input	Decision	Input	Decision	Input	Decision
Business Monarchy								IMSG Director of info.		IMSG Director of info.
IT Monarchy			Arch. comm.	Director of info. IM leaders		Director of info. IM leaders				
Feudal										
Federal	Business owners IM leaders	IMSG Director of info. Mgmt. board								
Duopoly					Business liaison		IM leaders Business liaison Business owners		Budget Portfolio	

☐ Most common pattern for all firms.

Governance mechanisms:
Arch. comm.—Architecture committee
Business liaison—Business liaison officers
Business owners—Business program/project owners
Budget—Enterprisewide IT budget management
Director of info.—Director of information

IM leaders—Information management leadership group
IMSG—Information management steering group;
  reports to management board
Portfolio—Formal IT portfolio approach

user representatives among its members. Critical to the decision-making and management process is the focus at MPS–Scotland Yard on benefits management and realization. The business sponsors, also known as the senior responsible owners, are held accountable for the benefit management and realization of the projects they promote.

Infrastructure projects sought by the Information Group face the same type of scrutiny as IT-enabled business projects. For smaller projects, there is now a simplified process. "We found that the procedures we developed brought transparency and accountability into the process," explained Beaton. "However, the requirements became overly complex for small projects. Some developments were set in train [initiated] outside our processes as we had made the process too complex. We now have a group that authorizes small projects between meetings."[3]

In contrast to the IT investment decision-making process, the Information Group drives the infrastructure strategy decisions. "I have drawn a strong line between infrastructure and applications in terms of decision rights," states Beaton. "When the business wants to do something, it is their decision, and we work with them. But with infrastructure projects, I am the sponsor—and a bidder like everyone else."

MPS–Scotland Yard had many different networks. As a result, senior officers needed three different workstations on their desks— for finance, e-mail, and Internet access. The Management Board accepted a proposal from Beaton to consolidate the infrastructure and gradually eliminate the need for multiple workstations. To date, the consolidation moves have taken several million pounds out of the cost base. Costs will continue to drop as officers need fewer machines. This success is a strong indicator of a successful IT governance process in an organization where measuring performance is very challenging. The learning from governance efforts so far positions MPS for forthcoming decisions on how to most effectively deploy IT throughout the organization.

Framework for Value in Not-for-Profit Organizations

The successful efforts of MPS–Scotland Yard in implementing IT governance illustrate many of the challenges facing not-for-profit organizations—measuring performance and value, a culture of formal committees, limited budgets, and endless opportunities to create value. A frustration facing not-for-profit executives is that many of the management frameworks and measures are designed for profit-seeking organizations where the performance measures of profit, shareholder value, and good corporate citizenship are clear. In addition, well-accepted strategy and management frameworks such as Michael Porter's five-factor model don't translate well for not for profits where there is often little competition and no marketplace with multiple buyers and sellers (for example, government services).[4] Leaders of not-for-profit organizations need a different management framework to help strategize and govern. Mark Moore and others have developed a very helpful value framework for executives of not for profits, which we adapt here (figure 7-3).[5]

Authorizing Environment

Moore's framework identifies three key interconnected factors that must be aligned to generate value in any organization: environment, capabilities, and value (the three circles in figure 7-3). Not for profits have some unique characteristics related to value creation, shown in

FIGURE 7-3

Value Framework for Managing Not-for-Profit Organizations

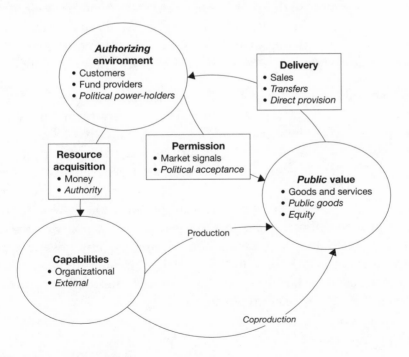

Note: Italics are for not for profits only.
Source: Adapted from John Alford, Melbourne Business School, University of Melbourne, 1993.
Used with permission.

italics in figure 7-3. A for-profit organization's environment is the
market conditions in which it generates capital, finds a market for
its goods, and adjusts to regulatory or resource constraints. In contrast, a not-for-profit organization has an *authorizing environment* of
potential clients or customers (who may or may not pay for services), funding sources, and political influences. The not for profit
is authorized to fulfill its charter by its funding sources, by the
political bodies or legislation who initiated it, and by its clients. For
example, the authorizing environment of a government-owned
and -run water utility has three parts:

- *Customers*—including citizens, businesses, and others
  who use water, wastewater, sewerage, and information
  services

- *Funds providers*—including federal and local governments,
  water rate payers, and banks

- *Political power holders*—elected officials and the citizenry
  who exercise their democratic rights to influence the elected
  officials or the utility directly. Legislation empowers the
  water utility to provide monopoly services and specifies
  their geographical regions, service levels, and price points.

The addition of the political power holders increases the complexity of the not for profit's authorizing environment compared
with the environment of a for-profit organization. In a for-profit retail store, for example, managers can analyze their industry position using Porter's five factors (customers, suppliers, basis for competition, substitutes, and potential new entrants) or a similar
framework. The government water utility must meet the letter of
its legislation and respond to the interests of the political power
holders including its elected board of directors and government
minister. If the citizens using the water utility are unhappy, they
cannot take their business elsewhere. Instead, they put pressure on
the utility via their elected officials.

Capabilities

Every organization needs capabilities to create goods and services.
For-profit enterprises develop some capabilities internally and pur-

chase or partner to obtain other capabilities to deliver products and services to their customers. Profits, long-term debt, and equity fund resources develop and leverage those capabilities.

In not-for-profit organizations, the authorizing environment provides resources (see arrow in figure 7-3) in the form of money and authority to create capabilities. The water utility has many organizational capabilities, including people who run water plants, do water testing, and connect new homes and businesses to the water infrastructure. In addition, the utility has information important to builders, developers, and other utilities about how to connect to the utility's infrastructure.

A unique feature of not for profits is that through legislation, regulation, or influence they can require other organizations to add capabilities that help the not for profit meet its goals. For example, MPS–Scotland Yard can influence corporations to use particular types of security procedures. The fire department sets and enforces rules and codes about fire protection systems in buildings that require the building owner to invest in safety measures. The water utility can require particular filtration systems be used in factories connected to the utility's wastewater systems. These external capabilities add *coproduction* (see the arrows in figure 7-3) to the production of the not-for-profit organization. For example, MPS–Scotland Yard's internal capabilities produce goods with *public value* (see circle on right of figure 7-3). The *external capabilities* of firms' security systems coproduce with MPS a safer environment, which also has public value. For-profit firms generally cannot require other organizations to create external capabilities or generate coproduction.

Public Value

For-profit firms generate value through goods and services purchased by customers. Successful firms also generate value for their owners. This value is measured and represented in financial statements. Not-for-profit organizations generate public value in addition to the private value represented by goods and services, such as, in our water utility case, water, sewerage, wastewater, and information services.

Public value has two additional parts illustrated for the water utility:

- *Public goods*—goods and services all citizens receive, even if they don't directly pay for them—for example, clean beaches with no effluent flow, clean and sustainable water catchment areas, public drinking fountains, and published statistics on water quality.

- *Equity*—correcting market failures—such as prosecuting water polluters or providing discounts for water services to the unemployed or aged.

Other organizations such as MPS–Scotland Yard also provide public value by ensuring social order—an important precondition not only for citizens engaging in community affairs but also for the operation of the market—by protecting property rights and enforcing contracts.[6]

Public value in not for profits extends beyond the organization like a series of concentric circles. Schools or water utilities providing excellent services will attract new people to live in the area or new businesses to open. These businesses in turn generate value, pay taxes, and employ workers who further increase prosperity. Thus, the performance of the water utility is not captured in the financial surplus (or deficit) the utility produces each year or in the physical infrastructure the utility creates. The utility's performance is also reflected in water quality, sustainable environmental management, and the effect of its services on the community. For schools, the measurement of performance is even more complicated and includes potential lifetime value created by students even beyond the local area. For MPS–Scotland Yard, the total measurement of value is virtually immeasurable—avoidance of crime, feeling of security, justice, opportunity to conduct businesses, and so on.

The public value created by a not for profit results in delivery back to the authorizing environment in the form of *transfers and provision of services* (see the arrow in figure 7-3). The authorizing environment grants permission back to the creators of public value in the form of market signals (increased demand) and *political acceptance*. Every not-for-profit organization, whether government agency or NGO, operates with this type of complexity and interconnected environment. The task for its managers is to create public value to the maximum extent possible given expectations of the authorizing environment and the available internal and external capabilities—in other words, to align the three factors represented by the circles in figure 7-3.

Particular Challenges for Governance in Governments and Not for Profits

The complex environment of not-for-profit organizations creates challenges for IT governance. We will focus on four complexities common to all not for profits here, but there are often several others to consider, for example, freedom of information acts, national security, encouraging the local technology industry, transparency, shrinking budgets, and democratic rights to voice opposition.

Measuring Value and Performance

The broad concept of public value in not-for-profit organizations makes measuring value and performance very complex. For example, the Tennessee Valley Authority (TVA) is one of the largest producers of public power in the United States. TVA is a wholly owned, self-supporting corporate agency of the U.S. government, responsible for developing the resources of the seven-state Tennessee Valley region and supporting its economic development.[7]

Similar to other utilities, TVA assesses performance with measures including power generation and distribution costs per unit, service quality levels, and debt reduction. TVA must also be self-supporting and manage its cash flow, debt, and infrastructure reinvestment while charging fair prices. With TVA's responsibilities for developing the resources of the Tennessee Valley region and supporting its economic development, broader measures of performance beyond the organization must also be considered. These broader value measures are always tough to quantify—for example, what is the value to the Tennessee Valley of an affordable, uninterrupted power supply?

The difficulty of measuring value and performance makes IT investment, already an uncertain science, more of an art. For example, calculating the net present value for an IT investment within the center of TVA's concentric circle of value is only the starting point. The impact and thus net present value of the investment must also be assessed for the outer concentric circles—how do you value a reliable source of cheap power in attracting new businesses to the valley? One governance approach is to provide a voice to people in the authorizing environment who are outside the organization. Either an input or decision-making voice is possible. Perhaps a representative of the governor's office is on the IT investment committee of the state-owned utility. Broadening the representation on the mechanism used for IT governance in several of the five IT decisions is a common and effective approach to dealing with complexity in not for profits.

IT Infrastructure Investment

Infrastructure investments can be justified in three ways: They are mandated (there is no need to cost justify), they reduce costs (can quantify and value and thus cost justify), or they enable new capabilities (often hard to quantify and value and thus option value is used). For example, at MPS, the infrastructure consolidation produced measurable IT savings but should also lead to quicker solving of crimes—a benefit that is much harder to value or predict. Not for profits typically have more mandated enabling infrastructure investments than do for-profit organizations. And enabling investments, particularly in government, are often political and attract public attention and debate. For example, schools fund computers in classrooms because parents insist on it. Countries, states, and cities fund mobile networks for police agencies because saving time in transmitting information about crime or criminals can save lives. Not-for-profit infrastructure investments also enable others to create public value through facilitating external capabilities and co-production. Infrastructure investment justification requires valuing and balancing all three ways infrastructure can be justified. How should a not for profit make infrastructure decisions? Who should make those decisions? Who should pay for the infrastructure?

In some cases, such as utilities, rates for users of the infrastructure can be adjusted to reflect operating costs to pay for the infrastructure. But very often, rate adjustments are not possible or practical. Balancing their prices, infrastructure investment, debt, and service levels to create broad public value is the critical infra-structure governance issue for not-for-profit executives. If revenue comes from budget allocations, as it does for organizations like the police, armed forces, immigration, and prisons, arguments (that are sometimes successful and sometimes not) are made to the funding authority based on demonstrated need (such as homeland security or flood prevention).

When funding comes from fees, not for profits are likely to use similar analyses to those of for-profit organizations. For example, all utilities make significant infrastructure investments, both physi-cal and IT. Due to the capital-intensive nature of the electric utility industry, TVA rigorously evaluates and selects which capital, opera-tions, and maintenance projects to fund. Funding for IT projects is subject to the same process as requests for steam generators and turbine overhauls. All TVA projects are reviewed by the Project Re-view Committee, which is sponsored by the chief operating officer and composed of key executives including the CIO. The expected value of IT projects is meant to be directly comparable to the ex-pected value of the other types of business investments.

Where coproduction or broader public value is created by other entities using the not for profit's infrastructure, justification and the question of who pays can be a barrier that stops sensible value creation. John Glaser, CIO of Partners Healthcare, explains: "It is difficult to NPV these projects across the board. The why and how of IT justification in different circumstances applies different val-ues. There are difficult issues in terms of who should be responsible for costs. If quality of care is the goal, should the insurance pro-viders be paying for it? It is difficult to align the value systems with resource responsibility. There are misaligned incentives in our busi-ness models. A lot of things don't get implemented because a lot of the value is to society rather than to the person who forks over the capital."[8]

Despite these challenges, not-for-profit organizations do suc-ceed in aggregating resources for infrastructures whose public value extends beyond organizational boundaries. Joe Adamski, CIO of Barwon Water, the largest regional water authority in the Aus-tralian state of Victoria, outlined his vision for a regional computer center for the greater Geelong area:[9] "Barwon Water covers over eight thousand square kilometers. Within this region, there has recently been an amalgamation of a number of councils. These organizations serve the same customers as ourselves. We have articulated the benefits of using common databases, mapping, and other information to serve these customers. Benefits include a service one-stop shopfront where customers could pay rates and water tariffs and apply for property approvals. The systems we now have at Barwon Water would be a good starting point in building this regional concept. Data is one of our region's most valuable assets, and there is no point in duplicating it."

This vision is slowly being realized. Adamski says: "With the geographic information systems (GIS), there is some hope of having a regional concept for this area, which would give the whole region a competitive advantage. There are many organizations that have expressed an interest in working with us. On top of that, we have many day-to-day queries wanting access to data. For example, we are using our IT infrastructure to do floodplain management for a number of consultants undertaking work for several councils in Melbourne and VicRoads in Gippsland. They supply the data or we capture it and do the analysis in partnership with the consultants."[10]

Governing IT infrastructure in not for profits requires different tools and mechanisms than in for-profit organizations. Funding for mandated infrastructure must be linked back to the mandate or legislation. Cost-saving infrastructure can be valued using traditional NPV approaches. The enabling investments must take into account the value created in the concentric circles of constituencies defining public goods. Invariably, the potential value-adding projects far exceed resources available. Project prioritization must consider the extended public value of projects to understand their relative worth. Again, external representation on committees for infrastructure investment decisions can be valuable.

Coproduction and Architectures

Coproduction provides unique opportunities and responsibilities for not-for-profit organizations. Well-designed coproduction can increase many times the effectiveness per dollar invested in IT.

Poorly designed coproduction is confusing, frustrating, and bureaucratic and creates little value. More recently, coproduction requires the coproducing organization to electronically connect to the not-for-profit organization. At the simplest level, this connection may involve posting regulations and information on the not-for-profit organization's Web site. More integrated coproduction enables the coproducer to download tools and directly interact with the not for profit's systems to coproduce.

For example, the Australian Tax Office (ATO) has achieved nearly 100 percent online individual tax return submission. Tax preparation agents are required to submit returns electronically using specified standards. The software firms building tax preparation tools for tax agents follow the ATO architecture guidelines to ensure compatibility for their customers. This coproduction by tax agents has simplified the ATO processes, removing the need for data entry and facilitating online tax assessment. Benefits of this coproduction have been passed back to the taxpayer in that tax refunds are typically received in two weeks rather than six.

To achieve this type of coproduction, IT architecture decision makers must consider many issues outside the organization. For the ATO's electronic filing to succeed, the tax agent had to be computerized. The agent's systems had to comply with the ATO's standards for electronic filing and the agent had to be trained to use the system. We expect to see many more creative efforts by not-for-profit organizations to encourage coproduction using IT. A key dilemma for governance and decision makers is the willingness and capability of the coproducers to invest in standard compliant systems. Does the not for profit have the power to encourage, cajole, or force coproducers to comply to create broader public value? How broad should the representation be on the IT governance decision-making mechanism?

Citizens, Clients, and Customers

Virtually all government organizations operate in some type of legislative authorizing environment that requires the organization to provide services. Some consumers of these services pay the not-for-profit organization; an example is householders paying for water or electricity consumed. Other consumers are clients who receive the services—welfare or public education, for example—because they are eligible. Other consumers are citizens who may consume services such as police and national parks and pay for these services indirectly via income taxes typically not related to their levels of consumption.

Making IT decisions requires balancing the needs of the three types of consumers—customers, clients, and citizens. Meeting the needs of clients rather than customers requires a broader market perspective and involves different market dynamics of supply and demand than it does in the for-profit sector. Recognizing the specific beneficiaries of any IT investment project and knowing who foots the bill for any particular consumer group can help align investment projects with funding sources. For example, many welfare agencies around the world could double their budgets and still not meet all legitimate demand. The direct beneficiaries of welfare programs are not the people who fund them (taxpayers and legislators, in most cases). Thus, attaining IT investment funds for welfare programs requires either demonstrating that the investment will lower program administrative costs or persuading taxpayers and legislators that the public value accrues back to them. This complex market for services influences all investment decisions in not for profits, including IT. To understand demand, satisfaction, and performance, it is particularly important for many not for profits to collect data on their clients. Online service delivery significantly increases their ability to collect client data.

These four factors and many others influence the way not-for-profit organizations govern IT, resulting in slightly different IT governance patterns relative to for-profit firms. All four factors lead toward broader representation often from outside the organization on many governance mechanisms. The broader representation ensures a voice for multiple stakeholders, but broad representation typically slows down decisions and makes consensus agreement on value much more difficult.

How Not-for-Profit Organizations Govern

The two bell-shaped distributions of governance performance in figure 7-4 illustrate a similar performance distribution in the

FIGURE 7-4

Comparing Governance Performance of Not-for-Profit and For-Profit Organizations

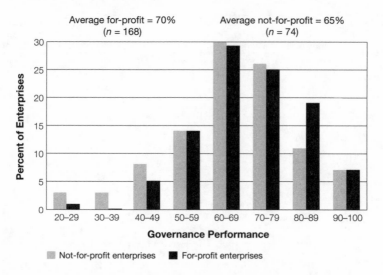

Average for-profit = 70%   Average not-for-profit = 65%
(n = 168)   (n = 74)

Governance Performance

Not-for-profit enterprises   For-profit enterprises

© 2003 MIT Sloan School Center for Information Systems Research (CISR). Used with permission.

for-profit and not-for-profit sectors. However, governance performance in not for profits is statistically significantly lower than in for-profit organizations.[11] Perhaps IT governance is less mature in not-for-profit organizations, but we doubt it. More likely, the complexity described earlier makes performance measurement, organization goal setting, and thus IT governance more difficult in not for profits, resulting in an average 10 percent lower governance performance.

The comparison between for-profit and not-for-profit IT governance (figure 7-5) reveals more similarities than differences, but five patterns of IT governance in not-for-profit organizations are notably different:

- More business monarchies in all decisions except architectures
- Significantly fewer IT monarchies in all decisions
- More federal arrangements in all decisions except investments

FIGURE 7-5

Comparing IT Governance Arrangements in Not-for-Profit and For-Profit Organizations

Decision / Archetype	IT Principles		IT Architecture		IT Infrastructure		Business Application Needs		IT Investment and Prioritization	
	Input	Decision	Input	Decision	Input	Decision	Input	Decision	Input	Decision
Business Monarchy	0 / 0	35 / 23	0 / 0	5 / 5	0 / 0	11 / 5	0 / 1	15 / 11	0 / 0	36 / 27
IT Monarchy	0 / 1	9 / 21	9 / 24	67 / 78	4 / 10	58 / 61	0 / 0	3 / 8	0 / 1	5 / 11
Feudal	1 / 0	1 / 3	0 / 1	0 / 1	0 / 0	1 / 2	3 / 1	20 / 17	0 / 0	1 / 4
Federal	86 / 84	15 / 14	49 / 45	5 / 3	66 / 58	8 / 4	82 / 80	43 / 25	95 / 93	24 / 28
Duopoly	12 / 15	37 / 37	42 / 31	23 / 11	30 / 32	22 / 25	14 / 18	15 / 33	5 / 6	31 / 30
Anarchy	0 / 0	0 / 1	0 / 0	0 / 1	0 / 0	0 / 1	1 / 0	4 / 4	0 / 0	3 / 0
No Data or Don't Know	1 / 0	3 / 1	0 / 0	0 / 1	0 / 1	0 / 2	0 / 2	0 / 2	0 / 0	0 / 0

☐ Most common input pattern for all enterprises.

The percentage in the top left of each cell is not for profits (*n* = 74) and in the lower right is for-profits (*n* = 168). Both sets of percentages add to 100 percent in each column.

- More federal arrangements for inputs to all decisions
- More duopolies for IT architecture

All the differences reflect the broader representation of decision making we recommended in the previous section. For example, fewer IT monarchies and more federal arrangements lead to broader involvement in decision making. Top governance performers find ways to deal with this complexity and govern differently from the average not-for-profit organization.

How Top Performers Govern

Top not-for-profit governance performers exhibit three major differences from other not for profits. They have aligned value creation and IT governance design, they use slightly different patterns of governance arrangements, and they use particular governance mechanisms very effectively.

Aligned Value Creation and Governance-Designed Frameworks

Just as a clear strategy is a prerequisite for effective governance in for-profit enterprises, effective governance design for a not for profit requires clarity about how value is created (see Figure 7-3). In all the not for profits with effective IT governance in our study, the process began with understanding and communicating the way value was to be created. The top performers articulated their required capabilities both internally and via coproduction to create maximum value within the limits of their authorizing environment. Clarifying value creation provides the input needed to create a well-harmonized IT governance design framework (for example, refer to MPS–Scotland Yard in figure 7-1).

Top Governance Performers Govern Differently

Studying the best and worst governance performers in not-for-profit organizations provides some general guidelines when using our two frameworks.[12] These general guidelines are a starting point, without considering factors such as sector, principles, culture, funding, and so on. All else being equal, we would recommend following these guidelines.

Use Joint Business and IT Decision Making for Principles

Joint business and IT decision making combines the strategic input on value creation from senior management with the IT leaders' understanding of the technology and organizational capabilities. Together they can find the right balance of aligning IT to the business needs and shaping the business strategies by what is possible technically. For example, many government agencies around the world are successfully innovating with online government (or e-government) to both improve services and reduce costs but also to encourage IT use in their communities. The Prime Minister of England, Tony Blair, mandated that all government services would be on line by 2008 and then backed up the target date to 2005.[13] Setting IT principles in not for profits often requires coordination with objectives or mandates set outside the organization. This requirement limits local flexibility but increases overall value.

Consider IT Infrastructure Principles to Be Strategic Business Decisions

In all not for profits, but particularly government organizations, infrastructure decisions are strategic and should be made by business monarchies or arrangements with strong business input. Typically, services are information-based, making IT the key infrastructure. For example, many governments are striving to provide life event servicing. Imagine that you have just experienced a life event, such as buying a house, turning eighteen, getting married, or moving to a new residence. Rather than contact each government agency independently, life event servicing enables you to interact through a single point of contact. Therefore, if you move you can provide the new address on a government Web site and identify, from a list, all the agencies you wish to instruct to update your details. IT infrastructures are critical to these strategies, and there are many opportunities to consolidate and reduce cost by sharing. Business monarchies for making infrastructure decisions are unusual (only 11 percent) and time consuming but often used by top performers. Even though the IT leaders may be better equipped technically, they often don't represent the broader constituencies required in not for profits. More important, business involvement ensures buy-in at the top level to making and utilizing infrastructure investments. Organizations entrusting infrastructure decisions to IT monarchies need strong business input.

Don't Use a Feudal Model for Business Application Needs

Over 20 percent of not-for-profit organizations use a feudal model for business application needs. For many not for profits the natural tendency is to use feudal models to specify the needs for different agencies, regions, or departments as they try to best serve their local clients. However, the central leadership of most not for profits is also striving to implement organizationwide programs such as improving service quality or reducing cost by removing duplication. The tension between the dual pressures of autonomy and centralized strategic focus results in poorer governance performance. We suggest avoiding feudal models for business applications needs except in the rare situation where there is no synergy between business units and no organizationwide initiatives.

Use Joint Decision Making for IT Investments

As with IT principles, duoplies for IT investment decisions combine the strategic input of senior management with the technological understanding and the organizational capability of the IT leaders. The top governance performers often use this approach to IT investment and prioritization. Where business monarchies are well informed about IT issues and include the CIO playing a leadership role, they are also very effective for investment decisions.

Mechanisms Used by Top Performers

Committees and other formal organizational mechanisms are often a strong part of the culture in not-for-profit organizations. Organizations such as MPS–Scotland Yard effectively use committees to ensure representation and transparency in difficult policy and operational decisions. Top governance performers use a relatively large number of formal mechanisms to implement their governance and reinforce the governance arrangements with a lot of communication. The result is a high percentage of senior executives who can accurately describe IT governance and use it effectively. The relatively large number of mechanisms adds overhead and, potentially, delays to making IT decisions but results in more commitment and higher performance.

Senior management of not-for-profit organizations with good IT governance performance identified the following mechanisms as highly effective in implementing their governance arrangements:[14]

- Executive committees focused on all key assets including IT
- IT council comprising business and IT executives
- IT leadership committee comprising IT executives

- Architecture committee
- Tracking of IT projects and resources consumed
- Business/IT relationship managers

Just having these mechanisms is not enough. We heard a number of horror stories about mechanisms being ineffective. For example, a common complaint was that senior executives would agree to serve on committees but then would not attend meetings or would send lower-level nominees who didn't want to make hard decisions, resulting in delays and frustration.

UNICEF Case Study

To learn from the experience of a much admired and effective global not-for-profit organization, let's turn to a case study of UNICEF.[15] UNICEF moved from an organization using IT in a very limited way until the mid-1990s to an organization in which IT is fundamental to its operations today.

UNICEF aligns its environment, capabilities (internal and external), and value creation. Using the value framework in figure 7-3, we can analyze how UNICEF creates value from its capabilities within its authorizing environment.

Authorizing Environment—Customers, Funds Providers, and Political Power Holders

The United Nations Children's Fund (UNICEF) is the only United Nations organization mandated to advocate and act for and with children to protect their rights and to help meet their needs. An extract from UNICEF's mission statement provides insight to some of its objectives: "UNICEF mobilizes political will and material resources to help countries, particularly developing countries, ensure a 'first call for children.'"[16] UNICEF conducts "programs of cooperation" in 162 countries, areas, and territories. These programs are planned and implemented in cooperation with governments, nongovernmental organizations, other UN agencies, and local communities. UNICEF is governed by a thirty-six-member Executive Board. Board members are elected by the United Nations Economic and Social Council and normally serve a three-year term. UNICEF is funded by voluntary contributions, two thirds from governments and one third from the private sector. Income in 2002 was U.S. $1.454 billion. UNICEF's funding and authority enable the building of significant capability both within and external to UNICEF.

Capabilities—Organizational and External

UNICEF's 7,100 staff members represent a powerful organizational capability delivering services worldwide including immunization such as polio vaccines and tetanus, school refurbishment, AIDS education, early childhood development, and programs to protect children from violence. In Afghanistan, a vast effort by UNICEF and its partners to get the country's seven thousand schools up and running cleared the way for 3 million children to attend school—one third of them girls—many of whom had never seen the inside of a classroom. In Kenya, the largest-ever national immunization effort undertaken in Africa succeeded in immunizing more than 13 million children against measles. In Swaziland, UNICEF joined with communities to provide care and support for children orphaned by HIV/AIDS, who are among the world's 14 million children under fifteen who have lost one or both of their parents to the disease.

Besides direct production, UNICEF encourages coproduction of value by other organizations to benefit children. UNICEF lobbies, influences, and educates governments and other authorities to improve conditions for children. UNICEF has many partnerships with other not-for-profit organizations such as GAVI (Global Alliance for Vaccines and Immunization) to create value. In addition, UNICEF works with many for-profit firms (for example, AEON, MasterCard International, IKEA, and Starwood Hotels and Resorts Worldwide) to raise money for children and provide services. For example, Starwood Hotels and Resorts Worldwide, Inc., continues supporting UNICEF programs through the flagship program Check Out for Children, which has raised more than $7 million since 1995 and in addition participated by raising funds for immunization programs.

Public Value—Goods and Services, Public Goods and Equity

The public value UNICEF creates is immeasurable. The goods and services provide education, relief, support, opportunity, and hope for children. The public good reduces illness, ignorance, suffering, and despair. If UNICEF is successful, not only do the children benefit but so does the world's economy. UNICEF's equity value objectives attempt to right many wrongs—injustice, poverty, prejudice, sexism, and exploitation.

With such broad-based value creation objectives, governing IT and all the other key assets at UNICEF demands tradeoffs. Spending on infrastructure to manage UNICEF leaves less for directly providing services to children. Total management and administration costs in 2002 were 6 percent of total expenditure.

IT Governance at UNICEF

UNICEF's business objectives include achieving results for children, sharing and reusing information globally, and achieving operational excellence under difficult field conditions with limited budgets (figure 7-6). Performance goals include operational, program, and social development targets. Program and social development targets are far-reaching and difficult to measure and quantify. The outcomes of a UNICEF intervention into children's lives may not be apparent for years.

UNICEF also operates in very unpredictable and dangerous settings. UNICEF has long-term presence and operates on site before, during, and after armed conflict, natural disasters, and other tragedies. In emergencies, UNICEF must rapidly set up field offices and communications infrastructures. For example, in such environments the UNICEF office is provided with a set of rapidly deployable "fly-away VSAT" stations delivering the maximum connectivity and IT suite: voice, fax, data, electronic mail, and even video conferencing. It also provides access to voice communications (VoIP), Lotus Notes, the public Internet, and the UNICEF corporate intranet, using the full suite of IT core office business applications, while at the same providing the safety and security of staff implementing UNICEF program objectives. Using this creative and mobile IT infrastructure enables UNICEF to quickly establish a base that can grow to a more substantial station over time.

Operating in so many countries with highly autonomous field representatives makes global governance a constant issue. Says

FIGURE 7-6

UNICEF Governance Design Framework

Enterprise strategy and organization

Financial drivers
- Operational excellence (efficiency and effectiveness)

Business maxims
- Achieve results for children
- Share and reuse knowledge globally
- Decentralize decision making and accountability
- IT is an enabler and competitive differentiator

IT organization and desirable behavior
- One overall strategy and framework
- Standardized global infrastructure
- Commercial orientation of IT
- Redeploy staff worldwide
- Support new collaborative ways of working (internally and externally)
- Management internalization of IT's role, costs, and processes
- Functional/business ownership of IT investments

IT governance arrangements

Business monarchy decides
- IT principles
- IT infrastructure strategies
- IT architecture
- IT investment

Duopoly decides
- Business application needs

Duopoly input to all

IT governance mechanisms
- IT council of IT and business executives
- Project portfolio management to maximize returns
- Central IT supports global operations and roll-outs
- Intranet as knowledge repository
- Semiannual executive review
- Annual global IT consultation on strategy and implementation validation with all constituents

Business performance goals
- Program and social development targets
- Fund-raising targets
- Operational cost targets
- Improvement in information sharing, reuse, and flow

IT metrics and accountabilities
- Business heads justify IT spending and investments
- Percent of regional plans endorsed and percent implementation of global plans
- Percent adherence to standards
- Percent of IT staff up-skilled and redeployable due to standards
- Percent of field offices linked to the global IP network
- Reuse and sharing of best practices

↔ **Harmonize what?**   ↔ **Harmonize how?**

Andre Spatz, UNICEF's CIO, "As a CIO, I invest a lot of my time in making governance work at all levels, to educate, coach, mentor, and lobby. In a global organization, governance is quite a challenge. We face high pressure for synergy across UNICEF, and at the same time, we have high pressure for local autonomy from the regional and country offices. CIO leadership in a global IT organization is not just command and execute. We must continually empower people with a vision and execution strategy and position governance elements within a global framework. Part of my role is to ensure that we do not centralize too much and that our IT organization adapts to the different cultural environments we work in."[17]

Until the mid-1990s, there was little IT in UNICEF offices, and IT was far from a CEO-level concern. The IT organization dealt primarily with headquarters (HQ); the field offices were basically on their own. There were few LANs, no common desktop environment, stand-alone, custom-built applications, no global network, and little use of the e-mail system, due to high long-distance dial-up costs. An executive-sponsored management reengineering program to streamline UNICEF was launched in 1995 and 1996 to improve efficiency and effectiveness and to decentralize decision making and accountability to the regions and countries where field activities take place. These changes were accompanied by recentralization of UNICEF IT—and its use as an integral and enabling part of the management transformation.

Over the past few years, IT has fundamentally transformed the way UNICEF operates and has improved global knowledge, information flow, transparency, and communication. Field offices now have transaction-level information and value-adding information they did not have before. IT has become a true differentiator for UNICEF.

Evolving IT Governance

The UNICEF governance arrangements are presented in figure 7-7. Officer-level executives, including the CIO and the global management team, make decisions for IT principles, IT infrastructure strategies, IT architecture, and IT investment and prioritization. This centralized approach is balanced with broad-based inputs via a duopoly of business unit leaders and functional unit heads working

FIGURE 7-7

UNICEF Governance Arrangements Matrix

		DECISION									
		IT Principles		IT Architecture		IT Infrastructure Strategies		Business Application Needs		IT Investment	
		Input	Decision	Input	Decision	Input	Decision	Input	Decision	Input	Decision
GOVERNANCE ARCHETYPE	Business Monarchy		CxO		CxO		CxO				CxO
	IT Monarchy										
	Feudal										
	Federal										
	Duopoly	IT exec. BU lead Business process owners Portfolio		IT exec. BU lead Business process owners		IT exec. BU lead Business process owners		IT exec. BU lead Business process owners	IT exec. BU lead Business process owners	IT exec. BU lead Business process owners Portfolio	

▢ Most common pattern for all firms.

Governance mechanisms:

Business process owners—Functional division heads
BU lead—Regional/county/HQ heads
CxO—CxO and global management team
HQ IT—Central IT supports global operations and roll-outs

Intranet—Intranet as knowledge repository
IT exec.—HQ, regional, and county IT managers/officers
Portfolio—Project portfolio management
Review—Semiannual executive review

with IT managers. Business application needs are decided using a duopoly of IT executives, business unit leaders, and business process owners. To achieve this level of governance sophistication, there were three main stages of evolution at UNICEF. First was project-level governance. Second was adoption of a global IT strategy and infrastructure. Third was implementation of a global IT portfolio management process. Educating management about recurring IT costs, operating costs, and mandatory system upgrades has been a challenge through all three stages.

Governance evolved initially from ad hoc fragmented management to individual project governance. The first major example
was delegated authority from the CEO to four division directors,
who became fully accountable for implementing the HQ financial,
logistics and private sector-related modules of SAP's enterprise
resource planning system. They delivered on time and within
budget—replacing more than a hundred legacy Wang systems. This
success would not have been possible without project-level governance and ownership. This governance/ownership process has become the model for all major IT investment projects in UNICEF. To
sustain operational governance, a regular weekly meeting of both
HQ functional and IT heads was established to address process and
IT issues. The decisions are reviewed by senior management twice a
year or as required. IT is cosecretary and codriver of this process,
but it is not the process owner.

IT infrastructure has been a major investment area at UNICEF.
Today, everyone has a standard desktop or laptop and applications,
office automation tools, and Internet and intranet access. The intranet is used as a global knowledge repository for UNICEF information, including IT procedures. One of the major infrastructure
initiatives was the deployment of a global IP network in 80 percent
of the countries, with guaranteed bandwidth services, quality of service, and local Web caching. This deployment was not a trivial task,
given the global reach of UNICEF's operations. The network forms
the foundation of UNICEF's new Web-based applications. Field staff
members who formerly felt isolated are now far more connected
and can leverage real-time information. The infrastructure has
democratized and changed the information culture of UNICEF and
is providing more transparency for the governance process.

Another major infrastructure initiative, the "Organization Management Systems," contributed to the organizational change process
by creating common tools, systems, and user support processes like
the global services desk or IT staff training and certification in ITIL
standard IT services management. The systematic collection of
data, coupled with processes such as call monitoring and problem
management to conduct quantitative analysis, allows resources to
be targeted to areas that require correction quickly and effectively.
At the same time, to keep HQ IT staff members in touch with field

operations, they spend nine to twelve months on the global service desk, which runs 24/7/365 and supports all UNICEF locations. This rotation program significantly improves their understanding of the complexities of supporting such a culturally diverse population. And the rotation is used in career development and advancement planning. The service desk has become an integrated business/IT help facility that provides transparency and information to overall governance.

A corporate-level IT portfolio management process was implemented when demand for IT services grew to be several times larger than the IT budget. Now the executive management team, division heads, and business heads, rather than IT alone, present and justify IT investment requests. This approach provides a clear organizationwide framework for investment priorities. While some local flexibility and adaptability are necessary, strong governance on IT standards, infrastructure, and global applications has facilitated staff and skills redeployment around the globe.

Managing Information Is Key

Managing knowledge and information are crucial governance elements at UNICEF because both must be shared between countries on many topics. Five years ago, representatives or country heads shared documents and knowledge in person or by distributing paper. Today, UNICEF's intranet has become the information and knowledge repository for the entire organization.

At first, there was great debate about ownership and governance of the Internet, and UNICEF had up to twenty-five individually run country Web sites. However, the infrastructure was consolidated for cost and security reasons in 2000. Content is provided locally, but it is centrally hosted and under a corporate umbrella, which provides the global touch while maintaining local involvement.

Today, governance is accepted throughout UNICEF. There's one overall IT strategy encompassing headquarters, regional, and local levels. That strategy is periodically validated with a broad constituency. Nevertheless, IT must coach, educate, and push the business to understand how to govern IT. Transformation takes time, but IT—in a relatively short time—has become a fundamental enabler and mission-critical part of the organization. UNICEF competes for funds from governments, private corporations, and individuals. IT governance has become important in achieving focus and flexibility to be competitive.

What Is Different in Not for Profits

In many ways, IT governance in not-for-profit organizations is the same as for profit-seeking firms. But the differences are important and stem from a more complex value creation setting. The broader definition of public value and the ability to develop external capabilities and coproduction result in different approaches to IT governance. Add the cultural norms of not for profits, with more focus on consensus, transparency, and equity—all of which affect IT governance design. Successful IT governance in not for profits relies even more on partnerships and joint decisions between business and IT leaders as well as heavier use of formal mechanisms such as committees. More and more not for profits will include representation from outside the organization on their IT governance mechanisms to reflect their broader definition of value. Changing governance arrangements less often in not-for-profit organizations is even more important as the time to communicate and implement new procedures is often longer.

8

Leadership Principles
for IT Governance

IN CHAPTER 1 we asked:

- Do your IT capabilities enhance your business competitiveness—or throttle it?
- Do managers throughout your organization recognize their responsibilities for the effective management and use of IT—or do they assume the IT unit will take care of such things?
- Do your IT investments target enterprisewide strategic priorities—or are resources frittered away on diverse tactical initiatives?

We now add a new question:

- Is your IT governance encouraging desirable behavior in the use of IT?

The premise of this book is that the difference between negative and affirmative responses to these questions is a reflection of IT governance. Simply stated, enterprises with effective IT governance generate strategic benefits from IT through the IT-related desirable behaviors of their people. IT governance requires senior management leadership. This chapter addresses leadership first by identifying the urgency for action. We look at symptoms of ineffective IT governance—the more symptoms like these you see, the more urgent the need for senior management action. Then we briefly review the steps to designing or rethinking IT governance. Next we identify the top ten leadership principles for effective IT governance and provide a checklist for leaders. Because good IT governance inevitably stipulates a significant leadership role for the CIO, we then review criteria for assessing and motivating the CIO. We then leave you with some predictions for the future of IT governance.

Symptoms of Ineffective Governance

IT governance is an issue whose time has come. Current investments of capital and management attention in IT compel careful evaluation of IT governance. In addition, the strategic impact of IT decisions raises the stakes for effective IT decision making and implementation. Good governance improves IT decision making and performance. Governance design is about getting the right people to make IT decisions and monitor performance. Good governance empowers the right people to make decisions even as needs change. Here are some common symptoms of governance not working. We have provided some simple yardsticks for each symptom to help assess urgency for intervention. How healthy is your IT governance?

Senior Management Senses Low Value from IT Investments. Do senior managers have a lingering, gut-level concern or doubt about the business value derived from their IT investments? Senior managers typically react in one of several ways to this concern. Some managers dive in to learn more about IT, making more IT decisions personally and centralizing control. Others abdicate responsibility to colleagues such as managers in the IT unit because they are unsure how to act or don't think it's important. Still other senior managers engage consultants or make new hires to "fix the problem." Rather than starting with increasing control, abdication, or bringing in new people, first look at IT governance. Perhaps the wrong people are making IT decisions or the people making those decisions need management education. Good governance will produce metrics supporting or contradicting management's gut feeling. If everyone on the senior management team cannot point to a record of how recent IT investments have been performing, governance is a problem.

IT Is Often a Barrier to Implementing New Strategies. Instead of acting as a strategic enabler, does IT often act as a barrier? If IT limits the ability to respond to new market opportunities, the IT infrastructure may be broken. As Delta Air Lines experienced with its infrastructure, IT cannot support new initiatives if those initiatives intend to integrate incompatible systems. This incompatibility could arise from obsolete technical platforms, redundant applications, or redundant data with nonstandard definitions. These problems typically arise from application silos where systems were developed independently, often on different platforms and at different times with no enterprise architecture. Fixing the infrastructure requires bringing IT leaders to the strategy table.

If IT learns about strategic initiatives after decisions are made, IT finds itself in the position of order taker. IT then builds a specific solution rather than a platform for the strategic vision. This sequencing prevents development of an enabling infrastructure. The result is that strategic initiatives are very slow to implement. A common cause of the delay is that the existing IT infrastructure, such as a customer database or network security, is not capable of supporting the new initiative. If new infrastructure has to be installed before every major application supporting the new initiative, governance is failing. A governance process that fails to bring IT into strategy discussions limits the opportunity to fix the infrastructure. If competitors are faster to introduce new IT-enabled initiatives, IT governance is a problem.

The Mechanisms to Make IT Decisions Are Slow or Contradictory. Effective governance comes from a set of well-designed and well-executed mechanisms that reinforce desirable behavior. Are different mechanisms sending contradictory messages to executives? For example, one firm we studied had IT principles set by senior executives encouraging the strategic use of IT and specifying that to fail early and often was good. However, we were repeatedly told of unsuccessful attempts to shepherd IT-enabled business initiatives through the capital investment committee. The committee was led by the CFO, who approved only projects with clearly documented and guaranteed cost savings. The result was a plethora of small, often nonstrategic, IT-enabled local projects in the business units. The projects were below the dollar threshold requiring approval from the CFO's committee. These contradictory messages led to suboptimal behavior for the firm.

Just as troubling are mechanisms that obstruct rather than support project implementations. For example, an architectural exception process demanding multiple approvals can delay projects—particularly if the responsible individuals or committees are not motivated to act quickly or if criteria for exceptions are not clear. If the exception process is not fast and predictable, individuals will be motivated to act outside the system. If renegade exceptions are in evidence, governance is a problem.

Senior Management Cannot Explain IT Governance. Do senior managers understand how IT is governed? We know from our research that the more managers in leadership positions there are who can accurately describe IT governance, the better the governance performance. In top-performing enterprises, accountabilities are clear. In particular, senior managers know what decisions IT makes and what decisions they must make. If managers can't describe IT governance, how can they follow it? If fewer than 50 percent of managers in leadership positions can accurately describe IT governance, and the number is not increasing every month, governance is a problem.

Describing governance is only the starting point. Increasingly, managers at top-performing enterprises not only understand their responsibilities for IT; they understand the enterprise architecture. Several senior IT staff people have told us that senior managers regularly ask how proposed projects would affect or leverage their enterprise architectures. The ability to articulate the key components of the enterprise architecture and understand how they enable and constrain business processes is becoming an important managerial competency.

IT Projects Often Run Late and over Budget. A number of studies over the last ten years in several countries found that the percentage of IT projects completed on time and on budget is typically less than half. Effective IT governance should provide consistency in project management and program design. Project management should ensure allocation of dedicated resources, a disciplined sequence of stages, and formal project tracking. Good project management leads to predictable project delivery. If 90 percent of projects are not delivered on time and on budget, governance is a problem.

Senior Management Sees Outsourcing As a Quick Fix to IT Problems. Selective outsourcing of IT capability can be a very effective management strategy. Many enterprises outsource commodity IT services and insource or perhaps cosource (develop systems cooperatively with a leading-edge producer) other services. However, some outsourcing decisions result from frustration with IT. Concerned about IT costs or lack of value, managers turn to outsourcing as a quick fix to control the problem. Outsourcing effectively places a contract between the IT consumer and provider. If the service can be well specified in a contract and the price fairly compared with the internally sourced cost, outsourcing often leads to reduced IT costs. To be effective, outsourcing should result from a decision that particular competencies or services are better provided externally. The enterprise should have clear expectations for the performance of the provider and how the externally provided services fit into the enterprise architecture. Outsourcing as a quick fix motivated by frustration with IT outcomes suggests that governance is a problem.

Governance Changes Frequently. Governance need not be changed with every small strategic change or shift in emphasis. The executives working within the IT governance mechanisms make decisions implementing the strategic changes. For example, when Amazon.com added electronics and then clothing to its product lines, the firm was changing its strategy to include nonprinted products. But its fundamental strategy of providing online services to customers had not changed. Amazon needed some new functionality on its site, vendor relationships, and even systems to support the business processes, but the shift in strategy did not change desirable behaviors. Thus, no change in governance was necessary.

Managers operating in the existing governance arrangements made necessary adjustments to the enterprise's IT principles, investment, application needs, infrastructure, and architecture.

This distinction reinforces the difference between governance and management. Management is what decisions are made. Management decisions typically change as strategies change. Governance is who makes the decisions, and thus changes less often than strategy. Changing governance every time you change strategy should not be necessary as many of the governance mechanisms, such as committees and budgets, are independent of strategy. Governance should change only when a change in strategy prompts a change in desirable behaviors. For example, a shift from a customer intimacy to a product leadership discipline would signal a change in how much business unit collaboration is valued. This more radical shift in strategy—a change in strategic intent—would be likely to drive changes in governance.

Frequent changes in IT governance almost guarantee ineffective IT use. Unable to comprehend or keep up with the changes, managers are likely to completely ignore governance. If governance of one or more of the five key IT decisions changes very frequently—more than once a year—governance is a problem.

We have listed seven common symptoms of poor IT governance. If an enterprise reached the threshold described on any one symptom (for example, 10 percent late or overbudget projects), we would be concerned about IT governance. The more symptoms observed in an enterprise, the sicker the governance and the more urgent the need for management attention.

Steps for Reviewing and Designing IT Governance

This section presents a brief summary of the steps for attacking the symptoms by designing or rethinking governance.

1. Map the enterprise's current governance onto both diagrams—the Governance Design Framework and the Governance Arrangements Matrix (as for State Street Corporation

in chapter 6). The inability to quickly create either of these two diagrams is symptomatic of a lack of clarity in IT governance.

2. Compare the two diagrams and ask how well the objectives on the Governance Design Framework are achieved by the arrangements of the Governance Arrangements Matrix. Focus on performance goals not being achieved. How might governance arrangements be tweaked to address performance goals?

3. Audit IT governance mechanisms.

   a. How many mechanisms are in use? Do they overlap across more than one key IT decision? Are they also used to govern the enterprise's other key assets (for example, human relationships; see figure 1-1)?

   b. Are they effective independently and together (see chapter 4)?

4. In a senior management team meeting, debate the upper left and right boxes of the Governance Design Framework. Then determine your preferred Governance Arrangements Matrix (also the middle box of the Governance Design Framework) based on your strategy and performance goals. A good approach is to study the governance patterns of top performers (chapter 5). For example, if your enterprise wants to focus on industry-leading revenue growth, consider the governance arrangement patterns of top performers on growth as a starting point. Then tailor the governance template to your enterprise's culture, structure, strategy, and goals (chapters 5 and 6). This step is the art form of governance design. We don't know of any concrete rules that work here. Rather, be guided by your instincts as to what works (or perhaps what should work) in your enterprise. Be sure to align incentive and reward systems with IT governance.

5. Lead the change using the "to be" versions of the Governance Design Framework and Governance Arrangements Matrix for your enterprise. Use these diagrams to communicate, teach, convince, refine, and measure the success of IT governance.

Top Ten Leadership Principles
of IT Governance

From studying and working with hundreds of enterprises, we have distilled the lessons from many outstanding leaders into ten principles of IT governance. We intend these principles to provide leaders with a succinct summary to use as a primer, refresher, or checklist as they refine their IT governance.[1]

1. Actively Design Governance

Many enterprises have created disparate IT governance mechanisms. These uncoordinated mechanism "silos" result from governance by default—introducing mechanisms one at a time to address a particular need (for example, architecture problems or overspending or duplication). Patching up problems as they arise is a defensive tactic that limits opportunities for strategic impact from IT. Instead, management should actively design IT governance around the enterprise's objectives and performance goals.

Actively designing governance involves senior executives taking the lead and allocating resources, attention, and support to the process. The diagrams in this book enable an analysis of all the governance mechanisms and enterprise goals. For some enterprises, this will be the first time IT governance is explicitly designed. Often there are mature business governance processes to use as a starting point. For example, the Tennessee Valley Authority (TVA; described in chapter 7) piggybacked its IT governance on its more mature business governance mechanisms, such as its capital investment process. TVA's IT governance included a project review committee, benchmarking, and selective chargeback—all familiar mechanisms from the engineering side of the business.

Not only does overall governance require active design, but each mechanism also needs regular review. Focus on having the fewest number of effective mechanisms possible. Many of the enterprises we studied had as many as fifteen different governance mechanisms, all varying in effectiveness. Fifteen mechanisms may possibly be needed but it's highly unlikely. All fifteen will certainly not be very effective, integrated, and well understood. Many enterprises with effective IT governance have between six and ten integrated and well-functioning mechanisms. One goal of any governance redesign should be to assess, improve, and then consolidate the number of mechanisms. Early in the learning cycle, mechanisms may involve large numbers of managers. Typically, as senior managers better understand IT value and the role of IT, a smaller set of managers can represent enterprise needs.

2. Know When to Redesign

Rethinking the whole governance structure requires that individuals learn new roles and relationships. Learning takes time. Thus, governance redesign should be infrequent. Our recommendation is that a change in governance is required with a change in desirable behavior. For example, State Street Corporation, JPMorgan Chase, Carlson Companies, and UNICEF all changed their governance to encourage desirable behaviors resulting from significant changes in strategy. All four enterprises designed governance to achieve their desired balance of business unit autonomy and commonality. State Street, JPMorgan Chase, and Carlson were all attempting to generate more synergies. UNICEF used IT to transform its operations and improve global sharing, information management, transparency, and communication. These transformations involve many other issues besides IT and take many months to implement.

In these types of transformation, IT governance can be used as one of the levers to encourage change. For example, State Street Corporation introduced enterprisewide IT budgeting, encouraging a shift in perspective from the business unit to the corporation. JPMorgan Chase's buy-hold-sell process accomplished the same objective at a technology level. These governance processes communicate and enforce new desirable behaviors to facilitate organizational transformations.

3. Involve Senior Managers

In our study, firms with more effective IT governance had more senior management involvement. CIOs must be effectively involved in IT governance for success. Other senior managers must participate in the committees, the approval processes, and performance reviews. For many enterprises, this involvement is a natural extension of senior management's normal activities. For example, MPS–Scotland Yard used its strong existing management committee structure to improve IT governance and gain greater synergies across all its operations. The Information Management Steering Group (IMSG) is one of fourteen strategic committees that connect to the top-level executive committee. This interlocking committee structure ensures senior management attention to IT in the context of the whole enterprise.

Senior management necessarily gets involved in strategic decisions. This means that senior management is rarely concerned with the exception process. However, if an exception has strategic implications, it may reach the executive level IT Steering Committee. UPS CEO Mike Eskew explained the top management role: "At some point, if it comes to you, then you say, 'This is the answer.' It's part of our jobs to make those kinds of decisions. Our CIO, Ken Lacy, almost always has it solved by the time it gets to me."[2] In firms like UPS, senior management occasionally gets involved in exception decisions because those decisions represent strategy decisions. If the exception request escalates to the CEO, then it's no longer a technology issue. At that point it's a strategic choice.

Many senior managers are willing to be involved but are not sure where to best contribute. It's very helpful for the CIO and his or her staff to communicate IT governance on one page with a picture like the Governance Arrangements Matrix. The matrix provides a vehicle for discussing each senior manager's role and any concerns they have.

4. Make Choices

Good governance, like good strategy, requires choices. It's not possible for IT governance to meet every goal, but governance can and should highlight conflicting goals for debate. As the number of tradeoffs increases, governance becomes more complex. Top-performing enterprises handle goal conflicts with a few clear business principles. The resulting IT principles reflect these business principles. Old Mutual South Africa's (OMSA) six IT principles, or "nonnegotiables," as they are called, provide a useful framework for how to use IT. The first principle, which all OMSA business units must observe, states: "The interest and needs of the Group/OMSA come first when exploiting technology or when contracting with suppliers."[3] Appropriate stakeholders must be involved in the approval process prior to contracts being signed.

Some of the most ineffective governance we have observed was the result of conflicting goals. This problem was often observed in the government sector, where directives come from many agencies. The result was confusion, complexity, and mixed messages, so the governance was ignored. The unmanageable number of goals typically arose from not making strategic business choices and had nothing to do with IT. We observed that good managers trying diligently to meet all these goals became frustrated and ineffective.

5. Clarify the Exception-Handling Process

Exceptions are how enterprises learn. In IT terms, exceptions challenge the status quo, particularly the IT architecture and infrastructure. Some requests for exceptions are frivolous, but most come from a true desire to meet business needs. If the exception proposed by a business unit has value, a change to the IT architecture could benefit the entire enterprise. We have described the exceptions process of UPS, State Street Corporation, and other enterprises. All these exemplars have three common elements to their exceptions procedures:

1. The process is clearly defined and understood by all. Clear criteria and fast escalation encourage only business units with a strong case to pursue an exception.

2. The process has a few stages that quickly move the issue up to senior management. Thus, the process minimizes the chance that architecture standards will delay project implementation.

3. Successful exceptions are adopted into the enterprise architecture, completing the organizational learning process.

Formally approved exceptions offer a second benefit in addition to formalizing organizational learning about technology and

architecture. Exceptions serve as a release valve, relieving the enterprise of built-up pressure. Managers become frustrated if they are
told they can't do something they are sure is good for business.
Pressure increases and the exceptions process provides a transparent vehicle to release the frustration without threatening the governance process.

6. Provide the Right Incentives

There has been so much written about incentive and reward systems
in enterprises that we feel the topic is well covered and understood.
Nevertheless, a common problem we encountered in studying IT
governance was a misalignment of incentive and reward systems
with the behaviors the IT governance arrangements were designed
to encourage. The typical concern: "How can we expect the governance to work when the incentive and reward systems are driving
different behavior?" This mismatch is bigger than an IT governance
issue. Nonetheless, IT governance is less effective when incentive
and reward systems are not aligned with organizational goals.

A major governance and incentive alignment issue is business
unit synergy. If IT governance is designed to encourage business unit
synergy, autonomy, or some combination, as discussed in chapter
6, the incentives of the executives must also be aligned. For example, in a large consumer products firm, the CEO wanted to increase
synergies between business units to provide a single face to the
small number of important customers that did business with several business units. The CEO and CIO worked together to design
IT governance to align the enterprise IT assets to support the
new objective. The new IT governance encouraged sharing of customer information, contact logging, pricing, and order patterns
across business units. However, it was not until the business unit
executives' incentive system was changed from being nearly 100
percent based on business unit performance to being 50 percent
based on firmwide performance that the new IT governance gained
traction.

Avoiding financial disincentives to desirable behavior is as
important as offering financial incentives. DBS Bank in Singapore
does not charge for architectural assistance to encourage project
teams to consult with architects (see chapter 3 for details). When-

ever incentives are based on business unit results, chargeback can be a point of contention. Enterprises can manipulate charges to encourage desirable behavior, but chargeback pricing must be reasonable and clearly understood.

It is hard to overestimate the importance of aligning incentive and reward systems to governance arrangements. If well-designed IT governance is not as effective as expected, the first place to look is incentives.

7. Assign Ownership and Accountability for IT Governance

Like any major organizational initiatives, IT governance must have an owner and accountabilities. Ultimately, the board is responsible for all governance, but the board will expect or delegate an individual (probably the CEO or CIO) or group to be accountable for IT governance design, implementation, and performance—similar to the finance committee or CFO being accountable for financial asset governance. In choosing the right person or group, the board, or the CEO as their designate, should consider three issues.

First, IT governance cannot be designed in isolation from the other key assets of the firm (financial, human, and so on). Thus the person or group owning IT governance must have an enterprisewide view that goes beyond IT, as well as credibility with all business leaders.

Second, the person or group cannot implement IT governance alone. The board or CEO must make it clear that all managers are expected to contribute to IT governance as they would contribute to governance of financial or any other key asset.

Third, IT assets are more and more important to the performance of most enterprises. A reliable, cost-effective, regulation-compliant, secure, and strategic IT portfolio is more critical today than ever before. The person or group owning IT governance must understand what the technology is and is not capable of. It is not the technical details that are critical but a feel for the two-way symbiotic connection between strategy and IT.

The CIO owns IT governance in the majority of sizable firms today.[4] Other enterprises have chosen either another individual (the COO or occasionally the CEO) or a committee (say, of senior business and IT leaders) to own IT governance. We have not observed any one approach that always works best. It takes a very business-oriented—and well-positioned—CIO to deliver on the first consideration and a very technically interested COO or CEO to deliver on the third. Committees have the problem of meeting only periodically and dispersing the responsibility and accountability.

Our recommendation is that the board or CEO hold the CIO accountable for IT governance performance with some clear measures of success. Most CIOs will then create a group of senior business and IT managers to help design and implement IT governance. The action of the board or CEO to appoint and announce the CIO as accountable for IT governance performance is an essential first step in raising the stakes for IT governance. Without that action, some CIOs cannot engage their senior management colleagues in IT governance. Alternatively, the board or CEO may identify a group to be accountable for IT governance performance. This group will then often designate the CIO to design and implement IT governance.

8. Design Governance at Multiple Organizational Levels

In large multibusiness unit enterprises it is necessary to consider IT governance at several levels. The starting point is enterprise-wide IT governance driven by a small number of enterprisewide strategies and goals. Enterprises with separate IT functions in divisions, business units, or geographies require a separate but connected layer of IT governance. JPMorgan Chase (see chapter 6) has IT governance at the enterprise, division, and business unit level. Usually the demand for synergies increases at the lower levels, whereas the need for autonomy between units is greatest at the top of the organization.

The lower levels of governance are influenced by mechanisms designed for higher levels. Thus, we advocate starting with the enterprisewide IT governance, as it will have implications for the other levels of governance. However, starting enterprisewide is sometimes not possible for political or focus reasons, and starting at the business unit level can be practical. Assembling the governance arrangements matrixes for the multiple levels in an enterprise makes explicit the connections and pressure points.

9. Provide Transparency and Education

It's virtually impossible to have too much transparency or education about IT governance. Transparency and education often go together—the more education, the more transparency, and vice versa. The more transparency of the governance processes, the more confidence in the governance. Many firms like State Street Corporation use portals or intranets to communicate IT governance. State Street's portal includes under the section "IT Boards, Committees, and Councils" a description of the Architecture Committee and all the other governance bodies. The portal includes tools and resources, such as a glossary of IT terms and acronyms and the "Computer Contract Checklist." Often portals include lists of approved or recommended products. Templates for proposing IT investments complete with spreadsheets to calculate the IT business value are often available.

The less transparent the governance processes are, the less people follow them. The more special deals are made, the less confidence there is in the process and the more workarounds are used. The less confidence there is in the governance, the less willingness there is to play by rules designed to lead to increased firmwide performance. Special deals and nontransparent governance set off a downward spiral in governance effectiveness.

Communicating and supporting IT governance is the single most important IT role of senior leaders. The person or group who owns IT governance has a major responsibility for communication. Firms in our study with more effective governance also had more effective governance communication. The more formal vehicles for communication were the most important. For example, CIOs on average assessed their enterprises' documentation of governance processes as ineffective. However, the firms with successful IT governance had highly effective documentation. Highly effective senior management announcements and CIO offices were also important to successful governance.

When senior managers, particularly those in business units, demonstrate lack of understanding of IT governance, an important opportunity is presented. Working with managers who don't follow the rules is an opportunity to understand their objections. These discussions provide insight on whether the rules need refinement as well as a chance to explain and reinforce the governance.

10. Implement Common Mechanisms Across the Six Key Assets

We began the book by describing how IT governance fits into corporate governance (see figure 1-1). We contend that enterprises using the same mechanisms to govern more than one of the six key assets have better governance. For example, executive committees that address all enterprise issues including IT, such as the one at MPS–Scotland Yard, create synergies by considering multiple assets.

Recall the exercise in chapter 1 of listing all the mechanisms implementing each of the six key assets. Each asset may be expertly governed, but the opportunity for synergistic value is lost. For example, a firm implementing a single point of customer contact strategy must coordinate its assets to deliver that uniform experience. Just having good customer loyalty (that is, relationship assets) without the products to sell (IP assets) will drain value. Not having well-trained people (human assets) to work with customers supported by good data and technology (information and IT assets) will drain value. Not having the right buildings and shop fronts to work from or in which to make the goods (physical assets) will drain value. Finally, not coordinating the investments needed (financial assets) will drain value.

Put this way, the coordination of the six assets seems blindingly obvious. But just glance back at your six lists of mechanisms and see how well coordinated—and more importantly, how effective—they are. Many enterprises successfully coordinate their six assets within a project but not across the enterprise via governance. In designing IT governance, review the mechanisms used to govern the other key assets and consider broadening their charter (perhaps with a subcommittee) to IT rather than creating a new, independent IT mechanism.

These ten management principles highlight many of the key findings in our work with enterprises. Attention to all of them should lead to greater value from IT. The leadership of the CIO is also critical to creating IT value. Thus, assessing and providing incentives for the CIO is our next topic.

Assessing the CIO

An important part of setting incentives is the assessment of the enterprise key executives. There has been a lot of debate on how to assess the performance and establish incentives for the CIO. Here are our suggestions based on conversations with CIOs and other senior executives. Assessing the CIO requires assessing multiple dimensions of the CIO's impact:

- Responsibilities of the CIO that are clearly under the CIO's control
- Decisions and behaviors influenced by the CIO
- Contributions made by the CIO as a member of the senior management team generating value for the enterprise

Therefore, assessing the CIO ultimately takes account of the business value created by IT.[5] We suggest the CIO assessment include three factors:

1. IT unit cost and service levels
2. Business and IT process management
3. Business value

Figure 8-1 illustrates CIO assessment showing these three important factors in vertical sections separated by dashed lines. The vertical axis of figure 8-1 represents the accountability and influence of various groups—business, IT, and joint.

The first factor contains both the IT unit cost and service levels that are clearly the responsibility of most CIOs. The IT unit cost is the cost to the business for each IT service used per unit consumed. The CIO and his or her team through architecture, sourcing, IT management, and many other activities heavily influence IT unit cost and should be held directly accountable. The unit cost, not total IT costs, is the right metric as other people (as described in IT investment governance) typically are involved in making IT investment decisions and thus determining total IT cost. The IT service levels

FIGURE 8-1

Assessing the CIO

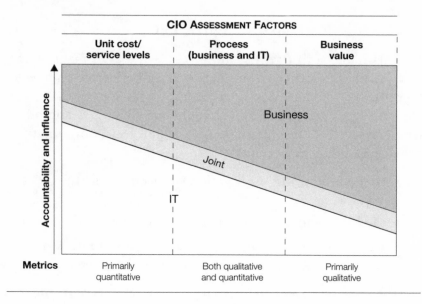

resulting from the IT investment are also part of the calculation and an important deliverable of the CIO. Assessing IT unit cost and service levels is primarily quantitative based on benchmarks, year-to-year comparisons, user satisfaction, and meeting service-level agreements.

The second factor relates to converting IT investment into business value by enabling business processes. Successful conversion requires at least two types of process management: business and IT. Business process owners, not the CIO, typically own the business processes. Therefore business process design and operation are only partially influenced by CIO activities. The CIO typically has more direct responsibility for the disciplines of managing and implementing systems, including project management, integration, migration, training, security, and facilities management. These systems are fundamental to how the business processes are performed, so the relationship between process and IT management is symbiotic and thus hard to assess separately. For this part of the CIO assessment we suggest a combination of quantitative and qualitative metrics. Peers, managers, and subordinates can provide quali- tative input on questions like the contribution, professionalism, and impact of IT in process management. Quantitative measures include a wide variety of process and project performance measures tailored to the business.

The third factor assesses the CIO and his or her team's contri- bution to business value through leadership and teamwork. How has the CIO influenced strategy and helped deliver business value? The CIO and his or her organization should identify strategic op- portunities and recognize potential synergies in the enterprise, par- ticularly exploiting existing IT capabilities. In addition, the CIO should help business managers conceive, specify, and implement their business strategies. Actual business value results from unit cost, service levels and process management, plus business leader- ship and teamwork.

Measuring and rewarding the business value created by the CIO should be based partly on the usual enterprise profit and share val- uation measures used for most senior executives. Another compo- nent of business value is assessing IT's contribution to business value and the leadership and teamwork role of the CIO in achiev- ing it. Again, some parts of the value may be assessable quantita- tively. For example, in financial services, the total cost per business transaction (claims processed, credit card transactions, and so on) are heavily influenced by IT and the CIO's team. Less quantitative is the contribution of the CIO and his or her team to the enterprise strategy. More and more, we expect CIOs to be held accountable for a firm's strategic agility—at least the IT infrastructure components, but perhaps some part of process agility also. These more strategic assessments are necessarily perceptual and qualitative.

The bottom line in figure 8-1 summarizes the metrics for CIO assessment. The three must be weighted for importance. Weighting the CIO's performance to the unit cost and service-level part will motivate a cost focus and service orientation. Weighting more heavily to the business value will motivate more of a business lead- ership and influence orientation. Weighting to process manage- ment will motivate integration between IT and business processes and a business operations focus.

Particularly if the CIO has responsibility for IT governance, the weightings on how he or she is assessed and thus rewarded are critical. The CIO will naturally focus the IT governance arrangements to encourage the behaviors encouraged by his or her incentives. For example, if the CIO's assessment is based solely on IT unit cost and service levels, asking the CIO to design IT governance to achieve other behaviors is a mismatch. Senior management must either change the way the CIO is rewarded or find another owner for IT governance.

Current and Future Challenges of Governance

As we gaze into our crystal ball, we see a number of trends that will influence IT governance; indeed several are already beginning in some enterprises. IT will play an increasingly important role in all industries. Information about products, services, and customers will continue to drive business processes. Information about customers and their needs will be even more precious, particularly as the huge changes in privacy legislation take hold around the world. More and more of the cash flow of an enterprise will be online. For some enterprises like UPS and Charles Schwab, online revenue is well over 50 percent. For other enterprises, it is rising rapidly. All these changes will only raise the stakes for the importance and effectiveness of IT governance. Understanding and refining IT governance now will be a good investment for the future.

We see enterprises consistently striving to be more strategically agile. Enterprises wish to increase the breadth of business initiatives they can implement quickly—thus being more responsive to market shifts. Because enterprises can't predict the future, strategic agility is crucial. The traditional approach of changing the organizational structure for each change in strategy will no longer work. Changing structure is too cumbersome, slow, and imprecise to meet tomorrow's or even today's needs for agility. Instead, agility will be achieved by recombining modular business processes and activities to meet the new need.

Business process modularity will increasingly depend on an enterprise's ability to create standardized, reusable systems, business processes, and data components. These components will build on core processes and infrastructure. Consequently, an enterprise's IT capability, particularly IT architecture and the resulting infrastructure capability, will be a strong predictor of an enterprise's strategic agility. Making IT infrastructure and architecture decisions, once the sole responsibility of IT professionals in enterprises, will continue to evolve to become more of a joint responsibility. These decisions must become part of the general management tool kit and more and more integrated into the enterprise's DNA.

At the same time, enterprises will have to make decisions more quickly. The need for speed will increase pressure on governance, particularly joint business and IT decision making. This pressure means that leaders will continually streamline governance decision-making structures. Alignment processes will require tweaking to ensure appropriate incentives, and communication processes will need refreshing. Duopoly models will become more dominant. In a duopoly, both roles are critical—a business person or team must take the lead on strategy, process changes, prioritization, and implementation. The more technical person or team must ensure technical integrity, project management, reliability, and integration. Heightened concerns about security are already creating more alliances between technical experts and business operations leaders.

Enterprises will continue to outsource more commodity IT services. Pricing and delivery of outsourced services will become more like an electric utility, with a connection charge and fees based on consumption. As the outsourcing industry increases in sophistication, the definition of a commodity service will continue to broaden. Consequently, enterprises will have smaller IT staffs. Many IT specialists without strong industry-specific skills will migrate to service providers such as Accenture, CSC, EDS, HP, IBM, and Microsoft. The remaining IT executives in enterprises will take more strategic roles. Clarifying strategy and the role of IT as well as managing vendors will become increasingly critical for internal IT staff.

In the future, describing how much an enterprise spends on IT will be meaningless. IT will be imbedded in every process and budget, just like capital. It will no longer be helpful to measure or benchmark IT investment levels. As a result, just like financial governance, IT governance will continue to increase in importance. Effective governance allows enterprises to extract maximum value from IT—and ultimately all six key assets of the enterprise. Effective governance delivers on a longtime management paradox—encouraging and leveraging the ingenuity of all the enterprise's people while ensuring compliance with the overall enterprise vision and principles.

In short, don't just lead, govern!

Appendix A

Research Sites

THE AUTHORS gratefully acknowledge all the participants who gave so generously of their time and insights.

The research for this book was conducted at over three hundred enterprises, as follows:

- CIOs at 256 enterprises in twenty-three countries spanning the Americas, Europe, and Asia Pacific—mostly Gartner EXP members—completed a survey designed by MIT Sloan Center for Information Systems Research.

- Case studies were conducted at thirty-two enterprises:
  Abbey National Group*
  Air Products Inc.
  Brady Corporation
  Campbell Soup
  Carlson Companies
  Citigroup
  DBS Bank*
  Delta Air Lines
  Dow Corning
  DuPont
  ING*
  ING Direct

---

*Case studies completed by Gartner's EXP research group led by Marianne Broadbent.

Johnson & Johnson
JPMorgan Chase
Manheim
Marriott
MeadWestvaco
Merrill Lynch
MetLife
Metropolitan Police Service–Scotland Yard*
Motorola
Nestlé USA
Old Mutual South Africa*
Panalpina
Partners HealthCare
Pfizer
State Street Corporation
Tennessee Valley Authority*
Toyota USA
UNICEF
UPS
USAA

- Thirty CIOs participated in one-hour telephone interviews about their IT management practices.

Appendix B

Measuring Governance Performance

TO QUICKLY ASSESS IT governance performance for an enterprise, ask the senior management team—we recommend at least ten managers—to answer the following questions. Then average the results and look at variation by business units and level of management. The formula for calculating governance performance follows the questionnaire.

Governance Performance Survey

The goal of this survey is to assess the effectiveness of your enterprise's IT governance. We define IT governance as *specifying the decision rights and accountability framework to encourage desirable behavior in the use of IT.* Please answer these questions for the part of the enterprise for which you are responsible.

1. How important are the following outcomes of your IT governance, on a scale from 1 (Not important) to 5 (Very important)?

Governance Outcome	Not Important 1	2	3	4	Very Important 5
Cost-effective use of IT	☐	☐	☐	☐	☐
Effective use of IT for growth	☐	☐	☐	☐	☐
Effective use of IT for asset utilization	☐	☐	☐	☐	☐
Effective use of IT for business flexibility	☐	☐	☐	☐	☐

2. What is the influence of the IT governance in your business on the following measures of success, on a scale from 1 (Not successful) to 5 (Very successful)?

Success Measure	Not Successful 1	2	3	4	Very Successful 5
Cost-effective use of IT	☐	☐	☐	☐	☐
Effective use of IT for growth	☐	☐	☐	☐	☐
Effective use of IT for asset utilization	☐	☐	☐	☐	☐
Effective use of IT for business flexibility	☐	☐	☐	☐	☐

3. What are the areas where IT governance works best? Why?
4. What are the areas where IT governance is not effective? Why?

Calculating Governance Performance

Question 1 assesses the importance of a particular outcome and question 2 assesses how well IT governance contributed to meeting the outcome. Since not all firms rank the outcomes with the same importance, the answers to the first question are used to weight the answers to the second question. Then the weighted scores for the 4 questions are added and divided by the maximum score attainable by that enterprise. Therefore, mathematically, governance performance =

$$\frac{(\Sigma_{n=1 \text{ to } 4} \text{ (importance of outcome\{Q1\}} * \text{influence of IT governance\{Q2\})) * 100}}{\Sigma_{n=1 \text{ to } 4} \text{ (5 (importance of outcome))}}$$

Given that there were four objectives, the maximum score for all enterprises is 100 and the minimum score is 20. The average score from 256 enterprises was 69 with the top one third of enterprises scoring over 74.

Notes

Chapter 1

1. We broadly define the term IT to encompass all the ways an enterprise invests to generate business value from IT—by cutting costs, automating or supporting business processes, gaining competitive advantage, meeting regulations, and using information to manage, sell, account, control, inform, share with customers, suppliers and partners, imbed in products, and so on.

2. Peter Weill and Marianne Broadbent, *Leveraging the New Infrastructure: How Market Leaders Capitalize on IT* (Boston: Harvard Business School Press, 1998), chapter 3.

3. Profitability was measured by three-year average industry-adjusted return on assets (ROA). See later in this chapter and chapter 5 for details.

4. Peter Weill and Richard Woodham, "State Street Corporation: Evolving IT Governance" working paper 327, MIT Sloan School of Management Center for Information Systems Research, Cambridge, MA, revised August 2002.

5. Stephen Labaton, "S.E.C. Pushes Companies to Disclose Data Faster," *New York Times,* 28 April 2002. Describes changes by the Securities and Exchange Commission in response to the announcement of President George W. Bush four weeks before.

6. Roberto Newell and Gregory Wilson, "A Premium for Good Governance," *McKinsey Quarterly,* no. 3 (2002): 20–23.

7. "Global Investor Opinion Survey," McKinsey & Company, July 2002.

8. See "The Corporate Governance Site" (www.corpgov.net/links/links.html), which contains an excellent list of links to many sources of information on corporate governance. One interesting source, for exam-

ple, is COSO (Commission of Sponsoring Organizations of the Treadway Committee), which published a draft of its "Enterprise Risk Management Framework" (www.coso.org) in July 2003.

9. Organization for Economic Cooperation and Development, Directorate for Financial, Fiscal and Enterprise Affairs, *OECD Principles of Corporate Governance,* SG/CG(99) 5 and 219, April 1999.

10. Inspired by the work of Michael Porter, Henry Mintzberg, and Constantinos Markides. For an excellent overview see Constantinos C. Markides, "In Search of Strategy," *MIT Sloan Management Review* 40, no. 3 (Spring 1999): 6–7.

11. For a description of how organizations develop and enact beliefs and values, see chapters by Janice Beyer and Lee Sproull in *Handbook of Organization Design,* Volume 2, ed. Paul C. Nystrom and William H. Starbuck (New York: Oxford University Press, 1981).

12. Johnson & Johnson corporate Web site, posted 17 April 2003, http://www.jnj.com/our_company/our_credo/index.htm (extracted 13 May 2003). The J&J corporate credo, which is too long to reproduce here, begins with the statement "We believe our first responsibility is to the doctors, nurses and patients, to mothers and fathers and all others who use our products and services."

13. The meeting took place in May 2003 using an anonymous audience response system. One of the authors, during a presentation of figure 1-1, posed a series of questions to the group.

14. A number of useful definitions and sources of information on IT governance are generally consistent in purpose with our definition. For example, see the IT Governance Institute (www.itgi.org), which defines IT governance as a "structure of relationships and processes to control the enterprise to achieve the enterprise's goals by adding value while balancing risk versus return over IT and its processes." This definition is from the IT Governance Institute's "COBIT 3rd Edition Executive Summary" of July 2000. The COBIT model describes the "control objectives" for thirty-four IT processes and the management guidelines and outcome measures for the processes. COBIT also proposes a five-stage maturity model of IT governance and a series of tool kits, audit guidelines, and education offerings to support use of the frameworks. The materials are detailed and comprehensive and very operationally focused on implementation and control. Another useful definition and perspective is by Wim Van Grembergen: "IT governance is the organizational capacity exercised by the board, executive management, and IT management to control the formulation and implementation of IT strategy and in this way ensure the fusion of business and IT" (Wim Van Grembergen, "In-

troduction to the Minitrack: IT Governance and Its Mechanisms," 35th HICSS conference, http://computer.org/proceedings/hicss/1874/track8/ 187480242.pdf).

15. Stilpon Nestor (Head, Corporate Affairs Division), "International Efforts to Improve Corperate Governance: Why and How," Organization for Economic Cooperation and Development, 11 January 2000.

16. For an excellent discussion of the political perspective and the source of several of these archetypes, see chapter 5 of Thomas H. Davenport and Lawrence Prusak, *Information Ecology: Mastering the Information and Knowledge Environment* (New York: Oxford University Press, 1997).

17. This was the strongest statistically significant relationship in the entire study. It is explored in detail in chapter 4.

18. This result is from the 116 for-profit firms in our study listed on U.S. exchanges. Governance performance is the effectiveness of governance assessed by the CIO to deliver four IT objectives weighted by importance: cost-effective use of IT, effective use of IT for asset utilization, revenue growth, and business flexibility. Governance performance has statistically significant positive relationships with several measures of financial performance (for example, ROE and market cap growth). The financial performance metrics such as ROA were three-year average industry-adjusted measures.

19. B. Gormolski, J. Grigg, and K. Potter, "2001 IT Spending and Staffing Survey Results," Gartner R-14-4158, 19 September 2001. Includes both IT budget and "hidden" IT spending outside the IT budget.

20. Estimate by Peter G. W. Keen, a leading author and consultant, in the foreword to Sarv Devaraj and Rajiv Kohli, *The IT Payoff* (New York: Prentice Hall (Financial Times), 2002).

21. This discussion of IT bombarding enterprises with opportunities draws on Jeff Sampler and Peter Weill, "Core Incompetencies," MIT Sloan School of Management Center for Information Systems Research, Research Briefing, vol. III, no. 1B, March 2003. These paragraphs were also influenced by the insightful discussion of the role, value, and management of information in enterprises from an economic perspective in Carl Shapiro and Hal Varian, *Information Rules: A Strategic Guide to the Networked Economy* (Boston: Harvard Business School Press, 1999).

22. The Standish Group's *2001 Chaos Report* estimates that only 28 percent of IT projects succeed.

23. See Jeanne W. Ross and Peter Weill, "Six IT Decisions Your IT People Shouldn't Make," *Harvard Business Review* (November 2002): 84–91, for a description of the roles senior managers should accept in IT decision making.

24. The discussion of UPS throughout this book comes from a series of interviews by the authors between January 2000 and February 2002 with UPS senior management including Mike Eskew, Jim Kelly, Ken Lacy, and Joe Pyne, among others. Some of these interviews were also referenced in Jeanne W. Ross, "United Parcel Service: Delivering Packages and e-Commerce Solutions," working paper 318, MIT Sloan School of Management Center for Information Systems Research, 2001.

25. Personal interview with Frank Erbick, former UPS CIO. Also referenced in Jeanne W. Ross, "United Parcel Service: Delivering Packages and e-Commerce Solutions," working paper 318, MIT Sloan School of Management Center for Information Systems Research, 2001.

Chapter 2

1. See James D. McKeen and Heather A. Smith, *Making IT Happen: Critical Issues in IT Management* (Chichester, UK: Wiley, 2003) and Robert W. Zmud, ed., *Framing the Domains of IT Management: Projecting the Future . . . Through the Past* (Cincinnati: Pinnaflex, 2000).

2. For example, see Thomas H. Davenport, Michael Hammer, and Tauno J. Metsisto, "How Executives Can Shape Their Company's Information Systems," *Harvard Business Review* (March–April 1989): 130–134; and Peter Weill and Marianne Broadbent, *Leveraging the New Infrastructure: How Market Leaders Capitalize on IT* (Boston: Harvard Business School Press, 1998), 58–62.

3. References to MeadWestvaco are drawn from a personal interview conducted by Jeanne Ross with the CIO of MeadWestvaco, September 19, 2002.

4. Metropolitan Life Insurance Company, *IT Principles* (Metropolitan Life Insurance Company, September 2001).

5. ACORD is an insurance industry standards body specifying data formats and technical standards for electronic exchange. For more information, see <http://www.ACORD.com>.

6. For this section we draw heavily on Peter Weill, Mani Subramani, and Marianne Broadbent, "Building IT Infrastructure for Strategic Agility," *MIT Sloan Management Review* 44, no. 1 (Fall 2002): 57–65; Peter Weill and Sinan Aral, "Managing the IT Portfolio (Update Circa 2003)," MIT Sloan School of Management Center for Information Systems Research, Research Briefing, vol. III, no. 1C (March 2003); and Weill and Broadbent, *Leveraging the New Infrastructure*.

7. In studying large enterprises, we identified a total of seventy different IT infrastructure services in these ten clusters. For a full list of the

infrastructure services in each infrastructure capability cluster and details of patterns of capability found in different enterprises, see Peter Weill, Mani Subramani, and Marianne Broadbent, "IT Infrastructure for Strategic Agility," working paper 329, MIT Sloan School of Management Center for Information Systems Research, Cambridge, MA, 2002.

8. For an excellent discussion of applying real options to technology investments, see Martha Amram and Nalin Kulatilaka, *Real Options* (Boston: Harvard Business School Press, 1998).

9. For more information on these implementations, see Jeff Bailey, "Trash Haulers Are Taking Fancy Software to the Dump," *Wall Street Journal*, 9 June 1999; Joseph B. Cahill, "Whirlpool Experiences Shipping Delays Over Computer Glitches in SAP Software," *Wall Street Journal*, 3 November 1999; and E. Nelson and E. Ramstad, "Trick or Treat: Hershey's Biggest Dud Has Turned Out to Be Its New Technology—At the Worst Possible Time, It Can't Fill Its Orders, Even as Inventory Grows—Kisses in the Air for Kmart," *Wall Street Journal*, 29 October 1999.

10. For further information, see Todd Datz, "Portfolio Management: How to Do It Right," *CIO*, 1 May 2003, 1.

11. For more information on the IT portfolio framework with benchmarks and historical returns, see Weill and Aral "Managing the IT Portfolio (Update Circa 2003), MIT Sloan School of Management Center for Information Systems Research, Research Briefing, vol. III, no. 1C (March 2003); and Weill and Broadbent, *Leveraging the New Infrastructure*, chapter 2. For an alternative approach, see Jeanne W. Ross and Cynthia M. Beath, "Beyond the Business Case: New Approaches to IT Investment," *MIT Sloan Management Review* 43, no. 2 (Winter 2002): 51–59.

12. A 2003 study by DiamondCluster International and Kellogg School of Management of 140 firms found that 24 percent of the firms actively used IT portfolio approaches for IT investment with 78 percent expecting to have a program operational by 2004. Ingmar Leliveld and Mark Jeffery, "IT Portfolio Management: Challenges and Best Practices," DiamondCluster International *Research*, Spring 2003.

13. The discussion of State Street, including quotes, is drawn from Richard Woodham and Peter Weill, "State Street Corporation: Evolving IT Governance" working paper 327, MIT Sloan School of Management Center for Information Systems Research, Cambridge, MA, 2001.

14. The discussion on Delta Air Lines is drawn from "Delta Air Lines: IT Infrastructure," a videotape produced by MIT Sloan School of Management Center for Information Systems Research and Melbourne Business School, The University of Melbourne, 2001.

Chapter 3

1. The average of eight business units was calculated after removing the top and bottom 5 percent of enterprises in terms of the number of business units to correct for very large and very small enterprises, thus giving a better picture of the average. The average without trimming was eleven business units.

2. The feudal entity varies by enterprise and industry with our estimate of the most to least common being business unit, region, function, and business process.

3. For an excellent discussion of the federal model of organizations, see Charles Handy, "Balancing Corporate Power: A New Federalist Paper," *Harvard Business Review* (November–December 1992): 59–72.

4. By duopoly we mean "control or domination by two persons or groups," as defined by the *Oxford English Dictionary,* Second Edition, 1989 http://dictionary.oed.com/cgi/entry/00070944?single=1&query_type =word&queryword=duopoly&edition=2e&first=1&max_to_show=10 (accessed 30 May 2003).

5. Discussions of IT governance at Commonwealth Bank of Australia draw on a personal interview with Peter Reynolds, then Chief Technology Officer, on January 30, 2003.

6. Tables showing industry and regional differences among the enterprises in our study are available at the following Web site: <http://web.mit.edu/cisr/itgovbookreferencelinks.htm>

7. Discussion of DuPont's IT governance draws on a set of interviews with four DuPont executives conducted by the authors during the period September–November 2001.

8. For an excellent discussion of "Big Rules," see Peter G. W. Keen, "Information Technology and the Management of Difference: A Fusion Map," *IBM Systems Journal* 32, no. 1 (1993): 17–39.

9. Personal interview between the authors and William Kirkey, DuPont's Chief Technology Officer, October 19, 2001.

10. Personal interview with DuPont IT executive, October 1, 2001.

11. This material is adapted from Marianne Broadbent and Peter Weill, "Effective IT Governance. By Design," EXP Premier Report, January 2003, and is used with permission.

12. Discussion of IT governance at Motorola draws on personal interviews with Motorola IT executives on and before April 24, 2003.

13. Excerpted from the Chairman and President's Letter to Stockholders in the Motorola 2002 Annual Report as listed at Motorola.com on April 23, 2003.

Chapter 4

1. The role of senior managers in the effective management and use of IT has been written about extensively. The importance of senior management involvement was noted early by John F. Rockart, "The Line Takes the Leadership," *MIT Sloan Management Review* 29 (Summer 1988): 57–64.

2. Marianne Broadbent and Peter Weill, "Effective Governance By Design," Gartner EXP Premier, January 2003. References in this chapter and elsewhere in the book to governance at Abbey National Group, DBS, ING, Scotland Yard, Old Mutual South Africa, Tennessee Valley Authority, and part of the UNICEF case study in Chapter 7 are excerpted with permission from the Gartner report cited above.

3. Jeanne W. Ross, "Dow Corning Corporation: Business Processes and Information Technology," *Journal of Information Technology* 14, no. 3 (September 1999): 253–266.

4. Jeanne W. Ross and Natalia Levina, "Brady Corporation: Delivering Customer Value Through Multiple Channels," working paper 315, MIT Sloan School of Management Center for Information Systems Research, Cambridge, MA, 2001. See also www.bradycorp.com.

5. The discussion of Campbell Soup IT governance mechanisms is drawn from interviews conducted by Jeanne Ross and Nils Fonstad with IT executives at Campbell Soup on September 11, 2002. These interviews also form the basis for George Westerman and Jeanne W. Ross, "Case Vignette of Campbell Soup," MIT Sloan School of Management Center for Information Systems Research, 2003.

6. References to MeadWestvaco are drawn from a personal interview conducted by Jeanne Ross with the CIO of MeadWestvaco, September 19, 2002.

7. C. Suzanne Iacono, Mani Subramani, and John C. Henderson, "Entrepreneur or Intermediary: The Nature of the Relationship Manager's Job," in *Proceedings of the Sixteenth International Conference on Information Systems*, ed. Janice I. DeGross, Gad Ariav, Cynthia Beath, Rolf Hoyer, and Chris Kemerer (Amsterdam, 1995): 289–299.

8. Jeanne W. Ross and Christine M. Lentz, "IT Governance at USAA: Implementing Enterprise-wide Synergies," working paper 339, MIT Sloan School of Management Center for Information Systems Research, 2004.

9. Peter Weill and Richard Woodham, "State Street Corporation: Evolving IT Governance," working paper 327, MIT Sloan School of Management Center for Information Systems Research, Cambridge, MA, 2002.

10. Jeanne W. Ross, Michael R. Vitale, and Cynthia M. Beath, "The Un-tapped Potential of IT Chargeback," *MIS Quarterly* 23, no. 2 (June 1999): 215–237.

11. The Capability Maturity Model (CMM) is a five-level model for judging the maturity of an organization's software processes. See Mark C. Paulk, Bill Curtis, Mary Beth Chrissis, and Charles V. Weber, "Capability Maturity Model, Version 1.1," *IEEE Software* 10, no. 4 (July 1993): 18–27.

12. Jack Welch, CEO at General Electric for many years, popularized the notion of intense focus on a few key initiatives. See, for example, Harris Collingwood and Diane L. Coutu, "Jack on Jack: The HBR Inter-view," *Harvard Business Review* (February 2002): 88–94.

13. Jeanne W. Ross and Richard Woodham, "Chase Global Markets: Defining New Business Models in the Investment Banking Industry," working paper 316, MIT Sloan School of Management Center for Infor-mation Systems Research, Cambridge, MA, August 2001.

14. Marianne Broadbent and Peter Weill, "Effective Governance By De-sign," Gartner EXP Premier, January 2003, p. 41. Used with permission.

15. This vignette was developed from interviews conducted by Jeanne Ross and George Westerman at Carlson Companies headquarters No-vember 22, 2002. The same interviews form the basis for Nils Fonstad and Jeanne Ross, "Case Vignette of Carlson," MIT Sloan School of Man-agement Center for Information Systems Research, January 2003.

Chapter 5

1. The following sources summarize many studies measuring enter-prise performance that informed our choice of measures and provide excellent references: Noel Capon, John U. Farley, and Scott Hoenig, "Determinants of Financial Performance: A Meta-Analysis," *Management Science* 36, no. 10 (1990): 1143–1159 (an issue focused on the state of the art in theory and method in strategy research); David J. Ketchen Jr., James B. Thomas, and Charles C. Snow, "Organizational Configurations and Performance: A Comparison of Theoretical Approaches," *Academy of Management Journal* 36, no. 6 (December 1993): 1278–1313; The Encyclo-pedia About Corporate Governance, http://www.encycogov.com.

2. We used three years of financial data for the 116 firms listed on U.S. exchanges in the study and measured average performance and per-centage change per annum. To compare across industries, we calculated relative firm performance by subtracting the three-year industry-average performance from the firm's three-year average performance. We divided the result by the three-year industry-average performance, taking into account that some industries had negative three-year averages. Like all

approaches to industry adjustment this analysis is not perfect but gives a good indication of industry-adjusted performance. The average annual percent change over the three years in each measure was also used in our analysis but not industry adjusted as the percent change is more readily compared from industry to industry.

3. The rankings and leverage are approximations derived from the strengths of the coefficients in regression equations and correlational analyses and thus are very rough estimates.

4. The three broad strategies used in the analysis are based on the idea of value disciplines in Michael Treacy and Fred Wiersema, *The Discipline of Market Leaders* (Reading, MA: Addison-Wesley, 1995).

5. The figure is based on statistically significant correlations between governance performance and the archetypes enterprises used for each IT decision and input considered separately.

6. Quotation from video of interview with Mike Eskew, Chairman and CEO of UPS, discussing IT governance and investment with Jeanne Ross and Peter Weill, MIT Sloan School of Management Center for Information Systems Research, Cambridge, MA, February 2002.

7. To understand which archetypes were classified as business, technical, and joint, refer to figure 3-2. Business decisions were business monarchies, feudal, and the bottom line in the federal model. IT decisions were the IT monarchy. Joint decisions were the duopoly and the top line in the federal model. We excluded anarchies and determined top and bottom performers by statistically significant correlations between governance performance and who made the decision.

8. Based on statistically significant correlations between three-year (1999–2001) industry-adjusted averages (and changes) in financial performance and governance archetype for each IT decision considered separately. In a couple of instances the probabilities of significance for the correlations were weaker than the usual accepted level for exploratory work but were consistent with the overall patterns for the performance metric and supported by case study analysis. Again, we claim no causality, but the patterns are interesting and should be regarded as indicative rather than strong evidence. As always with this type of analysis based on past performance, using such patterns to predict the future is problematic. Also there are many other factors that influence the financial performance other than IT governance that we did not consider.

9. Adapted from chapter 10 in Peter Weill and Marianne Broadbent, *Leveraging the New Infrastructure: How Market Leaders Capitalize on IT* (Boston: Harvard Business School Press, 1998) and drawing on Marianne Broadbent, "The Role of Information Technology in International Business

Operations: The Case of Citicorp," Melbourne Business School, The University of Melbourne, 1996.

10. Andrew Brand, Peter Weill, Christina Soh, and Pelly Periasamy, "Citibank Asia Pacific: Positioning IT as a Strategic Resource," case study, Melbourne Business School, University of Melbourne, 1999.

11. Peter Weill, Mani Subramani, and Marianne Broadbent, "IT Infrastructure for Strategic Agility," *MIT Sloan Management Review* 44, no. 1 (Fall 2002): 57–65.

12. Richard Woodham and Peter Weill, "Manheim Interactive: Selling Cars On Line," working paper 314, MIT Sloan School of Management Center for Information Systems Research, Cambridge, MA, 2001. For additional information, see http://www.manheim.com.

13. Ibid.

14. Ibid.

Chapter 6

1. We use the very insightful ideas of value disciplines developed by Michael Treacy and Fred Wiersema, *The Discipline of Market Leaders* (Reading, MA: Addison-Wesley, 1995).

2. JPMorgan Chase case study written from interviews with company executives during the period September 2002 to May 2003 and from Marianne Broadbent and Peter Weill, "Effective IT Governance. By Design," Gartner EXP Premier Report, January 2003.

3. Marianne Broadbent and Peter Weill, "Effective IT Governance. By Design," EXP Premier Report, January 2003, p. 53.

4. Ibid.

5. The bottom line in figure 6-3 is estimated from statistically significant correlations of the three-year adjusted performance of eighty-seven firms in our study.

6. Treacy and Wiersema, in *The Discipline of Market Leaders,* argue that customer intimacy is consistent with a profitability goal. We did not find evidence for a relationship between customer intimacy and profit in our study.

7. See Thomas H. Davenport, Jeanne G. Harris, and Ajay K. Kohli, "How Do They Know Their Customers So Well?" *MIT Sloan Management Review* 42, no. 2 (Winter 2001): 63–73.

8. Table draws on Jeanne Ross, David Robertson, George Westerman, and Nils Fonstad, "Aligning IT Architecture with Organizational Realities," MIT Sloan School of Management Center for Information Systems Research, Research Briefing, vol. 3, no. 1A (March 2003); Timothy R. Kayworth, Debabroto Chatterjee, and V. Sambamurthy, "Theoretical

Justification for IT Infrastructure Investments," *Information Resources Management Journal* 14, no. 3 (2001): 5–14; and Peter Weill, Mani Subramani, and Marianne Broadbent, "Building IT Infrastructure for Strategic Agility," *MIT Sloan Management Review* 44, no. 1 (2002): 57–65. The bottom line is estimated from statistically significant correlations of three-year adjusted performance of eighty-seven firms in our study.

9. The description of Pfizer's IT governance was drawn from interviews conducted by George Westerman and Jeanne Ross with four Pfizer IT executives between October 10 and October 21, 2002.

10. The State Street Corporation case study was based on Richard Woodham and Peter Weill, "State Street Corporation: Evolving IT Governance," working paper 327, MIT Sloan School of Management Center for Information Systems Research, April 2002; David Spina (State Street Corporation), "State Street Highlights Growth Strategy" at company's annual meeting, 18 April 2001; interviews with senior State Street executives; and published financial statements.

11. Richard Woodham and Peter Weill, "State Street Corporation: Evolving IT Governance," working paper 327, MIT Sloan School of Management Center for Information Systems Research, April 2002.

12. Ibid.

13. Based on a conversation between Peter Weill and State Street Corporation CIO Joe Antonellis at MIT on 22 January 2003.

Chapter 7

1. The MPS–Scotland Yard case study is adapted from Marianne Broadbent and Peter Weill, "Effective IT Governance. By Design," Gartner EXP Premier Report, January 2003 and Peter Weill and Marianne Broadbent, "Describing and Assessing IT Governance—The Governance Arrangements Matrix" MIT Sloan School of Management, Center for Information Systems Research, Research Briefing, vol. II, no. 3E, October 2002.

2. Weill and Broadbent, "Describing and Assessing IT Governance— The Governance Arrangements Matrix."

3. Broadbent and Weill, "Effective IT Governance. By Design."

4. For Porter's model, see Michael E. Porter, *Competitive Advantage: Creating and Sustaining Superior Performance* (New York: Free Press, 1985).

5. For more information, see Mark Moore, *Creating Public Public Value: Strategic Management in Government* (Cambridge, MA: Harvard University Press, 1995), chapter 3. See also John Alford, "Towards a New Public Management Model: Beyond Managerialism and Its Critics," *Australian Journal of Public Administration* 52, no. 2 (June 1993): 135–148.

6. John Alford, "Defining the Client in the Public Sector: A Social Exchange Perspective," *Public Administration Review* 62, no. 3 (2002): 337–346.

7. The TVA case study is adapted from Broadbent and Weill "Effective IT Governance. By Design."

8. Interview with John Glaser conducted by Jeanne Ross and Sinan Aral on June 24, 2002.

9. Paul Richardson, Peter Weill, and Joel B. Barolsky, "Barwon Water (B): Creating and Exploiting an IT Infrastructure," case 386 Melbourne Business School, University of Melbourne, 1999); and Paul Richardson, Peter Weill, and Joel B. Barolsky, "Barwon Water (A): Creating and Exploiting an IT Infrastructure (A Case Study of the Geelong and District Water Board and Their Innovative Approach to IT Infrastructure)," case 385 Melbourne Business School, University of Melbourne 1999).

10. Richardson, Weill, and Barolsky, "Barwon Water (B): Creating and Exploiting an IT Infrastructure."

11. Governance performance was determined by the CIO and is a four-factor measure of IT including cost-effective use of IT, use of IT for growth, use of IT for asset utilization, and use of IT for business flexibility. Each factor is weighted for importance to the organization to create a score ranging from 20 to 100.

12. Determined by statistically significant correlations between governance arrangements and governance performance as defined in the previous endnote.

13. "I want the U.K. to be the world's leading Internet economy. . . . I am determined that government should play its part, so I am bringing forward our target for getting all government services online from 2008 to 2005. This will mean that people and businesses will be able to access government services twenty-four hours a day, seven days a week." U.K. Prime Minister Tony Blair, 30 March 2000.

14. All the mechanisms mentioned in this section were statistically significantly used more effectively by top governance performers.

15. The UNICEF case study was drawn from discussions between Peter Weill and UNICEF CIO Andre Spatz; material adapted from Broadbent and Weill, "Effective IT Governance. By Design"; and www.unicef.org.

16. Source: www.unicef.org.

17. Broadbent and Weill, "Effective IT Governance. By Design." Used with permission.

Chapter 8

1. Many of the examples in this section are further descriptions or summaries of examples in earlier chapters where the sources are identified.

2. Marianne Broadbent and Peter Weill, "Effective IT Governance. By Design," Gartner EXP Premier Report, January 2003, p. 60.

3. Quotation from video of interview with Mike Eskew, Chairman and CEO of UPS, discussing IT governance and investment with Jeanne Ross and Peter Weill, MIT Sloan School of Management School Center for Information Systems Research, February 2002 MIT Sloan School of Management.

4. A survey taken by one of the authors using an audience response system at a meeting of fifty CIOs in May 2003 found the following patterns of IT governance ownership: CIOs 56 percent, CEOs 8 percent, COOs 13 percent, committee of senior IT leaders 3 percent, committee of senior business and IT leaders 13 percent.

5. This section draws heavily on the discussion at the MIT CIO Summit attended by twenty CIOs and CTOs on 22 May 2003. The diagram in figure 8-1 was jointly developed in a breakout session and then discussed with the entire group.

Index

Abbey National (UK), 93–94
accountability
  assigning of, 227–228
  of CIOs, 228
  clarifying, 116
  IT metrics and, 148, 154
  at MPS–Scotland Yard, 189
accounting, chargeback, 102–103,
  174
Adamski, Joe, 197–198
aggregators/aggregation, 15–16
alignment processes for decision
  making, 86
  architectural exception, 99–101
  Carlson Companies', 112–114
  chargeback accounting, 102–103
  formal tracking of business
    value, 103–104
  IT investment approval, 97–99
  project tracking, 103
  service-level agreements (SLAs),
    101–102
Amazon.com, 219–220
anarchy model, 12, 59, 60, 63
Antonellis, Joe, 182
applications
  coordination of development
    of, 156–157

infrastructure, 37, 38
strategic IT, 40
archetypes. *See also entries for each
  specific model, e.g., federal
  model*
  anarchy model, 12, 59, 60, 63
  business monarchy, 12, 58–59
  duopoly model, 12, 61–63
  federal model, 12, 61
  feudal model, 12, 60
  industry differences in use of, 81
  IT monarchy, 12, 59–60
  key players in, 60
architecture, 10
  component-based, 34
  committees, 91–92, 99, 138
  coproduction and, 198–199
  DBS Bank's, 76
  for decision-making principles,
    30–34
  Delta Nervous System, 51
  exceptions processes, 99–101,
    113–114
  integrity of, 43
  IT architecture and standards
    infrastructure, 39
  maintaining, in high-growth
    firms, 142–143

architecture *(continued)*
  MetLife's Enterprise
    Architecture, 32
  questions key for, 54
  typical governance arrange-
    ments for, 67
Asia-Pacific firms, 82
assessment
  analytical tools, 164
  of the CIO, 231–234
  of business value, 103–104,
    232–233
  how to assess governance,
    119–121
  measuring performance, 81,
    120, 195–196, 239–240
  of patterns across enterprises,
    64–65, 70–78
assets
  coordination of, 230–231
  IT asset classes, 47
  key asset governance, 5–7
  returns on assets (ROAs), 14
  utilization of, 136–139
audits of IT governance
  mechanisms, 221
authorizing environments,
    191–192, 194–195, 206–207

Beath, Cynthia, ix
Beaton, Ailsa, 186, 187, 190
  behavioral side of corporate
    governance, 9–10
benchmarks for governance
  performance, 124
BIC Graphics Europe, 159
bicycle wheel duopolies, 62,
    68–69
Blair, Tony, 204
Brady Corporation, 89–90

Broadbent, Marianne, ix
Brown, Steve, 110
business application needs
  decisions, 11
  feudal model for, 69, 75,
    204–205
  questions key for, 55
  typical governance arrange-
    ments for, 68–69
business/IT interactions, 93–94
business/IT relationship
  managers, 96–97, 138
business monarchy model
  for application needs decisions,
    69
  coordinating, with IT
    monarchies, 92–93
  decision-making structures,
    86–89
  for IT investment and prioritiza-
    tion decisions, 69–70
  in top performers, 136–143
  overview of, 58–63
  for IT principles decisions,
    65–66, 142
  use of, across industries/
    enterprises, 81–82
business objectives for IT
  investment, 126–127
business performance. *See*
  performance/performers
business process modularity,
    234–235
business unit autonomy and
  synergy, 105, 170–174

Campbell Soup, 91–92
Capital One, 164
Carlson Companies (Carlson),
    108–114

case studies. *See also entries for each specific company, e.g.,* UPS; research/studies
  Carlson Companies (Carlson), 108–114
  DBS Bank, 76–78
  Delta Air Lines, 49–53
  DuPont, 72–75
  Motorola, 78–80
  State Street Corporation, 175–183
  UNICEF, 206–214
  UPS, 18–21
centralized approaches
  to governance, 134, 140
  centrally managed IT, 15
  UNICEF's, 210
challenges
  to architectural integrity, 42–43
  governance, 234–236
  for government/not-for-profit organizations, 195–200
changes
  in designs, 223
  fewer governance, 128
  organizational, 44
  problems of frequent governance changes, 219–220
chargeback, 102–103, 174
Chase Manhattan Bank, 106. *See also* JPMorgan Chase
checklist for designing governance, 145–146
CIO offices, 106–107, 125, 126, 227–228, 231–234
Citibank, 15, 16
Citibank Asia, 140
Citicorp, 137–138
committees
  architecture, 91–92, 99, 138
  for communicating governance, 105–106, 125

Integration Steering Committee (USAA), 98
  MPS–Scotland Yard's, 224
  senior management, effective use of, 140
  structures of (MPS–Scotland Yard), 186–187
  use of, by top performers, 205
Commonwealth Bank of Australia, 69, 96, 101
communication approaches, 86
  coordinating multiple mechanisms, 108–114
  formal committees, 105–106
  office of CIO or IT governance, 106–107
  senior management announcements, 104–105, 125
  tools (Carlson Companies), 114
  Web-based portals, 107–108
  working with nonconformists, 107
comparisons
  governance versus management, 25, 220
  localized versus enterprise goals, 99
  not-for-profit versus for-profit governance, 201–202
  strategies versus behavior, 6, 154
component-based architecture, 34
consumers, types of, 199–200
control, through IT governance, 20–21
coordination issues, 92–93, 108–114
coproduction, 193, 198–199
corporate culture, 9, 71–72
corporate scandals, 4
councils, IT, 93–94

creativity, 40, 41–42
cross-functional business
    processes, 94
culture, corporate, 9, 71–72
customers
    authorizing environment of,
        192, 206–207
    consumers as, 199–200
    customer intimacy, 158,
        162–168
    customer relationship manage-
        ment (CRM) systems, 37
    loyalty of, 230

data standardization, 31
DBS Bank, 76–78, 88, 107,
    224–225
decentralized structures, 150
decision-making issues/structures.
    See also alignment processes
    for decision making; interre-
    lated IT decisions
    better decision makers, 133–136
    business monarchies, 86–89
    Carlson Companies', 110–112
    decision rights, 59, 136
    Delta Air Lines, 49–53
    designing effective mechanisms
        for, 115–116
    desirable behaviors and,
        153–154
    duopolies, 93–97, 132–133
    federal models, 89–90, 130–132
    governance arrangements for,
        130–136
    for implementing governance,
        114–116
    in infrastructure strategies,
        67–68
    IT monarchies, 90–93
    joint, for IT investments, 205

key IT governance decisions, 27
    mechanisms for, 217–218
    overlapping membership in,
        115
    power of CxOs for, 81
    processes for successful firms, 17
    speed of decision making, 235
    successful patterns of, 133–134
    top-down decision making, 26
Delta Air Lines, 49–53, 54, 105,
    217
descriptions of IT governance by
    leaders, 124
design issues/design frameworks
    active designing of governance,
        222–223
    checklist for, 145–146
    comparisons for design, 83
    components of effective,
        148–157
    coproduction design, 199
    designing at multiple organiza-
        tional levels, 228
    design proposal for linking cor-
        porate and IT governance, 5–6
    of governance arrangements,
        152
    IT Governance Design Frame-
        work, 13, 220, 221
    JPMorgan Chase's, 151
    leading enterprises' governance
        designs, 145–146
    MPS–Scotland Yard's, 188
    principles for effective
        mechanisms, 115–116
    redesigning, timing of, 223,
        219–220
    risks of designs, 157–158
    steps for reviewing/designing IT
        governance, 220–221
    strategic and structural drivers,
        designing for, 183–184

typical design profiles, 83
UNICEF's, 209
desirable behaviors, 6, 8–9, 148,
    153–154, 181–182, 183–184
differences among enterprises,
    71–72, 80–82
disciplined execution of decisions,
    42–45
disciplines, value. *See* value
    disciplines
disincentives, financial 224–225
diversity, of enterprises, 71
documentation, 125, 229
Dow Corning, 69, 88, 105, 138
duopoly model, 12, 59, 60
    for architecture decisions, 67
    by leaders on asset utilization,
        137–138
    bicycle wheel duopolies, 62
    decision making in, 93–97
    enterprise objectives and, 68–69
    for investment decisions, 70
    for IT principles decisions,
        65–66
    overview of, 61–63
    reasons for success in decision
        making of, 132–133
    T-shaped duopolies, 62, 65, 70,
        134, 137–138
    use of across industries/
        enterprises, 81–82
DuPont, 60, 72–75, 168, 169

e–business initiatives, 20
education and training, 39,
    229–230
effectiveness
    of architecture exception
        process, 100–101
    assessing IT governance,
        119–121

components of effective design,
    148–157
design principles for effective
    mechanisms, 115–116
documentation, 229
of duopolies, 97
effective IT governance as pre-
    dictor of value, 2–4
experience of IT governance
    and, 71
ineffective IT governance,
    216–220
of principles, 28
questions to address for, 10
e-government innovations,
    203–204
empowerment, 20–21, 104
enterprises. *See also by names of
    specific enterprises, e.g.,* UPS
architectures of, 31–34, 52
corporate governance, 5
customer-intimate, 164
enterprise-level governance,
    115–116
enterprise resource planning
    (ERP) systems, 17, 27–28, 34,
    41, 138
factors in, 71
high-growth, 142–143
leading, governance designs of,
    145–146
operationally excellent, 159
pattern analysis across, 70–78
product leadership, 168
strategy and organization of,
    148, 149–152
top not-for-profit versus other
    not-for-profit governance,
    202–203
typical IT governance in, 64–70
variations in governance across,
    122–123

equity, 194
Escarra, Vicky, 51
Eskew, Mike, 224
evaluation. *See* assessment/analysis
evolving IT governance, 184,
    210–213
exceptions
    exception-handling processes,
        99–101, 113–114, 156,
        225–226
    renegade, 127–128
    to normal policies, 17
expenditures, how much to
    spend, 45–46
expenses of IT governance, 14–15
experiments, 41–42

facilities management, 38
failure rates of IT projects, 17
Federal Express (FedEx), 45–46,
    164
federal model, 12, 59, 60, 61
    for application needs, 133–134
    decision-making structures,
        89–90
    for investment and prioritiza-
        tion decisions, 68–69
    for IT principles decisions, 65–66
    reasons for struggling with,
        130–132
    use of, across industries/
        enterprises, 81–82
Feld, Charlie, 50
feudal model, 12, 59, 60, 142.
    for business application needs,
        69, 204–205
    DuPont's use of, 77
    use of, across industries/
        enterprises, 82
financial assets, 6

financial disincentives, 224–225
Fiore, John, 178
firms. *See* enterprises
Fonstad, Nils, ix
formal committees, 105–106
formal tracking of business value,
    103–104
for-profit organizations, 81,
    192–193, 201, 202. *See also*
    government/not-for-profit
    organizations
frameworks, 160, 190–195.
    See also design issues/design
    frameworks
funding, 197, 200, 206–207
future challenges of IT
    governance, 234–236

Glaser, John, 197
goals
    alignment of IT decisions with
        organizational, 112
    business performance
        (JPMorgan Chase's), 153
    localized versus enterprise, 99,
        170–174
    strategic and performance, 71
governance. *See also* IT governance
    characteristics of leading
        enterprises, 145–146
    corporate, 4–7
    of government/not-for-profit
        organizations, 200–202
    versus management, 25
governance arrangements
    for architecture decisions, 67
    best governance arrangements,
        129–136
    for business application needs,
        68–69

industry and regional
  differences, 80–82
for infrastructure strategy
  decisions, 67–68
for investment and prioritization decisions, 69–70
of large enterprises, 89
leading financial performers'
  approaches, 136–145
matrixes, 10–14, 73, 189, 211
for principles decisions, 65–67
Governance Arrangements
  Matrix, 10–14, 224
  Carlson's, 113
  DBS Bank's, 77
  DuPont's, 74
  Motorola's, 79
  MPS–Scotland Yard's, 189
  State Street Corporation's, 180
  UNICEF's, 211
governance design. *See* design
  issues/design frameworks
Governance Design Framework,
  13–14, 148–157
  ING Direct's, 163
  JPMorgan Chase's, 150
  MPS–Scotland Yard's, 188
  Panalpina's, 166
  State Street's, 179
  UNICEF's, 209
governance mechanisms. *See also*
  by specific mechanism (e.g.,
  committees, chargeback)
  across key assets, 230–231
  common, 87
  coordinating multiple, 108–114
  design principles for effective,
    115–116
  high-impact, 109
  not-for-profit organizations,
    205–206

organizational, 7
overviews of, 85–86, 155–157
principles for, 114–116
slow/contradictory, 217–218
governance performance survey,
  239–240
government/not-for-profit
  organizations, 81
  challenges of governance for,
    195–200
  compared to for-profits, 214
  framework for value in,
    190–195
  governance of, 200–202
  Metropolitan Police Service
    (MPS)–Scotland Yard,
    186–190
  overview of, 185
  top performers, governance of,
    202–206
  UNICEF, 206–214
growth, leaders on, 141–145
guidelines, for good corporate
  governance, 4–5

Halbert, Keith, 53
Handy, Charles, 61
Harrison, William, Jr., 149–150
high-growth enterprises, 142–143
high-impact mechanisms, 109
human assets, 6

incentives, management, 226–227
industry differences, 71–72, 80–82
ineffective IT governance, symptoms of, 216–220
information assets, 6–7
information security governance
  (Motorola's), 78–80

infrastructures, 10
  cost-saving, 198
  decision making on, 26, 34–40
  investments in, 196–198
  questions key for, 55
  as strategic business decisions, 204
  typical governance arrangements for, 67–68
ING Direct, 88, 159, 161–162, 163
innovations, 9, 203–204
input to governance decisions, 64–65, 129–130
integration
  of formerly autonomous functions, 105
  of infrastructures, 37
  process, 30–31
  providing integrated solutions, 150
intellectual property (IT) assets, 6
interactions, business/IT, 93–94
interrelated IT decisions. *See also* decision-making issues/ structures
  Decision 1: IT principles, 27–30
  Decision 2: IT architecture, 30–34
  Decision 3: IT infrastructure, 34–40
  Decision 4: business applications needs, 40–45
  Decision 5: investment and prioritization, 45–49
  linking, 54–55
  overview, 26–27
intranets, 125
investment and prioritization, 11
  decision-making principles, 45–57
  questions key for, 54

typical governance arrangements for, 69–70
investment portfolios, 46–47
IT councils, 93–94
IT governance. *See also* governance
  call to action for, 22
  concepts of, 10–14
  definitions of, 2, 8–10
  empowerment and control through, 20–21
  importance of, vii–viii, 14–18
  research on, viii–x
  steps for reviewing/designing, 220–221
  symptoms of ineffective, 216–220
IT monarchy, 75, 90–93.
  for architecture decisions, 67
  coordinating, with business monarchies, 92–93
  decision-making structures, 90–92
  for infrastructure decisions, 67–68
  for IT investment and prioritization decisions, 69
  for leaders on profit, 139–141
  overview of, 58–63
  for IT principles decisions, 65–66
  use of, across industries/ enterprises, 81–82
IT principles, 10
  decision making on, 27–30, 135–136
  questions key for, 54
  typical governance arrangements for, 65–67

Johnson & Johnson, 67–68
joint business/IT membership, 93–94

joint decision making, 203–204, 205
JPMorgan Chase (formerly Chase Manhattan Bank), 104, 106, 149–158, 169, 228

Lacy, Ken, 40, 224
leadership, 90–91, 159, 222–231. *See also* managers
leading financial performers. *See under* performance/ performers
Levina, Natalia, ix
Logan, Hal, 143

management
of assets, 1
centrally managed IT, 15
change, 44–45
facilities, 38
versus governance, 25, 220
of information/knowledge, 213–214
paradox of, 236
principles for addressing strategic objectives, 183–184
services, 39
managers
better decision making of, 135
business/IT relationship, 96–97, 138
senior, 17, 124–126, 216–217, 218, 223–224
Manheim Auctions, 143–144
matrixes. *See* governance arrangements/matrixes
MeadWestvaco, 27–28, 29–30, 42–43, 94–96, 138, 159
measuring performance, 81, 120, 195–196, 239–240. *See also*

assessment/analysis; performance/performers
mechanisms. *See* governance mechanisms
MetLife, 28–30, 31–34
metrics and accountabilities, 148, 154, 182, 183, 233
Metropolitan Police Service (MPS)–Scotland Yard, 186–190, 193
models. *See* archetypes
monarchy model. *See* archetypes; business monarchies; IT monarchy
Motorola, 78–80, 129, 168, 169
Mullin, Leo, 49–53
multiple organizational levels, 115, 228

Nelson, Marilyn Carlson, 110
Nelson, Oz, 18–19
net asset values (NAVs), 182
new information technologies, 15–16
normative side of corporate governance, 10
not-for-profit organizations. *See* government/not-for-profit organizations

objectives, business, 68–69, 126–127, 183–184
"OECD Principles for Corporate Governance," 4–5
Old Mutual South Africa (OSMA), 90, 91, 224–225
online businesses, 143–144, 203–204
operational excellence, 158, 159–162

organization, enterprise strategy and, 149–152

organizational learning, about IT value, 16–17

Organization for Economic Cooperation and Development (OECD), 4–5, 9–10

outsourcing, 35, 219, 235

ownership, assigning of, 227–228

Panalpina, 164, 165–168

Partners Healthcare, 41

patterns
  analysis of, across enterprises, 64–65, 70–78
  factors in, 71
  of performance, successful, 133–134
  of top performers, 136
  variations in governance, 71–72

performance/performers
  assessing governance, 119–121
  best/worst, 131
  business performance goals, 148, 153
  calculating, 240
  leading financial performers, 136–145, 145–146, 176–177
  measuring performance, 81, 195–196, 239–240
  patterns of performance, successful, 133–134
  top governance performers, 123–128, 129–130, 133, 203–205, 205–206

Pfizer, 168, 169, 172–173

political acceptance, 194–195

political archetypes. See archetypes

political power holders, 206–207

portals, Web-based, 107–108, 125, 229

Porter, Michael, 190–195

portfolios, 46–47

predictors of top governance performance, 123–128

Price, Mark, 110–111, 113

principles, 10 See also IT principles
  for addressing strategic objectives, 183–184
  for choosing optimal IT governance, 146
  for designing effective mechanisms, 114–116
  leadership, 222–231
  "OECD Principles for Corporate Governance," 4–5

prioritization. See investment and prioritization

problems
  in aligning business and IT, 97
  of governing IT by default, 3
  inability to respond to technology–induced market, 16
  IT failure rates, 17
  of mismatches between desirable behavior and governance, 8–9
  outsourcing of, 67
  symptoms of ineffective governance, 216–220

procedures, documentation of, 125

processes. See also alignment processes for decision making
  architecture exceptions, 99–101, 113–114
  business process modularity, 234–235
  cross-functional, 94
  exception-handling, 225–226

governance/ownership, 212
integration of, 30–31
process organizations, 94–96
product (or service) leadership,
    159, 168–170
profits, leaders on, 139–141
public goods and services, 194,
    207–208
public value of not-for-profit
    organizations, 193–195

questions
    address for effectiveness, 10
    architecture, 54
    business application needs, 55
    choosing optimal IT gover-
        nance, 119, 145–146
    for each IT decision, 54–55
    for effective governance, 25–26,
        215
    for IT infrastructures, 55

realization, benefits management
    and, 189
redesigning, timing of, 223
regional differences, 71–72
regional differences among
    enterprises, 80–82
relationships.
    among assets, 7
    business/IT relationship
        managers, 96–97, 138
    customer relationship manage-
        ment (CRM) systems, 37
    strategy-governance, 174–175
research studies. *See also* case
    studies
    enterprises with superior corpo-
        rate governance, 22

IT governance, viii–x
premiums paid, 4
research sites, 237–238
value creation, 3–4
returns on assets (ROAs), 14,
    136–139
returns on investments (ROIs), 2,
    139–141
reviewing and designing IT gover-
    nance, steps for, 220–221
risk factors
    in business investment
        decisions, 47
    frustration levels and, 66–67
    security and risk capability
        issues, 37–38
Robertson, David, ix

scandals, corporate, 4
Schneider National, 68
security issues, 77
senior management, 17, 223–224.
    See also managers
    announcements by, 104–105,
        125
    engagement/involvement of,
        124–126
    of not-for-profit organizations,
        205–206
    selective outsourcing by, 219
    sensing of low value by, 216–217
    understanding of IT governance
        by, 218, 229–230
    use of committees by, 140
services
    in clusters, 38
    infrastructure, 35, 37
    outsourcing of, 235
service-level agreements (SLAs),
    101–102

service (or product) leadership,
159
shared infrastructures, 177–178
single business unit firms, 134
six sigma 104
Spatz, Andre, 210
Spina, David, 3, 176, 177, 182
standards/standardization
    centralized approaches for, 140
    and exception requests, 100–101
    exceptions to, 128
    IT architecture and standards
        infrastructure, 39
    process standardization, 31
    types of, 170–171
State Street Corporation, 48–49,
    58, 100, 175–183, 224
steps for reviewing/designing IT
    governance, 220–221
stewardship model, 94–95
strategic and structural drivers,
    158–170, 183–184
strategic IT applications, 40
strategic objectives, principles for
    addressing, 183–184
strategic priorities, 48–49
strategies
    barriers to implementing new,
        217
    versus behavior, for value
        creation, 6
    business unit synergies,
        170–174
    customer intimacy, 158,
        162–168
    differentiation of, 127
    enterprise, 149–152
    infrastructure, 39–40, 67–68
    linking components of gover-
        nance design, 148–158
    operational excellence, 158,
        159–161

product (or service) leadership,
    159, 168–170
strategy-governance relation-
    ship, 174–175
structural drivers. See strategic and
    structural drivers
structures. See also centralized
    approaches; decision-making
    issues/structures
    changing, 234
    decentralized, 150
    and desirable behaviors, 148,
        153–154
    duopoly, 138–139
    organizational, 71, 183–184
Subramani, Mani, ix
success
    decision-making processes for, 17
    indicators of, 46
    reasons for, 2, 132–133
    successful patterns of decision
        making, 133–134
supply chain management (SCM)
    systems, 37
surveys, governance performance
    survey, 239–240
synergies, 170–174, 175

teams, 74, 89–90
    contribution to business value
        of, 233
    leadership, 90–91
    senior management, 147
Tennessee Valley Authority (TVA),
    96, 195–196, 222
top-down decision making, 26
top performers. See also perform-
    ance/performers
    characteristics of, 123–128
    designing governance from,
        145–146

governance of, 18, 202–206
leading financial performers,
   136–145, 176–177
predictors of, 124
reasons for success of, 2
top three governance patterns,
   133
tracking of business value,
   103–104
transfers and provisions of
   services, 194–195
transformations. *See* changes
transparency in governance,18,
   115, 229–230
Treacy, Michael, 158
trends in IT governance, 234–236
T-shaped duopolies, 62, 65, 70,
   134, 137–138

UNICEF, 206–214
UPS (United Parcel Service),
   18–21, 42, 45–46, 59, 88–89,
   98, 131–132, 159
USAA, 98, 164

value
   business, 232–233
   creation, 3–4, 6, 41, 44,
      153–154, 203

framework for, in not-for-profit
   organizations, 190–195
from investment decisions,
   ensuring of, 69–70
of IT-related initiatives, 16–17
low, from IT investments,
   216–217
measuring, 195–196
tracking of business, 103–104
value disciplines
   customer intimacy, 158,
      162–168
   operational excellence, 158,
      159–161
   product (or service) leadership,
      159, 168–170
   relationship with governance,
      174–175
Vanguard, 15, 16
Vitale, Michael, x

Web-based portals, 107–108, 125,
   229
Weirsema, Fred, 158
Westerman, George, ix
Woodham, Richard, ix, x

Y2K, 50
Yodalee, 15

About the Authors

Peter Weill is Director, MIT Sloan School of Management Center for Information Systems Research (CISR) and MIT Sloan Senior Research Scientist. CISR's mission is to perform practical empirical research on how firms generate business value from information technology (IT). CISR disseminates this research via electronic research briefings, working papers, research workshops, and executive education and is funded by corporate sponsors and patrons. Peter joined the Sloan faculty in 2000 to become director of CISR, which was founded in 1974. Peter's research centers on the role, value, and governance of IT in enterprises. Peter has published widely, including award-winning books, journal articles, and case studies. Peter regularly advises corporations and governments on issues of IT investment. Peter cowrote a best-selling book entitled *Leveraging the New Infrastructure: How Market Leaders Capitalize on Information Technology,* published by the Harvard Business School Press in 1998. Peter cowrote another book for the Harvard Business School Press entitled *Place to Space: Migrating to e-Business Models,* published in 2001, which won one of the Library Journal of America's awards for best business book of the year.

Jeanne W. Ross is Principal Research Scientist at the MIT Sloan School of Management Center for Information Systems Research. At MIT she lectures, conducts research, and teaches public and customized courses on IT management. She has published widely, including journal articles, book chapters, and case studies. Her research examines organizational and performance implications of enterprise initiatives related to IT architecture, governance, and new IT management practices. Jeanne is a founding senior editor of the recently created *MISQ Executive.*